A HISTORY OF
NEGRO EDUCATION
IN THE SOUTH

From 1619 to the Present

A HISTORY OF
NEGRO EDUCATION
IN THE SOUTH

From 1619 to the Present

Henry Allen Bullock

Texas Southern University

HARVARD UNIVERSITY PRESS

Cambridge, Massachusetts

1967

To Merily, Merle, and Rodney

PREFACE

Every book is somewhat autobiographical in nature. Like an artist who paints a picture or a composer who scores a symphony, an author is moved to express an idea that haunts him and to share it with other people. A frank admission of this degree of personal bias is not dangerous, for reality is never absolute, but is always relative to the level from which it is observed. Though some element of the author's personality inescapably creeps into what he writes, his unique experiences within one of many private worlds may add another face to the multifaceted design that is human reality.

This book is concerned with the historical development of educational opportunities for Negroes in the South, and with the manner in which these evolving opportunities facilitated the desegregation movement now occurring in the United States. It is the result of an attempt to test a theory of history in which I have long been interested; more frankly I should say it represents the search for the vindication of a faith that I have long held.

During the early years of my college days at Virginia Union University, there developed within me the feeling that segregated education had some accidental purpose. The rather orthodox value system that Union imposed upon its students — not to smoke; not to play cards; not to drink; and, above all, not to refer to ourselves by that vulgar term with which racists were wont to identify Negroes — was selectively internalized, but the more fundamental belief that the system inculcated was embraced in full. It was the doctrine that the Negro college was to develop the leadership for the emancipation of the Negro American as a person. I shared this faith and sought its justification in a common denominator applicable to the development of all peoples. This was not a very diligent search, some intellectual crusade, that I waged; it was only a gnawing need to preserve and foster my self-respect.

Most Negro college students of this period felt this need. It was the time of the "Negro renaissance," when Langston Hughes, Claude McKay, Countee Cullen, and many other Negro writers were doing so much to improve the Negro's self concept. But the poetry, fiction, and essays of this period were not enough. They supplied no rationale that would justify the faith in Negro education which had been imposed upon us; they left us needing some order by which the promise could be fulfilled.

I guess I can say, with great humility, that the rationale for me came through the courses that I took at Union. In my study of the history of social thought with Gordon Blaine Hancock, our "Gloomy Dean" of economics, and H. J. McGuinn, whom we all knew as "Pat McGuinn," I became attached to the ideas of the German Romanticists and the generalized theories of the philosophers of history. These theories constituted for me a set of ideas that justified my faith in segregated education; they inclined my private hopes toward the belief that there is a divine purpose behind human society — even behind segregated education. Giovanni Batista Vico (*The New Science,* 1725) probably summarized it best for me, declaring the existence of a natural, universal, and eternal law of nations that joins societies in a great "world city," sends them on a trend toward moralization through eternally recurring cycles, and keeps them spiraling upward toward some divine goal. Though I came to look critically upon these views, the purpose theory of societal evolution was never completely erased from my mind.

When, almost one decade ago, I knew I would have sustained support for a study of the history of Negro education in the South, this theory emerged naturally as the guiding principle behind the organization of my accumulated facts. It provided a frame of reference by which Negro education as a force for social change could be tested; it now rests as a foundation for the thematic structure of this report.

My work has been made to hang heavily upon the concept of *historical accident.* I have done so because I believe that the changes in American race relations which we are now experiencing are the result of a "sneak attack" directed by the larger purpose of human society against the biases of individuals and through the force of a segregated educational system that was never created for such an end. Basic, therefore, is the central idea that our current educational and social revolution was never intended, but has developed instead out of liberating responses elicited by the nation's efforts to maintain the status quo; that Negro education in the South repeatedly served as the main leverage for this movement; and, despite purposeful efforts to the contrary, has been pushing the movement toward the complete emancipation of the Negro American as a person.

I searched for and believe I found the creative forces behind this type of emancipation. I believe I found them in the accidents of human purpose. The functions of any society have *intended* and *unintended* dimensions. More recent researches have supported this view. They have persistently shown that social functions of an unintended quality do arise and cause a society to veer in directions not necessarily set by the specific purposes of the majority. Events do occur "unofficially" in time and place where those acting "officially" never willed. Nevertheless, such events become a permanent part of man's past and an effective force behind his future, bringing into existence new social orders and more revolutionary alignments of peoples.

In no phase of our history has this process operated more freely than in the field of race relations. Inherent in each major racial issue has been a dimension of conflict — a dilemma, so to speak — pregnant with unintention. Western societies have frequently found themselves in the position where to do what they willed in their attempt to effect an interracial accommodation meant to do that which they did not intend. Carrying its own set of conflicts, therefore, each accommodation has tended to foster a new cycle that joined older ones to constitute a more equalitarian social practice. The process has been slow and heart-rending, but it has worked. Consequently, it is through the model of conflict–unintention–accommodation that I feel the dynamics of this phase of our history can best be explained, and it is to this model that I have turned in search of a vindication of my faith and an explanation for the educational and social revolution occurring in American race relations today.

Preface

If justification for my faith does exist, I hope that my method of inquiry has adequately revealed it. Selecting strategic periods of black and white contacts in American history, I attempted to identify the direct intentions and inherent conflicts involved in each; to derive the unintended and contrary interracial practices that resulted; to delineate the new and higher levels of interracial accommodation that progressively came into existence; and to establish the Negro American's developing educational opportunities in the South as the initiating force within each stage of the historical process.

Some of my sources are general and secondary, recording the historical asides of Negro life and education and revealing impressions of other scholars whose interests were mainly elsewhere. Many, too, are specific and primary. They are autobiographies, diaries, letters, news items, and reports of persons who lived during the periods of which I write and who were engaged in the activities from which I have attempted to glean deeper meaning. But I might not have handled all of these sources skillfully. In the midst of a great abundance of material dealing with this important phase of American history, I found that the making of judicious selections and the drawing of valid conclusions was difficult and not entirely susceptible to the guidance one tends to get from established research criteria. Nevertheless, I have tried to weigh the evidence with as much diligence as I have reported it, hoping that my efforts would come to rest upon conclusions that, in addition to being verifiable, are unbiased and unemotional.

I am deeply indebted to Texas Southern University and its President, S. M. Nabrit, for giving complete financial support to this study. It was W. R. Banks, President Emeritus of Prairie View Agricultural and Mechanical College of Texas, who first suggested the need for such an investigation. His sustained interest gave me buoyancy at times when the delay of tedious reading might have caused a sag.

Naomi Williams Lede, formerly my research assistant, gave significant aid. She assisted in the development of bibliographies; maintained contact with libraries owning rare sources; accumulated some of the notes from which many of my conclusions were drawn; and typed early drafts of the manuscript. Carolyn A. Wallace, Archivist for the Southern Historical Collection of the University of North Carolina, provided reading space; made the University's collection of plantation papers, diaries, and unpublished manuscripts available and freely offered suggestions that led to valuable sources. Dorothy Briscoe, Reference Librarian at Texas Southern University, gave indispensable aid in securing materials through the University's Hartman Collection and interlibrary loan services. The aid of Kenneth S. Tollett, Dean of the School of Law in Texas Southern University, cannot be overestimated. In addition to giving technical assistance in the selection of legal cases, Dean Tollett also served to prompt inquiry along many lines that otherwise would have been overlooked. Similar acknowledgment must be made of the kindness of Calvin L. Reese, my colleague, who critically reacted to so many of the ideas incorporated in this work. Without the help received from these friends and many others, this work could never have been completed. While such virtues as it may possess must be attributed to their kindness, I must take the blame for its vices. All final decisions are my responsibility; all mistakes are of my own making.

Henry Allen Bullock

Houston, Texas
March 1967

CONTENTS

TABLES

CHARTS

A HISTORY OF
NEGRO EDUCATION
IN THE SOUTH

From 1619 to the Present

I · INTRODUCTION:
A PRELUDE TO CHANGE

In the beginning there was no thought of educating the Negroes; yet the necessity to do so was always present. During the early part of the seventeenth century, Europeans and Africans, caught in the tide of empire, were joined in a system of economic interdependency — a system which would inevitably require that Africans would have to be educated and would aspire to become a part of a society that would encompass the two races.

Inherent in the circumstances under which the two races met was a contradictory motif that would render their relationship unstable for more than three hundred years. Soon after the establishment of the slave regime in the American South, there were set in motion unintentional processes destined to introduce the first of the many educational opportunities that the Negroes were to have prior to the Civil War. While the underground railroad was operating against the institution of slavery, a hidden passage was being created within the system and with the unwitting approval of the master class — a passage through which many of the slaves could gain access to educative experiences and become leaders.

A HIDDEN PASSAGE IN THE EARLY SOUTH

For purposes of the slave economy, no such passage should ever have come into existence. The plantation economy was intended as a completely rational institution in which the relationships between master and slave constituted a model much like that existing between plant and animal species occupying the same territory. These

1

were to have been purely symbiotic relationships, in which each black was to serve as a tool — was to have been used solely for the economic benefit and grandeur of his owner. It was intended, also, that the two races live in a system of economic interdependency devoid of personal sentiment and emotions. With Negroes conceived of as tools and investments, the rational model required that master-class relations be structured almost solely along functional lines: the profitable purchase, production, and utilization of slave labor.

As time passed, an institutional structure designed to serve these rational ends did in fact crystallize throughout the South. A slave code defining the rational relations between master and slave was made a part of the legal structure of every Southern state and was even strengthened — made more impersonal — after the Nat Turner rebellion of 1831. But long before the legal structure had matured, the practices of business enterprisers had become established as "good" plantation policy, and their ways of protecting the capital invested in slaves had become important institutional functions throughout the plantation South.

A few examples may suffice here. Historians have reported freely on the systems of liability insurance and slave care that were installed as means of protecting this capital. There were no gains without risky venture. After a trader had purchased Negroes from Africa or distant parts of the Americas, death could deplete his number during the passage; pirates could seize his ships; or storms could wreck his cargo. Reports of the reality of these risks and indemnification for such losses are found in the journals and account books of some of the most active traders of the eighteenth century.[1] Risk continued on the plantation itself, causing definite health practices to become standard managerial policies. Nothing illustrates these practices more clearly than the contents of the many plantation records now available to historians. In an extensive survey of these records, Ulrich B. Phillips reported that the initial topic contained in them was usually about the care of the slaves.[2] Some well-run plantations had their own hospitals, and there is some evidence that these health centers were more than mere names.[3] William Massie not only recorded his slave population each year but also closely observed their mortality and morbidity rates.[4]

2

Introduction: A Prelude to Change

The managerial practices of Francis Terry Leake of Mississippi indicated a similar concern, and the notation he made in his diary on October 6, 1852, subtly reflected the institutionalization of certain health practices as related to slaves and plantations throughout the South.[5] Owners judiciously recorded health remedies, which were published periodically in the plantation-oriented press.

Another expression of rational business practice appeared in the attempts of planters to utilize their labor efficiently. A complex system of division of slave labor was instituted on every plantation. In particular, there was an attempt to assign labor according to age, sex, physical strength, appearance, and intelligence. Efforts were made to coordinate all roles to take advantage both of a slave's skills and of the nature of the seasons. All this was done in pursuit of the maximum production per unit of slave labor. Also, each master was expected to maintain absolute authority over his slaves. Backed by law, his authority over them extended to the limits of life and death. Within these broad limits he was expected to require and get absolute obedience, loyalty, docility, diligence, and all other patterns of behavior considered essential for profitable production and the survival of the slave economy. The laws of every slave state backed the normative line which he could draw, and every slave was expected to fear the consequences of any deviation from the range of tolerance his master set.[6] These requirements, when executed to the letter of the slave laws, clearly defined the master as the traditional "economic man" at work within the classical capitalistic design. They also set a rigorous sociocultural matrix within which young Negroes were to be socialized and were to become the personality types required by the rational order. Indeed they set the unyielding slave regime that Frank Tannenbaum could contrast so sharply with the more lenient system in the West Indies and the other Americas. They made possible the patterns of "infantile regression" that Roger Bastide attributed to the slave's socialization process, and they encouraged the development of the "Sambo" personality that Stanley M. Elkins finds within the Negro population today.[7]

But there were points at which the rational order was to betray the best intentions of those who created it. Because its rational functions could not adequately satisfy certain emotional needs of the slaveholding class, interracial permissiveness sprang up outside the official structure of that order. Within the boundaries of social tolerance etched by these patterns of permissiveness, many Negroes were able to gain closer and more personal contact with the master class, acquire some degree of literacy, develop an unplanned-for leadership structure, and thereby experience upward mobility within Southern society. As the South passed through various strategic stages in its history, the intensity of this interracial permissiveness waned and was almost extinguished; yet the hidden passage was never completely closed.

At least in part the rational order carried its own defeat. As Walter Firey has so well stated, "Man has the capacity to develop sentimental attachments to almost any object, and sentiment frequently influences behavior to such an extent that questions of utility are disregarded." [8] The dynamics of slave management soon reflected this. Long before the fall of the slave regime, investment practices had lost much of their rationality. At first there were only faint signs that this was happening — that the plantation order would become somewhat laden with emotion and sentiment. However, as early as the 1650s, a pretentious economy under the dominance of the official colonial class had centered in Virginia and slowly spread along the coast. This was an economy that was firmly anchored in large estates and the influence of the colonial leaders who owned them. There was Stag Park, patented by George Barrington, the governor of the Province of North Carolina; there was the estate of Samuel Ashe who was later elected governor of the state. Another sparkling show place was Green Hill, owned by John Ashe who became a leader of the Southern patriots against the British. Many of these estates soon became fabulous show places and glittering examples of the dominance of a colonial class.[9] Although the pattern of class dominance began to change in revolutionary fashion near the close of the seventeenth century, when plantation leadership passed mainly to more rough-and-ready hands,[10] the use of plantation ownership as a symbol of "class" and power had already been set.

Individually, various members of the planter class trusted more and more of their economic future to their ownership of slaves. Many of them, like Guy M. Bryan of Texas[11] and James Crawford, a personal friend of Francis Terry Leake,[12] ventured beyond the boundary of rational judgment. The wheeling-and-dealing activities characteristic of many slave owners of the eighteenth and nineteenth centuries made it most difficult to determine whether the planters or their creditors owned the slaves and the plantations. Public anxiety about this was shown as early as 1738, when in a letter to the *South-Carolina Gazette* a reader expressed the fear that emotional slave buying "may prove the ruin of the Province." [13] The practice, so prevalent among the slaveholding class, of placing the most intelligent and likely of the slave crop in personal service to the master rather than in productive service to help his economy obviously violated the rational model.

As if by stealth, sentimental attachments between masters and selected slaves widened the hidden passage to significant proportions. Ironically, this change was caused by the society's official functions. All the slaves could not be efficiently utilized, as the rational system required, unless they were trained in ways that the system prohibited. As the power of individual planters expanded, many plantations tended to become self-sustaining worlds, and the slaves trained for effective service to the rational order came to have higher value. The food consumed, clothing worn, tools used, and houses inhabited were all produced by slave labor. This type of development caused an increase in the complexity of slave duties, and rising slave prices very quickly reflected this fact. A. T. Walker of North Carolina made over 25 percent profit in his purchase and sale of Burell and Patrick, two slaves who were trained as artisans.[14] On-the-job training programs developed within the formal structure in response to the rise in demand for and to the higher prices elicited in the markets where trained slaves were auctioned. Isaac Croom of Alabama trained his slaves in the construction crafts. His magnificent home, Magnolia Grove, stood as testimony of their building skills.[15] C. W. Tait and Thomas Blackshear of Texas provided opportunities for their slaves to learn a variety of skills. Many carpenters, blacksmiths, weavers, and seamstresses emerged from these training experiences.[16]

The inclination of certain owners to respond to the sheer challenge offered by a slave's brightness of mind and gift of talents gave added impetus to the invasion of the plantation society by sentimentalism. Many masters placed such slaves under the tutelage of master craftsmen. Henry Harris of Clarksdale, Mississippi, was sent by his master to an iron foundry in Tuscaloosa, Alabama, where he learned to mold iron. The slave Gregory, who was reared in Charleston, South Carolina, was observed by his owner to have a love for tools. He was apprenticed to a master carpenter who taught him the skillful use of the hammer and saw.[17] Frederick L. Olmsted noticed cases like these during his travels through the seaboard states. One slave he encountered, called "the watchman" by his owner, was entrusted with keys to all the store provisions of the plantation. He weighed and measured all the rations issued, supervised all the machines, and made all the machinery, including the steam engine.[18] He acquired these skills when his master took him to a steam engine builder and paid $500 to have him trained as a machinist. Records show, however, that production was not always the aim of these training opportunities.[19] The wills of many owners contained provisions for the education of their slaves and occasionally for their manumission.

It was not long before the growing number of highly trained slaves became redundant, exceeding the capacity of many owners to involve them in their productive enterprises. Consequently, these servants were often maintained as status symbols for their owners, who frequently found it necessary to provide some means of holding and supporting them. Out of the pressure of circumstances came a policy of "hiring out" slaves to employers who needed them. Although this policy was legally forbidden by every slave state, it was freely practiced, and instances of prosecution for this violation were extremely rare.[20] Despite continued opposition, the practice of training slaves continued to make the plantation what Booker T. Washington called an "industrial school." [21] What was to become one of the most controversial movements in the entire history of Negro education was actually begun within a system officially committed to the policy that Negroes should not be educated at all.

The informality and permissiveness inherent in these practices reduced the rigors of plantation life and produced leadership within the Negro population. It fostered a higher self-concept among the slaves and, because of the many manumissions that resulted, led to the rise of an aggressive and mildly secure middle class within the free Negro population. Some of the slaves so favored by these educational opportunities managed to develop their own business enterprises. Lydia Maria Child, a former slave in South Carolina, cited one such example in her grandmother, whose talents had been observed and developed by her master.* What was more important, however, was that the permissiveness contributed to the development of a group of skilled workers within the free Negro and slave populations. This fact is clearly evidenced by the number who were employed in skilled occupations during 1848. Using the industrial census of Charleston, Phillips showed that free Negroes were employed in all but eight of the fifty occupations composing the skilled group, and slaves were employed in all but thirteen.[22] Negroes were fairly dominant as carpenters and joiners, barbers, hairdressers, and bankers. Slaves represented between 47 and 67 percent of all such employed workers in the area.

By the opening of the nineteenth century, permissiveness had eroded the plantation society's rational policy, and new educational opportunities had opened for a select group of slaves. As an expression of the emotional needs and rugged individualism of the planter class, the institution of slavery had become infected with a form of indulgence that was eventually to create an educated group of slaves who would supply a leadership on behalf of their own freedom.

A familial pattern that placed household servants in direct personal contact with the master class and outside the direct restrictions of the slave laws developed. And, it should be added, this kind of relaxed sociocultural setting was not infrequently available to many of the slaves on the larger plantations of the South. The practice of keeping some of them close to the "Big House" was common. In the case of *Michan v. Wyatt,* for example, evidence

---

* After Lydia Maria Child's grandmother was trained as a cook and seamstress, she was allowed to go into business for herself and to use the profits to clothe herself and her children. She eventually accumulated enough funds to purchase her freedom. See Lydia Maria Child, *Incidents in the Life of a Slave Girl* (Boston, 1861), p. 12.

showed that Leah Michan was very much attached to certain slaves and reared most of them in the dwelling with her own children. Evidence in the case of *Randall v. Lang* revealed that a slave boy was born and reared in the family of the owner.[23] Some slaves slept in the same room with their owners in order to be handy for any need that might arise. Selected slave girls were the almost constant companions of the little mistresses to whose whims they catered, and body servants were equally inseparable from their masters, who indulged them as a kind of luxury. Although one could hardly build a case for slavery as a bed of roses, it was probably this relaxed setting that prompted Simon Phillips, an ex-slave from the Bryant Watkins' plantation in Alabama, to reflect, "Then there were the special privileges that made it so worthwhile being a servant on the old plantation." [24] W. Austin Steward, a slave for twenty-one years, recalled in 1859 that the slaves of Colonel Alexander were always better fed, better clad, and had greater privileges than any he knew in the Old Dominion. "And, of course," he added, "the patrol had long had an eye on them, anxious to flog some of those 'pampered niggers' who were spoiled by the indulgence of a weak owner." [25]

Historians have been inclined to underrate the sociohistorical significance of these patterns of master-slave relationships. Such relationships were more than instances of sheer physical proximity and the availability of slaves for exploitation by their masters; they carried a degree of personal intimacy that reached beyond the level of blood mixture and miscegenation into the area of cultural diffusion and acculturation. They constituted a way of life that transformed many Negro children into personality types quite unlike those prescribed by the rational order. There was a closeness of mind involved in them and a social nearness which helped give some of these children a special self-image — a feeling of worth and superiority. Slaves of the more wealthy usually referred to themselves as belonging to "quality folks," and established within the Negro American subculture in the South a tradition of looking down upon poorer white people.

In many instances psychological identification with the master class and its high-toned ways was firmly internalized by those slaves

8

who had access to these special experiences. There were actual cases in which some, influenced by persistent intimacy with their owners and their families, became very much like the quality folk with whom they lived. For example, Julie, the slave nurse in the family of William Alexander Hoke, was reared like the other girls of the Hoke family. She was married to a mulatto boy from the same plantation, and the ceremony was held in the Episcopal Church "in a big white-style wedding." [26] Accepted as a family member by all the Hokes, Julie embarrassed the family and fell from grace when she later shouted in a Negro church.

Neatness of dress and elegance of appearance quickly found their way into the value systems of personal servants, for the women who served in personal attendance to a mistress were given sound advice along these lines.[27] Indeed, some of them learned so well that advising the little mistress about her appearance became one of their duties. Assimilation in some instances was so complete that a slave could pass for white under the banner of master-class demeanor unless betrayed by his complexion or someone's knowledge of his condition. A mulatto slave girl purchased at Louisville and reared on the Affleck plantation in Texas ran away to the nearby town of Brenham, where she registered as a white woman. After receiving all the courtesies usually accorded an aristocratic Southern woman, she was pursued by her master and was returned to the bondage from which she had temporarily escaped. She never dropped her aristocratic demeanor, however. Though sold to another family and married off to their servant, she was later freed and lived to serve as hostess to her former master, who visited her at her home in Mississippi.[28] To slaves like these, being white or being special was the only life they really knew. They could not all be "Sambos."

Gradually and inescapably, the indulgence of their masters led many to literacy. Contrary to the implied assumptions of Stanley Elkins and Roger Bastide, personality results not from a one-way impact of a cultural setting upon the individual, who passively reflects its imprint, but from the interplay — a game, so to speak — between the child and those who train him. Many favored slaves wanted to *be* the quality people with whom they identified. They thought that being able to read and write made them such, and they used all the opportunities to become literate that the informal system afforded them. A house servant learned through necessity how to distinguish among the different newspapers his master ordered him to select, and slaves who served as foremen had to learn enough to keep a daily record. More generally, however, some slave children gained literacy through the "play schools" that grew out of the sociable relations maintained with their owner's children. Though starting in play, these schools were often taken seriously by both "teacher" and "pupil." Such was the case on a Mississippi plantation when a planter's son aspired to make scholars out of some of his father's slaves. Five of these slaves learned to read so well that they became ministers.[29] Recalling her life as a girl in Virginia before the Civil War, Letitia Burwell reported that she and her sister operated one of these "schools," and she emphasized the reward her father gave them for teaching arithmetic to the slave boys he was training as mechanics.[30] Richard Sinquefield experienced similar educational advantages through the literary enthusiasm of the white children with whom he played.*

As the spread of antislavery literature among the slaves grew more threatening, the official camp of the plantation order fought back, but the practice of teaching slaves to read and write merely moved underground. In fact, a play school for teaching slaves operated within the household of the Honorable John Fouchereau Grimke, judge of the Supreme Court of South Carolina. His daughters, Sarah and Angelina, took delight in teaching slave children at night and against continued legal opposition. In describing how she operated her school, Sarah reported lightly: "The light was put out, the keyhole secured, and flat on our stomachs before the fire, with spelling books in our hands, we defied the laws of South Carolina."[31]

The spirit of defiance expressed by these children spread to the slaves themselves. Thomas H. Jones pursued the freedom of self through a spelling book which became his constant companion.[32] The literary zeal of Frederick Douglass was nourished in this way.

* An account of these experiences may be found in *Life and Times of Rev. Richard Anderson Sinquefield, 1832–1908* (Nashville, Tenn.: Sunday School Union, 1909), pp. 7–8.

He kept crumbs of bread with which he bribed hungry white boys into giving him lessons from *Webster's Spelling Book*.[33] Thus, the boy who would become one of slavery's most bitter and eloquent enemies was not denied his destiny. Historical literature is replete with cases of slaves who struggled to gain literacy in this way.[34] Old slaves give mixed accounts of these educational escapades.[35] In the experience of some, learning was the expected thing — an apparently formal course of plantation life; for others, it was a forbidden and clandestine undertaking into which only the young would venture.

As various patterns of interracial permissiveness gained a foothold outside the official structure of the planter-dominated society, those anxious to establish schools for Negroes became more bold. Probably paving the way for such a courageous venture was the tolerant attitude that planters themselves took toward the religious education of their slaves. Motivated mainly by the desire to make them more obedient, large planters established Sunday schools for them and quite often required Bible reading as part of a home-study program.[36] There were even attempts, though much later, to institute these practices as a part of the official order. Despite the general fear that literacy would expose the slaves to abolition literature and stimulate revolt within their ranks, a group of Southern religious leaders insisted that, instead, literacy was the potential savior of the slave system. None of these was more persistent than the Reverend George F. Pierce, Bishop of the Methodist Episcopal Church, South.[37] In his sermon before the General Assembly of Georgia on March 27, 1863, he entered the strongest plea made by his colleagues in the interest of the toleration of literacy among the slaves. Although his declaration came late, it still indicates the sentiment that had developed before the Civil War.

Long before this conversion, however, signs that informal permissiveness would result in formal education for the South's Negroes were already abundant. The foreign missions that arose around slavery were never killed; they were allowed to form the nucleus of a movement for formal schooling among free Negroes and slaves. As early as 1620, when the slave trade began, English clergymen had expressed an interest in extending religious training to those "in bondage beyond the seas" and had made some progress in this direction.[38] One century later, the Presbyterians took even bolder steps toward developing religious leadership among the Negroes by making formal training directly available to them. In 1740, Hugh Bryan, a wealthy and deeply pious Presbyterian, opened a Negro school in Charleston. By 1755, other schools had been opened in Virginia, where Presbyterians were teaching the slaves to read and spell.[39] The movement even extended to college training for selected Negroes. Anxious to determine whether or not a Negro was capable of acquiring a college education, Presbyterians selected John Chavis of North Carolina as an experimental subject and sent him to Princeton University. After graduation he became a leading teacher in the South. However, once his school was established, Chavis was forced to make it available only to white children. He can be rightly classified as the first Negro to act as the headmaster of Southern children of aristocratic parentage. Many of his students became great leaders in government and politics. And, although Negro children were denied access to his scholarship, he did prove that Negroes were capable of acquiring a college education and that this kind of education for them could be profitable.

Educational work among the slaves was considerably augmented by other religious groups. Dr. Thomas Bray of England, organizing the Society for the Propagation of the Gospel near the opening of the eighteenth century, raised funds, aggregated teachers, and established schools for slaves and Indians in Charleston, Savannah, and other parts of Georgia.[40] The Southern Quakers soon joined Dr. Bray's associates in providing the rudiments of an educational system under the slave regime. Beginning merely as a missionary gesture aimed at improving the conditions of the slave under bondage, the Friends soon moved to a more liberal position of absolute adherence to the philosophy of radical abolitionism. The years between 1764 and 1785 marked the period of their most aggressive campaign. They established their first school in Virginia, where they began with 108 pupils who stood at a variety of academic levels. They founded a second school at Gravelly Run and by 1808 had instituted a trustee system by which slaves could receive individualized instruction on a familial basis, followed by eventual manumission.[41]

These educational opportunities, like all the others developed for Negroes prior to the Civil War, were neither available to all the slaves nor firmly established as an acceptable part of the official Southern society. They were privileges gained principally by household servants still under the slave regime or by the free Negroes who had escaped it.

Out of this indulgence and stealth there had developed for Negroes a greater trend toward freedom and a leadership that would keep the trend alive, though not always in great force. A free Negro population was allowed to grow up outside the walls that held the slaves. Between 1790 and 1860, this population had increased at rates significantly higher than the slave population.[42] It expanded from 32,523 or 4.7 percent of the total Negro population in the South in 1790 to 258,346 or 6.3 percent in 1860. And most of this increase was concentrated in those areas of the South where informal patterns of interracial permissiveness had been the most prevalent. Considerable interbreeding between the master and slave classes had resulted in a sizable mulatto population that included many who had apparently gained their manumission through the conscience of their white parentage. Some had been freed through master-class indulgence, and, of course, intermarriage between free Negroes had resulted in free births. Notwithstanding its source of origin, however, the free Negro population of the South gradually came to constitute a threat to the region's official way of life.

Of even greater threat was the literate and articulate Negro leadership that permissiveness had allowed to develop. This leadership was sometimes crude and bold, at other times more sophisticated and subtle. But at all times it was able to keep the official society off balance and on a collision course with the antislavery sentiments that were developing both within and outside the South. The Negroes in Charleston, for example, after reading the antislavery debates of the Missouri Compromise, became emboldened by the attacks upon slavery that it implied and revolted in an effort to effect the institution's extermination. They found their leader in Denmark Vasey, an educated Negro who had brought his ideas of freedom from Santo Domingo. They struck against their masters in the bloody insurrection of 1822. Although their attempt was crushed, there were to be others in other years and at other places led by Negroes who had gained some rudiments of education. David Walker, another Negro who had managed to acquire a high degree of literacy under slavery, emerged from the free Negro population of Wilmington, North Carolina, to use his knowledge against the existing regime. He published his *Appeal* in 1829 and through it urged all the slaves of the South to rise up against their masters. In a subtle and prophetic style, he made this promise to those of his people still in bondage: "For although the destruction of the oppressors, God may not effect by the oppressed, yet the Lord our God will bring other destruction upon them, for not infrequently will he cause them to rise up against the others, to be split, divided, and oppress each other, and sometimes to open hostilities with sword in hand." [43] Copies of the *Appeal* were widely distributed among the slaves, causing an increase in their spirit of revolt. This is evidenced by Governor John Forsyth's communication to the Georgia legislature in which he attributed the seriousness of the insurrectionary movement to the distribution of this type of literature.[44] Two years after its distribution, although no evidence of connection has been found, Nat Turner, the mystical and literate slave rebel of Virginia, led his famous insurrection against the slave masters. Despite stringent measures instituted by the formal plantation society, the fire of insurrection continued to smolder, kept alive by various kinds of appeals that were sent into the South by the educated Negroes who had left the area.

Probably the heaviest blow that Negroes struck against slavery came from those slaves who had gained their education under bondage and who had escaped North to join the antislavery movement. Through their personal narratives, the leaders of this movement found ready-made materials for their propaganda machines. William Wells Brown, Thomas H. Jones, Lunceford Lane, Frederick Douglass, Austin Steward, and the Reverend Richard Anderson Sinquefield are examples of those who had acquired their education while slaves and had escaped to serve the antislavery movement

14

in this capacity. The works they published through the antislavery press and the speeches they made from the antislavery platform were used not only as proof that Negroes could learn but also as a dramatization of the evils of slavery that was more graphic than any other type of antislavery literature. The activities of these Negro leaders make one conclusion clear: Many opportunities for the personal emancipation of the Negro American had come into being as early as 1860 with the unintentional help of those who dominated Southern society at that time.

EMERGENCY FUNCTIONS DURING THE CIVIL WAR

With the coming of the Civil War, the Negro's developing educational opportunities moved into a new cycle. A series of historical events began to push them from underground and to establish them as an official part of the new order imposed upon the South after its military defeat. But here, again, the change was not the result of initial intent.

As one looks back over these decades, it is apparent that the trend was operative in the South as early as the middle of the last century. Even by that time the continuous invasion of the official system by unofficial permissiveness had weakened the formal order and rendered it vulnerable to the pressures of a war in the making. Out of the rationality of societal organization had come an incompatibility between North and South that would make violent conflict between the two regions inevitable. Their diverse courses of economic development had removed all bases for interregional companionship at the equalitarian level.[45] The credit system upon which the South's agrarian economy had rested was itself the result of Northern industrial profits, causing the major portion of the plantation class to resent this dependency strongly. The system of slave labor so important to the Southern economy was causing the nation's tide of European immigrants to veer away from the South westward in the direction of national expansion. These newcomers, therefore, were continuing to swell the population of the free states and to create an imbalance in congressional representation unfavorable to slavery. The South's needs, in general, were radically different from those of the North; its position in national politics had not been strong enough to force through constitutional processes legislation favorable to its agrarian economy. Lacking the political power to effect relief, it turned to the force of arms.

But when "the irrepressible conflict" did occur, as William H. Seward had predicted it would, the conflict between the South's rational economic policy and the emotional needs of the slaveholding class backfired even further. The strong individualistic and informal character of the South, which had subtly grown up outside the official structure, had weakened the society for the ordeal that was ahead. Southerners had been relatively free of governmental interference, except for the responsibility of paying those taxes that were essential for the support of minimal public functions. They found it difficult to accept the idea that any government, at home or abroad, had the right to invade their social life or to regulate their economic interests. This attitude strengthened public suspicions of every step taken by the Confederacy toward organization for war through the extension of its power.[46] Despite the government's reluctance to cut into the people's customary liberties, the pressure of war made curtailment necessary and triggered the undisciplined individualism of Southern society.

Discord within the Cabinet of Jefferson Davis spread to the entire Confederacy, undermining the solidarity of purpose that had given it birth. The rapport that had developed between the wealthier and poorer classes gradually gave way under the strain of military conflict. As the hardships of war grew, small farmers, who had accepted their responsibilities with enthusiasm, became distrustful of the ruling class whose interests they felt were mainly being protected.[47] The exemption of slave owners and overseers from military service, and the tendency for many of the wealthier class to hire substitutes to take their places in the Confederate Army, served to justify a distrust and to generate even greater discord among the poorer Southern people, who had begun to call the conflict a "rich man's war." [48] Observing this breakdown of the morale once contained in the Southern class structure, William Howard Russell, Special Correspondent for the London *Times,* reported from New

Orleans on May 24, 1861, that military enthusiasm was proportional to the property interests of the various classes.[49] However, not all of those composing the dominant planter class remained firmly committed to the war effort. James Lusk Alcorn of Mississippi, one of the South's leading planters, certainly displayed instability in the letters he wrote to his wife, Amelia, at the early stage of the war.[50] On November 25, 1861, he advised her that the cause of the South was lost, and less than one month later he revealed to her his plans for liquidating his wealth, fleeing to New York, and leaving his homeland to its unfortunate fate.

When the official Southern society lost its control over the Negroes, a new set of problems arose. Without any intentional relation to education, the sequence began with a large-scale movement of the slaves away from the plantations and toward areas which to them symbolized greater freedom. The Emancipation Proclamation, which became final on January 1, 1863, merely added momentum to a tide of bondsmen already in motion. Hordes of wandering slaves formed one of the most picturesque aspects of the turmoil that resulted from the Civil War. "Many grotesque scenes were witnessed," wrote Elizabeth Botume of her days among the fleeing slaves of South Carolina. "When the steamer, *John Adams,* anchored at one of the plantations, the Negroes rushed along carrying every conceivable thing on their heads that could possibly be placed there." [51] Vincent Colyer, describing the refugee situation in North Carolina, reported that slaves from neighboring plantations fled in groups of 100 at a time.[52] By the summer of 1865, masses of Negroes had shifted to the cities. More than twenty thousand had reached Washington, D.C.; the great exodus had reached the plantations of Mississippi; and all the larger cities of the South had been overrun by deserting Negroes seeking the protection of invading Union forces.

These refugee concentrations introduced problems that the Union forces did not anticipate and therefore were not prepared to handle. Basically the problem was that of securing support for the hungry and destitute masses who had been uprooted by the change. The slaves, as a result of emancipation, could no longer depend on their former owners. The law that freed them also freed their masters.

Some owners, shedding their responsibility for the freedmen's plight, found consolation in this fact, and the *Southern Cultivator* so stated their sentiments in 1865.[53] The problem of support was made even more acute by the condition of the refugees themselves. All who deserted the plantations were not prepared for the ordeals of freedom that awaited them. Many among the early migrants were virtually helpless — either too old or too young to care for themselves. In addition, some were physically disabled, and even those able to work were so disoriented by their newly found freedom that they, too, required extended emergency care.

The problem in some way provided the basis for its own solution — the stimulus that would call forth leaders who would foster the organization of activities against it either because of the compulsions of their official responsibilities or because of the dictates of their moral conscience. In fact, both of these forces went into operation at the same time. The confusion resulting from the concentration of refugees within Union lines made some kind of official action essential to the successful prosecution of the war. And not without its blessing was the depth of misery which the sheer concentration of deprived masses brought into bold relief. The concentration generated a philanthropic concern that probably would not have developed so rapidly had those sharing a common misery remained scattered and uncounted.

Organization for the emergency grew informally and outside the more rational provisions of military design. Admittedly, however, the initial leadership in planning for the security of the refugees came from the Union military structure. Union generals faced the problem in its immediacy since it hampered their military operations, and they sought rather diligently to remove this obstacle by stimulating the public to accept the responsibility for meeting the pressing needs of the recently freed slaves. Apparently they did this well, through a series of emotional appeals. On February 6, 1862, when the emergency was in its earliest stage, General W. T. Sherman issued a declaration from Hilton Head, advising that the condition of the blacks in the vast area of his command called for immediate action on the part of "a highly favored and philanthropic people." Planting the idea from which a new educational movement for

Negroes would develop, he added: "To relieve the government of a burden that may hereafter become unsupportable, and to enable the blacks to support and govern themselves in the absence of their disloyal guardians, a suitable system of cultivation and instruction must be combined with one providing for physical wants." [54] Although many such appeals would be voiced by Union generals,[55] this one alone was to pierce the public conscience deeply enough to arouse the nation and to stimulate the development of an extensive emergency organization outside the military regime that was imposed upon a defeated South.

News of the various appeals spread rapidly to various corners of the North, and many people, even those who had been indifferent toward the antislavery cause, allowed themselves to become actively involved in fighting the conditions created by the emergency.[56] Benevolent societies sprang up in quick succession to form a complex of freedmen associations that reached such cities as Boston, New York, Philadelphia, Cincinnati, and Chicago in 1862–1863. The functions they carried out so well consisted mainly of providing clothing, food, money, religious leaders, and teachers for the refugees. Although these groups were nonsectarian, they were joined by church organizations that were to extend the program to include the freedmen's school system then in its germinal stage. Leading the entire group of these religious organizations was the American Missionary Association, which had been incorporated in 1849 for the purpose of operating Christian missions and educational institutions at home and abroad. The Baptist Church, North, was another of the many religious units that entered the field of freedmen's relief at this time. Its Home Mission Society, later to create many colleges for Negroes, was established in 1832 in order to preach the gospel in destitute regions. This society also entered upon the difficult problem of supplying trained leaders for work among the refugees. Joined by the Freedmen's Aid Society and the General Conference of the Methodist Episcopal Church, it helped dispense a great deal of money and many supplies through the Union Army.

The first phase of the emergency program was only indirectly related to education; by force of circumstance the program had to deal with problems of more immediate concern. Mainly, these were the conditions growing out of the quality of dependency so characteristic of many of the refugees. As a basic strategy designed to render them self-supporting, refugees were introduced to the free labor market through employment on the plantations then operating under Union control. General Nathaniel P. Banks, clearly specifying work conditions, announced that all employment of freedmen was to be on the basis of absolute freedom and gauged to prepare them for an independence "as complete as that enjoyed by any class of people." [57] The various organizations supplying relief supported this philosophy by requiring the freedmen to earn their livelihood like other people, but they also required that schools and churches be provided for them.[58] In a concentrated drive along these lines, therefore, many persons from the North were commissioned as teachers and superintendents for work among the freedmen. At the call of General Edward L. Pierce and the New England Freedmen's Society, numerous educators joined in the execution of the historic Port Royal Experiment in March 1862. They engaged heartily in the task of developing the economy, directing the Negroes toward economic independence, and organizing schools in the area. Such, in summary, was the general nature of the emergency program found operating wherever masses of refugees had concentrated. To Northern missionaries it was a remedy but not a cure.

After three years the program began to have a positive effect in two very important ways. First, there was an important increase in the proportion of freedmen who were self-supporting.[59] Although there was definitely an inadequacy of land in North Carolina, for example, the freedmen there earned $275,000 in 1865 through their labor on cotton and turpentine plantations. Of the 1,593 Negroes at Beaufort and Morehead City, North Carolina, less than 300 were receiving government assistance at that time. And Colonel George H. Thomas, Commissioner of Freedmen for the area, reported that only 3,000 of the 346,000 in the state were being supported by the government.

There were also signs that the program was encouraging a greater degree of responsibility among the former slaves.[60] The superintendent of the Department of Tennessee and Arkansas gave recognition of this in his report of 1864. He called this responsiveness a fine "public spirit" since it broke through brilliantly following his Order 63.[61] This order had imposed a temporary wage tax upon able-bodied workers for the support of the sick and dependent. The freedmen had gladly accepted the tax as another sign that the government was recognizing them as citizens. The spirit of responsibility extended to incorporate the development of relief measures by the freedmen themselves. Several Negroes who were ex-soldiers maintained a labor agency in Kentucky.[62] They boasted of sending laborers to almost every occupation in the state. They secured 3,000 jobs for Negroes during the first half of 1869, and celebrated the achievement with a "big thanksgiving dinner" on August 20 of that year.

Also helping were those Negroes who had received special training within the institution of slavery. Town life afforded many employment opportunities to those who had acquired the skills demanded by urban economies, and towns had long been a refuge for the free or manumitted Negro who had managed to forge ahead. The seamstress of the Hull family of Athens, Georgia, moved with her daughter into the Hull household and took in enough sewing to support the family.[63] Throughout the South there were Negroes who supported themselves and at times their former masters by the small businesses they had learned to organize and manage. Their economic independence had become a badge of freedom; it heralded the emergence of a middle class around whom an even greater drive toward self-respect and individual emancipation was to be developed.

FREEDMEN'S EDUCATION UNDER UNION GUNS

Nevertheless, the missionaries who worked among the freedmen held a strong conviction that emergency measures were not enough. They believed that some permanent plan should be installed and made an official part of the new order. They felt that this plan should be a school system of the New England style. Working al-

most independently of each other, though with the informal blessings of Union generals, these missionaries had tried the educative
process at the formal level and had found it more in keeping with
their missionary zeal. Consequently, they constantly worked with
Union generals to include formal education in a reform plan that
would create a medium through which Negroes could pass from
legal to natural equality of citizenship. Their opportunity came
when faults of the emergency program reached the point of public
concern: Some elements of corruption had seeped into the program,
and local officials, misusing the residual authority left them by military defeat, had not always dealt justly with the freedmen.

Nowhere were these faults more brutally exposed than in the report made to the Secretary of War by the Freedmen's Inquiry Commission.[65] As public awareness sharpened, more definite steps were
taken by the Union government to revise the program's structure
and harness its functions. The commission had recommended the
creation of an agency that would centralize the responsibility for
care of the freedmen. Discussions of this recommendation took
place in and out of Congress, and definite proposals were made from
January 12, 1863, to March 5, 1865. Congress passed an act creating
such an agency one month before the close of the war.[66] The agency
was the Bureau of Refugees, Freedmen, and Abandoned Lands.

The historical significance of this action was twofold. First, it
actually did meet some of the faults of the relief program; it made
the care of the freedmen a part of the official structure by which
Southern society was then being controlled. More specifically, it
committed the United States to the job of caring for the freedmen
and thereby placed the agency, commonly called the Freedmen's
Bureau, in the business of protecting the Negroes against mistreat-
ment by local officials. It located the Bureau within the War Department and gave it the responsibility of supervising all subjects
relating to refugees and freedmen of the rebel states. General Oliver
O. Howard, the first commissioner appointed by the President, immediately mapped a program aimed at securing "health, sustenance,
and legal rights for refugees" and at providing them with "the foundations of education." And so special care for the Negroes passed

into Federal hands and to the official structure of the society composing the South's military commands.

From the point of view of the Negro's educational opportunities, however, the act was of even greater historical significance. It was to coordinate the many relief programs in operation and was to give official backing to teachers of the benevolent societies, who in their persistent efforts had been trying desperately to establish a complete school system for the freedmen. By this official step, Northern teachers of Negroes in the South had gained the protection of Union guns. Although the protection would be challenged by an active spirit of rebellion that military defeat failed to kill, it would remain long enough for the freedmen's school system to become an institutional fact in the South.

What was the social character of the missionaries into whose hands the destiny of the former slaves had fallen? Were they sheer opportunists, or were they religious leaders seriously committed to the cause of their spiritual profession? These questions cannot be sloughed off but must be faced because of the many charges and countercharges that have since found their way into historical literature. Traditionalists' interpretations of the Reconstruction period present Northern missionaries and others who worked among the freedmen as persons aiming to humiliate Southern people by placing them at the mercy of former slaves; they charge them with imposing goals that ranged far beyond the freedmen's aspirations and with engaging in activities that actually blocked adjustments which the South either had instituted through its own initiative or would have done so without outside interference.[67] Historical records seem to best support the revisionist interpretations,[68] for there is evidence that the activities of Union generals and Northern missionaries were quite consistent with their expressed intentions. When in 1862 General Ulysses S. Grant appointed one of his chaplains, the Reverend John Eaton, "to superintend the colored people" throughout the area of his command, the chaplain straightway turned to the job of building a school system for those placed in his care. His system became the largest and most effective in the military district of the South.[69] On taking the helm of the Freedmen's

Bureau, General Howard once again publicly expressed his aspirations for the freedmen in terms of adequate formal education. "Education," he wrote, "underlies every hope of success for the freedmen."

But the direct responsibility for establishing the freedmen's educational system in the South was to rest with the strongly motivated people who composed the active teams of the benevolent and religious groups of the North. They were by moral orientation and training peculiarly prepared to shoulder the responsibility. They were in the main devout Christians. The spiritual aspirations that fed their missionary zeal also kept alive their antislavery belief that teaching the Negro to read and understand the Bible was absolutely essential to his religious and moral development. They were largely trained in New England colleges and universities and were probably some of the best prepared of the nation's small supply of common school teachers. They had interpreted the Emancipation Proclamation in terms of what it was supposed to mean — the freedom of Negroes to care for themselves and participate in a free society like other people.

Tradition had set no sharp and unfavorable image of the Negro in their minds. Their faith in his educability was unaffected by his previous condition. With abundant zeal, they often wrote as did Sarah G. Stanley, a teacher of the American Missionary Association: "The progress of the scholars is in all cases creditable and in some remarkable. . . . How richly God has endowed them, and how beautifully their natures would have expanded under a tender and gentle culture." [70] In general, the basic aspiration of Northern teachers was to effect the freedmen's transition to the state of absolute freedom through an educational institution of the only kind they knew — one of the New England style.

Contrary to the traditionalists' interpretations, also, the educational movement was not imposed upon Negroes by overzealous Northerners. It seems that wherever teachers carried their seeds of knowledge, they always found some fertile soil in which to plant them. They found in their Negro charges not only a desire for literacy but also a willingness to endure the hardships necessary to attain it. Years of servitude had generated an intense desire for knowledge among the freedmen who had come to them with some degree of literacy.

As the opportunities for formal education appeared on the horizon of the free world that began to open before them, the freedmen placed more pressure upon their supporters for the establishment of schools. General Banks encountered this pressure in Louisiana, where Negro leaders when asked what they most desired as a means of improving themselves put education foremost among their expressed wishes. Growing impatient with the slower development of educational opportunities in Alabama, Negro leaders published an appeal in the *Selma Times* on December 30, 1865, asking their friends and former masters to supply them with schools and teachers. After commissioners of education persistently reported this urgency expressed by the Negroes, the Freedmen's Bureau announced that the Negroes' desire for education had not been overestimated.

The foundation for a freedmen's school system was strong. With strong and obvious motivations had come white and Negro teachers whose past deeds in the field of Negro education left no question of their sincerity. They were of three kinds. First, there were those who through sheer courage and moral commitment had managed to maintain schools for Negroes throughout the crisis. One such educator, found in Savannah, Georgia, when the Union Army moved in, was a Negro woman whom tradition knows only as "Miss Deaveaux." She had been teaching a private school in the same building since 1838. Although quite advanced in years, she was still teaching with great earnestness and zeal.[71] Her stories of how she had carried out her work in secret, eluding for more than a quarter of a century "the lynx-eyed vigilance of the slave-holders," adequately reflected the tenacity of the leadership that kept the Negro's hidden passage open until revolutionary changes could bring it from underground. Many of her former students, then scattered throughout the South, were ready to join her in organizing a new educational system for the freedmen.

Another pioneer teacher was Mrs. Mary D. Price. When in April 1862, the guns of Farragut transferred the city of New Orleans from rebel to national rule, she and her school formed a base from which the freedmen's educational movement could be launched in that area. With her husband and little money she had moved to the city from Ohio in 1858 in response to a strong impulse to teach colored people in the South.[72] Threatened by signs placed before her door reading "death to nigger teachers," Mrs. Price, like many others of her spiritual breed, had persevered courageously until change could free her anxieties.

Second, some educators on their own initiative had started schools for Negroes during the emergency. The work of Miss L. Humphrey represents this group. In the autumn of 1862 she opened an evening school at Nashville, Tennessee, using a rod as a persuader and the "word system" as a curriculum.[73] Of the rod that striped the backs of many of her best pupils, one said, "Not once did I think this rod could ever point out to me the words of eternal life." Miss Humphrey later put the school in the hands of one of her best pupils and in November 1862 opened another just below the city. Like many of the others who had joined her in this work, she developed many Negro teachers for the emergency schools and the developing system.

Third, a group was formed by those educators who responded to the appeals of Union generals by setting up schools. The first of these schools opened at Fortress Monroe in Virginia in September 1861 under the leadership of Mrs. Mary Peake, an intelligent Christian woman born of a Negro mother and a white father — "an Englishman of rank and culture." [74] Through her readiness, the first Negro school of the slave states to have the legal authority and protection of Union guns was taught by a Negro woman.

Through the inspiration provided by the efforts of dedicated educators like these, "a favored and philanthropic people" were moved to supply the funds by which a freedmen's educational system could be supported in the South. At least we know that the funds were supplied. Some came in response to appeals by Northern religious groups which circulated calls for help everywhere and created subsidiary organizations through which aid was channeled to those working directly with the freedmen's schools. The New York Yearly Meeting of the Friends had great success along these lines. During 1863, contributions from the Quakers alone amounted to more than $20,000 in money and $19,000 in clothing.[75] Using a similar campaign, the National Freedmen's Relief Association met with even greater success.[76] Including all supplies and money sent to various centers where freedmen's education was going on, the association had contributed over $200,000 by June 1865. The ever-present American Missionary Association had given $240,000 by that time, and other church organizations had made the financial return even greater. Of the sixty-five benevolent societies organized to support Negro education between 1846 and 1867, financial receipts from sixteen are known.[77] These few, alone, contributed $3,933,278 to freedmen's education from 1862 to 1874.

Adding to the growing support was the Freedmen's Bureau. During its first year the Bureau derived $1,865,646 from the sale of crops and confiscated Confederate property and from school taxes and tuition.[78] Congressional appropriations for the period from 1866 to 1870 amounted to $11,084,750. Of the total amount obtained, $5,145,124 went to support the freedmen's schools. Joined in a common endeavor, benevolent societies and the Union government gave the schools an economic foundation whereby the goals of Northern teachers and their Negro teaching associates could be reached with greater ease.

In all fairness to the freedmen, it must be said that they carried a significant share of their own burden. They contributed $672,989 in taxes and tuition through the Bureau and donated approximately $500,000 through their church organizations.[79] In doing this, Negroes established a practice that was to be repeated less than a half century later: the tendency to match funds given in the interest of establishing schools for them.

In all fairness, it also must be recorded that they were limited in what they could do. Many of them were working for a share of the crops they produced, and most of the planters for whom they worked were unwilling to advance the amount necessary to support a teacher. However, some of the planters were far more cooperative. They advanced the money and charged the cost to the freedmen; other planters gave the teachers board and lodging, trusting to a good crop to pay their salaries at the end of the year. It seems only fair to say that some white Southerners did help. Despite apparent poverty, 1867 records show that freedmen of Louisiana, Tennessee, and Virginia had sustained forty-six schools entirely, contributed to the support of forty-two others, and had purchased thirty-three buildings — all through their own resources.[80] Of equal importance is the fact that they afforded sources of spiritual support and overt expression of faith without which not even the missionaries, with all their religious zeal, could have sustained interest.

These means of financial support gradually evolved into a series of endowed sources through which the schools could operate as an institutional system. As the Freedmen's Bureau neared its end, funds from the benevolent societies and religious groups grew larger. Negroes themselves became more economically secure in their freedom; more of them could pay the tuition necessary to keep their children in private schools, and their churches could contribute more to the maintenance of their educational institutions. Out of the benevolence of many people, therefore, came financial backing sufficient to support schools for Negroes until the system of free public education could be organized to give them relief.

Against the background of a developing financial structure, the institutionalization of the freedmen's educational system slowly began to take shape. First came the common schools. Beginning on the sea coast, an organizational scheme of schools spread inland to become an established part of the official society of a defeated South. The schools established in Virginia at Fortress Monroe, Norfolk, Portsmouth, Newport News, and on the plantations in their vicinity gradually gained some degree of stability. Reports of April 1864 revealed that more than three thousand pupils were enrolled in them and were receiving instruction from fifty-two teachers, including five Negroes. The organization swept southward. The night schools of the American Missionary Association operating at Wilmington were instructing eight hundred pupils at this time; and Francis Cardozo, a Negro of high education who had several years of teaching experience in the North,* had a school operating smoothly at Charleston.[81] The year 1865 saw the establishment of schools for Negroes as distant as the Southwest, where they had

---

* Only a very few of the Negroes who had gained an education under slavery and escaped North returned South to aid in the freedman's educational movement.

begun to operate at Antioch and Mount Zion Baptist churches and at Trinity Methodist Church in Houston.[82] Gradually white children began attending the freedmen's schools. They were taught in the same room and received the same attention as the Negro children.

From its small beginnings in 1861 and with the new push given by the Freedmen's Bureau, the school system was virtually completed in its institutional form some eight years later. Fourteen Southern states had established 575 schools by 1865, and these schools were employing 1,171 teachers for the 71,779 Negro and white children in regular attendance. The schools were not equally available to all the children of the South. Those of Louisiana, Virginia, and North Carolina were most greatly favored. These three states possessed approximately half the schools, teachers, and pupils in the region at this time.[83] In Louisiana, where General Banks' work had resulted in a very highly organized system of education, over 60 percent of all the Negro children from five to twelve years of age were enrolled in some school.[84] No other Southern state had an educational system that touched so many children. Even within these favored states, however, the children in the cities fared best. Nevertheless, the total number of freedmen enrolled and in regular school attendance had reached 114,522 by 1869.

As the stabilization process moved along, teachers became more and more preoccupied with the job of building academic curricula. At first, the methods and programs of instruction were varied, shaped almost individually according to the needs of each pupil and the ingenuity of each teacher. Later, many teachers began grouping students according to their reading levels and tended to move each through stages according to the speed and nature of his progress.[85]

The search for workable methods of instructing the pupils continued, and by the close of 1865 some degree of curricular standardization had evolved. Older schools like those at Beaufort, South Carolina, had become graded, and teachers were pursuing their work systematically.[86] The curricula continued to converge, finding common characteristics around reading, writing, grammar, geography, and arithmetic — the usual three Rs. But some mention should be made of number work, which was organized to serve a dual purpose. It was to supply mental discipline as well as to provide a practical skill. In general, one could say that the freedmen's school curriculum was designed to give Negro children the same kind of education given the white. It was classical in purpose, like the schools of New England.

Although they aimed to give Negroes a general training, the teachers were quite conscious of the special needs circumstance had imposed upon them. Here and there signs of this awareness showed through the methods that blanketed school operations. Much time was spent in the development of habits of industry through varied experiences. Curricula were sprinkled with nonliterary subjects. Needlework for the girls and woodwork for the boys were the most popular courses of the manual arts. Some schools emphasized these more than others, and some institutions were established specifically to teach the industrial arts.

The program as a whole was a powerful force in acculturation. It marked the point in history when Negroes began to be exposed to basic elements of the white man's values on a mass basis. Incidental to the sharp conflict between the old South that had been defeated and the new South that was being built under military rule, the acculturation process was carried to a personal level. Helping the process, of course, was the strong concern the teachers held for their pupils and the communities in which they lived. The teachers emphasized character and personality development in their pupils, and they tried to stimulate growth along these lines through personal contacts with the children.[87] But the social pressure to which teachers of Negroes were exposed also served to reduce the social distance between them and their charges. Often by community pressure as well as choice, Northern teachers kept largely away from whites as they went about their work. They were very close to Negro family life; they supplied a goodly portion of the leadership which Negro churches enjoyed; and there were times when Negro pupils lived in homes with them. This close contact gave a particular slant to the socialization of some Negro children, causing the development of qualities of gentility not prevalent in the Negro population before that time. Evidence is abundant that the freedmen's school experiences, at both the formal and informal levels, had a significant effect upon the children. Five years after the schools began to stabilize, the personalities of the children showed signs of changing, and illiteracy among the Negroes showed a definite decline.[88] Enthusiastic reports of these changes came from all corners of the South.

It was not long before the need for higher education among the freedmen became evident. It became obvious, too, that the supply of Northern teachers was inadequate and that even the number then available could not be expected to last. Therefore the need for types of schools in which Negro teachers could be trained became apparent. The Freedmen's Bureau, attempting to meet this need, influenced the establishment of normal schools, where Negroes could learn "the simplest elements of the teaching arts." Schools of this class came into existence at Norfolk, Charleston, New Orleans, and Nashville.

A natural process of segregation had set in as Negroes concentrated to compose racial communities in the various towns and cities. The inadequacy of leadership for the communities became apparent, and those directly responsible for the freedmen's welfare began visualizing higher institutions in which Negro preachers, doctors, lawyers, and others of a professional class could be trained along with potential teachers.

Before the freedmen's educational program reached its five-year mark, benevolent societies aided by the Freedmen's Bureau had begun to establish a system of colleges and universities which, under the rigors of reality, were to mature and become the Negro American's main avenue to higher education and more natural emancipation. The work was begun by the American Missionary Association, which in 1865 established Fisk University at Nashville, Tennessee, and Talladega College at Talladega, Alabama. At the same time, leaders of the association were also at work in other areas of the South. There was then begun the pioneer work which formed the basis for what now exists as the Atlanta University complex. The Reverend Frederick Ayer and his wife arrived in Atlanta from Bell Prairie, Minnesota, around November 15, 1865, and joined later by Rosa and Lucy Kinney, they took over the

Jenkins Street school, which two former slaves had been operating for Negro children. A second school, called the "Car Box," was later established on Ellis Street when the association purchased a railroad car for $310 to serve as a building. Additional structures were developed through association funds until the status of what was conceived of as a university was reached. Much is owed to Asa Ware, a Yale graduate whose leadership secured a charter for the fledgling university through the Superior Court of Georgia in 1867, and who went on to create a strong school that would open "opportunities of the highest advantages" to all.[89]

By the time Atlanta University had gained its legal status as an institution of higher learning, the American Missionary Association had already turned its attention to more extensive operations in this field. It had envisioned the Hampton Normal and Agricultural Institute of Virginia.[90] Inspiration to found the institute reached as far back as the time when the Union Army advanced upon Richmond and first made contact with the pitiable conditions suffered by the slaves whom it liberated. General S. C. Armstrong was later sent to Hampton as a representative of the Freedmen's Bureau to relieve the situation and adjust the difficulties that had developed there between the races. Finding an assortment of Negroes there who were basically wards of the government, he set about organizing the people into an effective community. His first step was to create a program whereby Negro teachers and leaders might be properly trained. This program actually marked the inception of Hampton Institute. In 1867, the association purchased "Little Scotland," a small plantation of 125 acres on the Hampton River, as a site for the school. From a manual labor school that he had been operating in the Hawaiian Islands, General Armstrong cut the pattern for this institute. His efforts were guided by a four-pronged educational concept. He wanted to make the Negroes of service to themselves and whites, to dignify human labor by reinforcing it with intelligence, to develop a sense of responsibility within each pupil by giving him specific tasks to perform, and to saturate the entire program with useful forms of manual training. He held to these ideals because he believed that the future role of the Negro was that of an industrial worker with strong moral and Christian principles.

Under Armstrong's leadership, Hampton Institute opened in 1868 with two teachers and fifteen pupils; and two years later, the Virginia Legislature granted it a charter. With support from the Freedmen's Bureau and from Northern philanthropists who virtually fell in love with the experiment, Hampton became the other horn of an educational dilemma that was to face Negro leaders for more than a half century. It introduced the idea of vocational education for Negroes and attributed to this type of training a value superior to that offered by the liberal arts colleges that were also being established at this time. Those interested in the advancement of Negro education would be placed in conflict by the two styles of training: They would debate the merits of one as against the other and find that accepting either would rob them of some advantage which the other offered.

The work of the association in the field of higher education for Negroes was joined by that of the American Baptist Home Mission Society. With special emphasis on training for religious leadership, the society established Wayland Seminary at Washington, D.C., in 1864, Richmond Theological Seminary in the following year, and later combined the two institutions to constitute Virginia Union University.[91] It helped establish Morehouse College, Shaw University, and other institutions that were to foster a more highly trained religious leadership for the Negro communities.[92]

The Methodist Episcopal Church likewise moved into the field of producing leadership by establishing colleges for freedmen in other strategic areas of the South. It founded Walden College, which later became Meharry Medical College, at Nashville in 1865 and had already created Claflin University at Orangesburg, South Carolina, shortly after the Civil War. These moves merely foreshadowed the great work in the education of Negroes that was still to be done by this religious organization.

Although most of these colleges were offering high school work during this period, one was established mainly for the purpose of catering to those who had been prepared for collegiate and professional training. This was Howard University at Washington, D.C., an institution conceived at an assembly of the Monthly Concert of Prayer for Missions held at the First Congregational Church in

Washington on November 19, 1866. On the following evening, ten persons assembled at the home of H. A. Brewster and decided unanimously to establish an institution of higher learning in that city. It was first decided that the school should be named the Howard Theological Seminary in honor of General O. O. Howard, but in January 1867 the idea was enlarged, and the name was changed to Howard University, an institution whose doors would be open to all races and to members of both sexes. Application for a charter was made to the Congress of the United States in February of that year and was approved by President Andrew Johnson the following month.

Gradually the university began to take shape. The normal and preparatory department opened on May 1, 1867, with four white girls as students. They were children of the trustees. The Reverend Edward F. Williams, a graduate of Yale College and Princeton Theological Seminary was appointed principal. Although the university began operation in a leased frame structure, the incorporators soon secured 150 acres of land for $150,000. With the aid of the Freedmen's Bureau and other sources of income, dormitories were built, and the plant was rendered free of debt by 1869. The theological department began operating the following September. November saw the establishment of a medical department, the beginning of a pharmacy department, and the opening of a general hospital. The law department opened in January 1869 with six students. Five years after the first students were admitted, the university had developed nine departments: normal and preparatory, music, theology, military, industrial, commercial, college, law, and medicine.[93] When General Howard assumed his position as the first president of the institution, the main divisions of a germinal university were available to him for future development.

In the main it can be concluded that change in Southern race relations is not a new phenomenon. The social fermentation caused by the presence of Negroes in the region during its early history enhanced an unintentional development of their educational opportunities and an increase in their social position among Southern white people. Through needs generated by the inadequacies of the efforts to maintain the interracial *status quo,* a hidden passage to education and freedom for the slaves was able to persist until the collapse of the official Southern society could bring it into the open. The freedmen's schools established within the official structure of the new order nourished the Negro's educational aspirations and provided the race with guidelines for its relations with the new state governments.

II · THE RISE OF PUBLIC SCHOOLS AND EQUAL EDUCATIONAL OPPORTU- NITIES IN THE SOUTH

Despite the fine services rendered by the Union government and the benevolent societies in providing freedmen with educational opportunities, there had to develop a more permanent institutional structure through which these opportunities could be continued. The historical process making this continuation possible, as before, involved activities that aimed to solve immediate problems but incidentally gave impetus to further development.

Impermanence, a condition that made the go-ahead necessary, was inherent in the freedmen's school system. The Union government could not remain in the business of supplying special guardianship to the former slaves forever. No constitutional provision justified it, and the rights reserved for the states could not be continuously invaded. The financial resources of the benevolent societies, although adequate to meet the emergent needs of freedmen and even sufficiently permanent to support some schools in perpetuity, were not capable of sustaining a private educational system for four million people. Therefore, permanent support for Negro education had to come through public funds.

Even here, although without official intention, conditions were to the Negro's advantage. A commitment to public schools had caught the fancy of some, partly because they believed education to be the Negro's vehicle to economic independence and moral maturity and partly because many had concluded that education

36

for all Southern children was better than education for only some. The many Negroes who had been attending the freedmen's schools had inspired a creative type of concern for the white children whom they had begun to leave behind. Also, the need for reconstructing the various Southern states still existed. Governments of the slave states had to be reborn because this was the condition upon which these rebellious states could rejoin the nation. Through the immediacy of such needs as these, public education for all Southern children crept in and settled at the equalitarian level of the reconstructed Southern society. Although the course of development of this new educational movement was circuitous and fraught with many blockages and frustrations, its momentum was never completely halted.

PRESIDENTIAL TOLERANCE

Presidential Reconstruction turned out to be unwittingly creative. This executive policy, by catering to the traditional needs of a people still in rebellion, virtually invited the South to exercise a control over the Negroes and their education which would exceed the range of tolerance set by Congress.

Begun by Lincoln and carried through by Andrew Johnson, Presidential Reconstruction showed a decided leniency toward the region. It communicated the idea that the South could exercise much of its own will in dealing with the Negro problem. Lincoln himself left many loopholes in his policy and etched a zone of great latitude within which white Southerners were left free to act. This was clearly expressed in his Amnesty Proclamation of December 8, 1863,[1] and in his letter to Governor Michael Hahn of Louisiana on March 13, 1864, when he proposed a limitation of Negro suffrage.[2]

Andrew Johnson showed no less leniency toward the seceded states. His amnesty of May 29, 1865, included more exceptions in qualifying for readmission to the Union, but he granted more pardons to those who had been involved in the rebellion. His position on Negro suffrage favored the preservation of the *status quo,* as expressed in the interview he granted G. L. Stearns on October 3, 1865. "It would not do to let the Negro have universal suffrage now," he said, "it would breed a war of races." [3] Although this position softened as the various constitutional conventions went into assembly, little attention was given his advice along these lines.[4] Through Governor William L. Sharkey of Mississippi, Johnson advised the various Southern states that the election franchise should be extended to all who could read the Constitution in English and who could write their names and to all who owned and paid taxes on real estate valued at $250. The Mississippi convention of 1865, ignoring such advice, did little more than recognize the abolition of slavery.[5] Feeling that the state and not Congress should have jurisdiction over the Negro, and with a rebellious spirit almost equal to that with which they left the Union, the various Southern states found easy readmission under the Johnson administration and comfort in their belief that they could continue their relations with the Negro on about the same basis as before. Although the Negro had been recognized as a freedman, his position as a citizen had not been accepted in the South.

Made confident by the leniency that President Johnson had shown, the South, in keeping with its traditional prejudices, hurriedly erected barriers against the realization of two of the Negro's most pressing aspirations: the aim to become a full-fledged citizen and the desire to educate his children. Out of each constitutional convention of this period came recommendations concerning the treatment of the freedmen, but all of them were designed to freeze the Negro's status just short of slavery. Legislatures of the various states very quickly enacted these recommendations into law, forming a set of Black Codes which gave Southern people an effective tool by which they could reestablish the traditional position of the Negro among them. Mississippi was the first state to forge such a tool, and its code became a model for other Southern states. Through its provisions, the complete assimilation of the Negro was made impossible. His identity became defined by law; the limitations of his rights before the courts were specified; his ownership and use of land was confined to incorporated cities and towns where civil authorities could maintain more strict control over him; interracial marriages were prohibited; and rape by a Negro of a white female was made punishable by death.

Laws affecting the Negro as a person were much more stringent and restrictive. The kind of work he was allowed to do fell far short of exhausting the capabilities which he had acquired in slavery. Nevertheless, he was compelled to work by force of the vagrancy acts of each state. According to these acts, all "persons of color" who possessed no "lawful employment or business" were considered vagrants and upon conviction were fined or imprisoned. Civil authorities were given the responsibility of investigating such charges and enforcing the laws that related to them. Orphaned children without "apparent support" were also to be apprehended and brought before the probate court, where they were to be apprenticed to some "competent and suitable" person (the former master usually having first preference) for whom they were to work until maturity. Most of the Black Codes prohibited the assembly of Negroes, especially with whites, and very often freedmen were required to secure permits when traveling from one county to another.[6]

And so the Black Codes replaced the Slave Codes with little difference between the two. Recognition of the Thirteenth Amendment imposed no greater responsibility upon the South than the region had experienced before the war. In fact, no phase of the situation made the freedmen's position less precarious than when they were slaves. They were no longer capital or wealth and were thereby rendered more expendable. Major General Carl Schurz made this observation in his report to President Johnson which revealed the sad condition of the freedmen in several Southern states.[7]

The freedmen's schools immediately began to feel the effects of the wave of anti-Negro sentiment released by the President's Reconstruction policy and the Black Codes. The wave first struck through the provincial governors whom Lincoln and Johnson had backed. It gradually spread through the various branches of government and involved a goodly portion of the public in acts so violent as to seriously hamper the entire educational program.

When Edward Stanley became governor of North Carolina in 1862, his first official act was to close the freedmen's schools that Vincent Colyer and others had worked so hard to establish in the state. On May 31, 1862, Colyer assembled the contrabands at the Methodist church on Hancock Street in New Bern and there conveyed the sad news to them. "These schools are now to be closed," he told them tearfully, "not by the officers of the Army under whose sanction they were commenced, but by the necessity laid upon me by Governor Edward Stanley, who informed me that it is a criminal offense, under the laws of North Carolina, to teach blacks to read, which laws he has come from Washington with instructions to enforce." [8] The school at the Baptist church, where the more advanced pupils had been studying, was closed for the same reason. Subsequent action showed that Stanley's intentions were not only to stop the freedmen's educational program but also to gain broader control over the Negro problem. The governor returned several fugitive slaves to their owners and generally manifested a hostile attitude toward the refugee problem. Many Northerners denounced him bitterly for his actions. Governor Benjamin F. Perry of South Carolina shared the sentiments of the head of his sister state. He expressed this in his official message after taking the office of provisional governor, to which Johnson had appointed him. He maintained that the government of the United States, including the privilege of suffrage that it guaranteed, was for whites alone, that his government was not bound to care for the blacks at all, and that the state government had the duty of adjusting the master-servant relations between whites and Negroes.[9]

The Florida legislature of 1865 passed an act that affected the schools even more directly. It imposed a special tax of one dollar upon all male Negroes, to be paid into the treasury to be used to establish and maintain schools for Negroes. The superintendent was authorized to collect tuition fees for each pupil, and these fees were also to be deposited to the freedmen's school fund. There were two disturbing features of this act. One was the great financial strain that it placed upon the freedmen, especially in the light of their limited opportunities to earn adequate wages. The act, in fact, made the schools no stronger than the general economy from which the Negroes were barely able to gain subsistence. The other disturbing feature was the amount of control placed upon the teachers. Individuals could not teach unless they were certified by the superintendent, who, by the act itself, was given the authority to refuse certification if he judged a teacher unfit or incompetent. This provision of the statute created much unrest in the ranks of the benevolent societies then supporting the schools. The societies feared that the action was an attempt on the part of the state to oust Northern teachers and to dictate what the freedmen were to learn.[10] They knew that the spread of such action to the other states would mean the death of their educational program. Their anxiety subsided only when the societies were assured that those who were to administer the law were in sympathy with Northern leadership. Nevertheless, the Florida act drew the reins of control tighter around the freedmen's schools.

Members of the Texas constitutional convention of 1866 had plans for Negro schools similar to those of the Florida legislature. They recommended that income derived from the public school fund be employed exclusively for the education of all white children and that all money raised from Negroes through a proposed school tax be used for the maintenance of a system of schools "for the Africans and their children."[11] Although the Texas legislature did nothing about these recommendations, the proposals did help encourage a hostile attitude toward the freedmen's schools in that state.

However, Southern opposition to Negroes and their schools was not uniform. Now and then a spark of human kindness showed through. Three years after Colyer announced the closing of schools in North Carolina, a group of Negroes who sought public support for their civil and educational aspirations directed a strong plea to the state's constitutional convention of 1865. They asked that laws be passed that would be helpful to them in their new condition of freedom and that education be provided for their children which would make them useful citizens. The convention responded favorably by directing a resolution to W. H. Holden, the state's provisional governor, asking him to appoint a commission to study the question and report to the legislature at its next session. A conservative committee reported but concerned itself with matters other than education.[12] These, however, were days when even silence was progress. The Mississippi constitutional convention of 1865, controlled by native whites, failed to modify the article on education, which had been written into the Constitution of 1832.[13] Although the convention made no provision for the education of Negroes, it did not openly oppose or limit it.

Nevertheless, the sympathetic ear and the silence that gave consent were not sufficiently forceful to stem the tide of hostility that the legislation under Presidential Reconstruction had released against the Negroes and their schools. The Southern fear that Northern teachers would plant the doctrine of social equality in the minds of Negroes was basic. It motivated a complete rejection of these teachers by many whites who lived in communities where freedmen's schools were located. This rejection is probably best illustrated by a letter that James C. Southall of the *Charlottesville Chronicle* of Virginia directed to a Northern teacher of that city. Southall frankly stated the case for the many Southern people who shared his views. On February 12, 1867, he wrote Anna Gardner:

> I take as deep an interest in the welfare of the Negro race as anyone. I am anxious to see them educated, and am prepared to give any aid to further these objects. The impression among the white residents of Charlottesville is that your instruction of the colored people who attend your school contemplates something more than the communication of ordinary knowledge implied in teaching them to read, write, cipher, etc. The idea prevails that you instruct them in politics and sociology; that you come among us not merely as an ordinary school teacher, but as a political missionary; that you communicate to the colored people ideas of social equality with whites. With your first objective we sympathize; the second we regard as mischievous, and only tending to disturb the good feeling between the races.[14]

The clergy added the weight of "divine authority" to the South's unrelenting attack on Northern teachers. A white minister of Columbus, Georgia, assembled a group of Negro ministers in his study and told them that they must employ Southern teachers since Northern teachers tended to "stir up prejudices between the races." His mission was partly effective, for some of the Negro clergymen spoke out against the Northern teachers during their services.[15] During a religious revival at the Walnut Street Baptist Church in Louisville a teacher from Pennsylvania was refused admission to the church's membership. The officials found no fault with her religious conversion except that she had not purged herself of the ambition to teach Negroes.

Community pressure was also placed upon pupils who attended freedmen's schools. One of the greatest obstacles the schools of Alabama encountered was the fact that many whites who employed Negroes as servants would not allow them to work if they attended school.[16] Peter Woolfolk, who was a slave at Richmond prior to the city's surrender, experienced this pressure while teaching there. He wrote on April 22, 1865, that landlords were seeking to prevent Negro parents from sending their children to school by threatening to put them out of their houses.

Antagonistic actions like these stripped the struggling schools of much of their public support and exposed them to an uncontrollable pattern of mob violence. The teachers felt it first. They were more obvious in the community and were thereby more exposed. When Fannie Woods entered Warrenton, Virginia, as a teacher of freedmen in 1866, hostile forces threatened to burn her school. Only the impending interference of Union forces dampened the rebel aggression directed against her. Some citizens of Georgetown, Texas, applied to the Freedmen's Bureau for a teacher, promising to provide her with a school and a place to board. A teacher was sent but was there only a short time before she was expelled from her boarding house and was unable to secure another.[17] Neither the teachers nor the pupils were absolutely safe at school. When marauding bands of irresponsible citizens attacked the schools, the teachers found little protection except where there were Union soldiers to defend them. Although rebellious citizens fired into the night school at Orangeburg, South Carolina, on several occasions, the culprits were never apprehended. A schoolhouse located in the northeast part of Haygood County, Tennessee, was burned by a group that had drifted in from border counties, and the school at Springhill in Maury County of that state was stoned several times by rebellious citizens of that vicinity.[18] Many of these incidents were mischievous pranks, but most were overt expressions of an intense resentment of any action taken to educate Negroes. Since they were more or less common to the entire South, they combined to keep the freedmen's school movement unstable and the pupils and teachers insecure. They were to set a pattern that would prevail for almost one hundred years: Where official rejection of Negro rights was apparent, violence against Negro rights movements was open.

THE MANIFEST FORCE
OF CONGRESSIONAL REPRISAL

Nevertheless the circuitous course of historical events continued. The reestablishment of the South's old social system triggered the wrath of Congress and unintentionally set in motion movements that would relieve the Negroes of their social limitations and the restrictions that had been directed against their educational opportunities.

Congress first showed open hostility to the Johnson plan when the President, in his annual message to that body on December 5, 1865, reported on the "progress" that had resulted from his efforts to restore the Southern states. Congressional leaders had not considered the President's Reconstruction job a progressive accomplishment. Thaddeus Stevens and other members of the House questioned the legality of the status of the states that had been reconstructed under the Johnson plan and contended that only Congress could define the conditions under which the seceded states could return to the Union.

Congressional reaction was rather firmly based. Not only had the Black Codes evidenced a return to the traditional order in the South, but the conditions of the freedmen as revealed in Carl Schurz's report vividly portrayed the region as reconstructed in state government only and not in its accommodations to the results of the war in point of spirit. Emphasizing the blockages that still remained in the Negro's path to full citizenship, Schurz drew this conclusion: "The emancipation of the slave is submitted to only insofar as chattel slavery in the old form could not be kept up. But although the freedman is no longer considered the property of the individual master, he is considered the slave of society, and all independent state legislation will share the tendency to make him such." Infuriated by the Black Codes and the conditions contained in Schurz's report, a Congress of conservatives, moderates, and Radical Republicans viciously nullified the Johnson plan and replaced it with a plan of its own.[19]

Congressional antagonism turned into action in February 1866. A new Freedmen's Bureau bill was passed, extending indefinitely the life of this agency and enlarging its power to include authority to seek military aid when rights of Negroes were denied. When the President vetoed the bill, Congress passed it over his veto, created a joint committee for the purpose of inquiring into the conditions of the Southern states, and passed, also over Presidential veto, a civil rights act that made Negroes citizens of the United States.

From the point of view of the development of the South's public school system and the enhancement of educational opportunities for Negroes this action was historically strategic. It gave the Negroes the political power necessary to write a goodly portion of their wants into the constitutions of the various reconstructed states. Despite Southern opposition to its influence and the region's development of strategies to combat its political weight,[20] universal suffrage placed a large number of blacks in the electorate of these states. Their numerical weight had its effect. For example, nearly 93,000 Negro voters were registered in Louisiana against 43,000 whites when the time to hold constitutional conventions came around. Registration in Alabama totaled 104,518 Negroes as compared with 61,295 whites.

The Negroes voted solidly for holding conventions and the white conservatives were divided, but this did not mean that the conventions were Negro-controlled. Although a goodly portion of the white upper class did not vote, the conventions were basically composed of white conservatives who largely represented the poorest element of the South, Northern whites who had taken up residence in the South, and freedmen.[21] But congressional Reconstruction had given the freedmen a solid representation in the business of reconstructing civil government in the erstwhile Confederacy and had placed, incidentally, the destiny of public education largely in their hands.

This conclusion is rendered much more obvious by the barriers that the Negro delegates and their supporters had to overcome before they could legally provide for free universal education and bid for public acceptance. One of these barriers was the fact that many people of the various states did not consider the conventions representative; therefore they were not inclined to support their recommendations, even if enacted into law. Governor James I. Orr warned the South Carolina convention of its atypical representation and the hazards it posed soon after it was called into session. In a speech before the convention, he reminded the delegates that the white population had almost unanimously abstained from voting, and that the convention's membership was representative only of the colored population of the state. "This being the case," he admonished, "it cannot be denied that the intelligence, refinement, and wealth of the state is not represented by your body. Hence the very high duty is devolved upon you of discharging the important trusts confided to your care in such a manner as to command your action to the confidence and support, not only of those by whom you were elected, but by those who refused to go to the polls and vote in the election." [22] A similar interpretation of atypical representation sprang up at the Arkansas convention of 1868. J. N. Cypert of White County alluded to it when he introduced a resolution, proposing that the convention "cheerfully" adopt the state's constitution of 1864. He made the proposal on the pretext that the government of that state had been already agreed upon by "all the people" and that an attempt was being made to set the government aside by men who had no interest in the State of Arkansas.[23] His implication that the convention had been captured by outsiders was not well founded. Of the seventy-five members who had been elected as delegates to the convention, only eight were Negroes, and sixty-seven had been living in the state for six or more years. Some dared to label the Arkansas convention as "the bastard collection." A *New York Herald* correspondent dubbed the Alabama convention of 1868 the "Black Crook." [24] This kind of disrespect for the conventions that assembled during this period was evident throughout the South.

Another barrier that Negro delegates and their supporters faced was the South's unstable attitude toward public school legislation. This type of legislation was not entirely new to Southern people. Many of the Southern states made attempts to establish public schools as early as the first part of the nineteenth century. Tennessee established a school fund by an act in 1806 and created subsequent legislation for the purpose of strengthening it. Virginia followed with a similar act four years later, and there is evidence that public school legislation was popular prior to the Civil War.[25] But many of the school funds provided by the laws went for other purposes, keeping the various proposed public school systems almost entirely on paper. Only in a few instances were there free schools, and practically all of them were established for the poor.[26] They were poorly taught and operated only for a short period during each year. There were many private schools throughout the South, but these took care of the educational needs of the well-to-do.

Despite these earlier experiences with the public school question, the Southern mind offered severe obstacles to those who endeavored to make the free public school system an actual going concern. Owners of property were the most antagonistic. Since they were quite capable of caring for their own, they did not embrace, under any circumstance, the idea of being taxed for the education of the laboring class. They believed that laborers did not need education, that if any of them were worth educating, they would find some way to get an education by their own efforts. The laboring class offered a resistance almost as difficult to surmount. They saw no need for education, accepted their subordination to the propertied class, and generally regarded education as a luxury to be enjoyed only by that class.[27]

Getting an article on public education into the constitution of each state, however, did not prove a formidable task. It was the *kind* of article that caused the trouble. The conservative element of the various conventions fought hard to keep the social order as close to ante-bellum status as possible, and this fight naturally carried over into the education question.

On the fifth day of the South Carolina convention, W. B. Nash, a Negro delegate, introduced a vital resolution. He proposed that all schools — academies, colleges, and universities of the state —

47

which were to be endowed in part or whole from public funds would be open for the reception of scholars, students, and teachers of every grade without any distinction or preference whatever and that it should be the duty of the legislature, at its first session, to divide the state into school districts and establish free schools that would be open to all citizens of the state.[28] On the following day, A. J. Ransier, another Negro delegate, introduced a resolution that provided for a board of education, a thorough system of common schools, and a superintendent for each district. He, too, included a nondiscrimination clause in his resolution.[29] Both these resolutions gave impetus to the free school question and were referred to the committee on education.

The committee included the spirit of these and other pertinent resolutions in its report, but provoked much opposition and discussion on the questions of compulsory school attendance and mixed schools. The first source of irritation was embedded in the fourth section of the proposed article on education, which stipulated that it shall be the duty of the general assembly to provide for the compulsory attendance of all children between the ages of six and eighteen years, not physically or mentally disabled, for a term equivalent to twenty-four months.[30] Both white and Negro delegates objected to the word "compulsory," but for different reasons. White objection was motivated by the fear that this section was a mechanism designed to force mixed schools upon the people. A. C. Richmond made this fear obvious when he based his objection on the ground that white families unable to send their children to private schools would be obliged to send them to public institutions in which white and Negro children would be educated together.[31] J. J. Wright of Beaufort and R. H. Cain of Charleston, both Negroes, joined some white delegates in opposition to compulsory school attendance. Wright considered the plan "impractical" from the point of view of time — that the number of schools would be inadequate for the enforcement of compulsory school attendance at the start. Cain thought the measure "impolite to parents who should have freedom of decision in such matters involving their children." Another Negro delegate, F. L. Cardozo, sought to reconcile the differences by proposing an amendment to the effect that no such law should be passed until a system of public schools had been thoroughly and completely organized. The amendment was adopted.[32]

The question of mixed schools was even more bitterly debated. The leader of the opposition was B. O. Duncan, a conservative. This delegate reasoned that mixed schools, instead of reducing prejudice between the races, would serve to increase it. He accused the committee of trying to "build the house from the top upward." [33] Wright opposed Duncan's implication that mixed schools were being forced by the section under discussion. He countered that the section did not compel a mixture of white and Negro pupils. "This provision," he cried during the heated debate, "leaves it so that white and colored children can attend school together if they desire to do so; but I do not believe the colored children will want to go to white schools or vice versa."

Notwithstanding strong conservative opposition, the South Carolina convention of 1868 wrote into the constitution of the state the basic educational ideals for which the Negro delegates and their supporters had fought so hard. It established a system of public education, made school attendance compulsory when the system was fully formed, and opened all schools to all children and youths of the state without regard to race or color.

Similar action was taken by the constitutional conventions of other states, but reactions to the questions of compulsory attendance and mixed schools varied widely. The Alabama convention of 1867 side-stepped these vexing issues. When the article on education was presented, the mixed school question set off a fiery debate in which conservative delegates attempted to assure constitutional prohibitions against having Negroes and whites attend the same schools. The Negro delegates tried to keep the constitution silent on this issue, although they made it clear that they did not want to send their children to school with white children. In their sincere judgment, constitutional silence on the question would prohibit school officials from maintaining inferior schools for Negroes in case the section on education did provide for separate institutions. John Caraway, a Negro delegate from Mobile, backed up his colleagues by offering an amendment to the effect that should separate schools prove ex-

49

pedient, the board of education could make an equal division of the school fund in districts where such division was demanded.

The article on education that the Alabama convention finally adopted provided for the establishment of a free school system without mentioning mixed or separate schools and without making school attendance compulsory.[34] The Georgia convention, assembled at Atlanta in December 1867, acted likewise: It created a system of general education and made it forever free to all children but made no mention of mixed schools or compulsory education.[35]

The eight Negroes who were delegates at the Arkansas convention of 1868 were concerned much more with suffrage than with mixed schools. Consequently, the report of the convention's education committee, on which William H. Grey and James W. Mason, both Negroes, served, stirred up no commotion. The article on education simply provided for a system of free schools that was to be open to all children of the state between five and twenty-one years of age. It was required by law that the schools run three months in order to get public support, but it was also required that every child of sufficient mental and physical ability attend school for three years or until his eighteenth birthday.[36] It is apparent that the absence of the mixed school question forestalled any discussion of compulsory school attendance.

The trend in other states generally took the middle course between the provisions for and provisions against mixed schools. The North Carolina convention of this period made education compulsory but made no mention of mixed or separate schools.[37] The Mississippi convention was silent on both issues; however, a proposition to incorporate provisions for separate schools was voted down as a result of the influence of the Negro delegates.[38] The Texas convention permitted no discrimination. It incorporated a provision in the constitution that allowed mixed schools.

The Virginia constitutional convention of the year 1867–1868 was composed partly of men who had come from states where public education had become popular. It was also composed of twenty-five Negroes and some middle-class whites, all of whom were anxious to educate their children at state expense.[39] This element, although strong enough to get a comprehensive system of free public education adopted, did not have sufficient force to institute mixed schools. Not enough of the middle-class whites were in favor of such schools. When the report of the committee on education was made, a conservative delegate offered an amendment to the report, specifying that in no case should white and Negro children be taught in the same schoolhouse at the same time. The Negro members of the convention were agitated by this amendment and spoke vehemently against it. They were not capable, however, of securing sufficient support from the Republicans to defeat this issue. Their provision for mixed schools failed by a large majority.[40]

But the South had already shown that the hearts of men cannot remain forever hard. The idea of educating freedmen had begun to grow more acceptable to Southern people even before some of the conventions were held. J. L. M. Curry introduced a resolution at Marion, Alabama, in 1866, calling for the education of Negroes by the whites of the South. The Mississippi State Teachers' Association, during the following year, went on record as favoring public schools for the "blacks," and Southern politicians urged that they be given decent treatment and adequate schooling.[41] Such statements were not all a matter of words. Some definite action accompanied them. Prominent planters, like William D. Bloxham of Florida, had opened schools for freedmen on their plantations and, to some extent, even the hostility toward Northern teachers had begun to wane. Eventually it became a common remark that the "Yankee school marm," with her twang, abominable pronunciation, and other faults, was par excellence the successful teacher and disciplinarian.[42] Southerners themselves began to take more interest in teaching the former slaves. They felt that only in this way could the Negroes be directed in the way whites believed they should go. So the stigma once attached to Southern educators who taught in the freedmen's schools lost some of its venom. In fact, some of the teachers took great pride in their work.[43] The Reverend James Burke, a Southerner by birth, reported from Houston to the American Missionary Association that about fifty thousand freedmen in Texas had learned to read and write. He made an earnest appeal for books, primers, spellers, first readers, Testaments, and hymnals.[44] So, widely scattered as they were, these declarations and positive steps in behalf of the freedmen's schools indicated a sharp turning point in the whole matter of race relations in the South. They indicated that some kind of accommodation between whites and Negroes was developing. Whether both groups could be proud of the adjustment was yet to be revealed.

By 1870, some sign of the coming pattern had appeared. White Southerners had developed a consensus concerning the Negro's status among them. They had accepted the Fourteenth Amendment under duress, but in spirit they had rejected the concept of racial equality. They had also begun to ponder ways of preventing universal suffrage from remaining a reality. About matters of public education, they were not so sure. They permitted the education of the Negro, but they rejected the idea that this should be done at public expense. Not all Southerners accepted the idea of public education for whites, but those who did accept it continued to oppose the mixed school policy that had been adopted by some states.

COMMON SCHOOLS AND COMMON PROBLEMS

The legislature of each Southern state passed some type of law establishing a free public school system soon after the conventions adjourned. Since the states were not prepared for this new institution, the problems they encountered were about the same. There was not any state that had a large number of native whites already trained in school administration or in the art of instructing pupils. Consequently, securing adequately trained personnel was a common problem. There was no tradition of paying taxes in support of schools. Therefore taxes were hard to collect, and minimal funds were hard to establish. Complaints against the expenses of running schools were frequent, and there was always the fear that public support of education would mean the imposition of mixed schools.

Just as the states faced common problems, so also did they have at least one common advantage. Each had inherited some form of a ready-made school system through the work of the various benevolent societies and the Freedmen's Bureau. Though bitterly fought, this system had persisted in its general framework. There were 2,677 such schools scattered throughout the South when government aid was withdrawn. Approximately 3,300 teachers were at work in them, and almost 150,000 pupils were in regular attendance.[45] Benevolent societies, pressed for teachers and motivated by a desire to see Negroes take over their own schools, had already turned to normal schools as a means of providing native teachers. High school, normal, and collegiate classes in cities like Charleston, Atlanta, New Orleans, Nashville, Berea, and Memphis not only refuted the Southern view that Negroes could not learn, but offered to the South a fairly well trained leadership with which to staff its infant public school system.

Arkansas was quick to capitalize on some of the experiences and resources of the freedmen's school system. The law establishing the state's system was approved on July 23, 1868, and the office of education was opened in August of that year. At the board of education meeting on January 11, 1870, Superintendent. M. H. Wygant offered a resolution accepting the recommendation that Major General Howard had placed in his circular of November 19, 1869 — that the Educational Division of the Bureau and the Arkansas State Department of Education be consolidated. Attached to the resolution was the additional proposal that teachers of the colored schools in the public system be instructed to report to the superintendent of freedmen's schools as well as to the trustees of the school board.[46] W. M. Colby, Superintendent of Freedmen's Schools, cooperated heartily with the state government and secured a large expenditure of money for the erection of school buildings.

Despite this type of cooperation, Arkansas still encountered serious difficulties in its first experiences with public education. Chief among its problems was the serious inadequacy of administrative personnel. As the superintendent so clearly stated in his first annual report, "It was not to be expected that capable trustees could be secured in every instance. The whole system was put into operation among people who were largely without education or experience in school matters." [47]

Nevertheless the state accepted these and other handicaps and took definite steps to overcome them. B. H. Farmer organized the

Arkansas Journal of Education and published the first number on January 1, 1870. This was fortunate for the state's newly created public school system since the *Journal* proved to be a good organ through which information concerning schools could be disseminated. It advised people on how to organize school districts and establish schools; it informed county officials concerning their duties and relations to the school fund; and it helped a good deal in popularizing public education.

Before the end of 1871, there were signs of the development of some type of professional attitude among the official and instructional staffs. Thirty-one teachers' institutes were held during that year, and twenty-five were held in 1872. There were also signs that the public was beginning to accept the responsibility of supporting the schools. The state had 240 schools that aggregated $82,741 in value before 1869, but 417 new schools were erected in that year, and 1,289 during the next. A total of $833,853 was collected in school revenues in 1870, and a total of $760,468 was spent for public education. This degree of public support naturally afforded the absorption of a greater proportion of the school-age children into the schools. The proportion of whites attending public schools in the state increased from 42 percent in 1869 to 63 percent in 1870. The proportion of Negro pupils increased from 28 to 50 percent.[48] The Negro children, having been given a significant start in the primary branches of education by the freedmen's schools, gradually passed under public support.

Alabama was not so fortunate as Arkansas or nearly so prudent in matters of public education. The state's school system was organized in 1868, and serious difficulties began immediately thereafter. A much needed supply of local school officials failed to materialize, and adequate school funds were not forthcoming. The schools were in continuous difficulty during their first five years as a result of the bitter opposition of the white citizens and their failure to pay taxes. When reactionaries began to ascend to power in 1873, the schools were temporarily closed. They did not have sufficient funds to operate for a creditable term.

A Mississippi legislature, composed largely of Negroes and Republicans, established a school system in 1870. The system first experienced some difficulty in getting funds since many whites violently opposed supporting education for Negroes. As in many other Southern states, most of this opposition resulted from the fear of mixed schools. There were also bitter complaints against the cost of education. It was thought that the expenditures for schools were too high and that much of the money was being squandered.

Unlike the Alabama situation, these conditions failed to stop the Mississippi free school system from growing. State Superintendent H. R. Pease reported that more than three thousand free schools were opened the first year and that they had an aggregate attendance of 66,257.[49] During the following year, 1871, there were 126,769 Negro school-age children, and 39 percent of them were enrolled in school. Of the 120,073 white school-age children, over 52 percent were enrolled.[50] There was some evidence that the influence of the freedmen's schools was being felt. Negro children, who had been oriented to schools earlier than most of the white children, were attending more regularly. Their average daily attendance was 79.3 as compared with 74.4 percent for the white children. Negroes who had been trained in freedmen's schools or who had been able to get schooling during the slave regime helped swell the teaching force. There were approximately 400 of them among the 3,000 teachers who served the Mississippi public schools at this time.

Georgia's public school law was passed in October 1870. It was largely the work of a committee from the state teachers association. Governor Rufus B. Bullock appointed J. R. Lewis as state school commissioner, and the schools began their first year of operation. The school debt very quickly climbed to $300,000 — a sum quite beyond the revenue on which the system could count. This discrepancy, of course, resulted from the failure of the state to collect the poll tax for the period from 1868 to 1870.[51] It is also true that much of the school fund had been diverted to other purposes. To correct the difficulty, a new school law was passed in 1872 on the recommendation of Gustavus J. Orr, who had become school commissioner by this time. Commissioner Orr stopped the establishment of new schools for this year, and the legislature in 1873 appropriated funds which, when mixed with those appropriated by the counties, put the schools in operation again. By the end of the year, Georgia had 1,379 schools for white children and 356 for Negro.[52] These schools helped accommodate an aggregate enrollment that expanded from 49,578 to 135,541 in 1874.[53]

The general assembly of South Carolina, also composed largely of Negroes, passed laws establishing a free school system in 1868 and 1870. This system probably operated more smoothly than that of any other Southern state. There were fears about expenditures and many claims of fraud. Nevertheless, the system grew significantly. Pupil enrollment expanded from 16,418 in 1869 to 30,448 in 1870. The number of public schools grew in similar proportion — from 381 to 769 during the same period.[54] In 1873 came the very important addition of a state normal school. Since the public schools of South Carolina were mixed by constitutional requirement, the state normal school was open to Negroes as well as whites. In fact, Negroes made up the majority of those enrolled. They also attended the university during this time. Henry E. Haynes, Negro and secretary of state, entered the medical school, and F. L. Cardozo, another Negro and state treasurer, enrolled in one of the branches of the university.[55]

The North Carolina school system, though set up well by the constitutional convention of 1868, immediately ran into trouble after becoming legal in April 1869. The people refused to accept the idea of taxation for schools. Consequently, funds were scarce and the number of school officials was inadequate. The Supreme Court ruled the school law unconstitutional, and the $100,000 appropriated when the law was passed could not be used. S. S. Ashley, a Northern white man who favored mixed schools, was made state superintendent. His position on the whole school question made him very unpopular with the conservatives of the state. There was a change for the better, however, when a new school law was passed in 1871. This law provided for property and capitation taxes for school purposes and made possible the rise of teacher-training institutions.

Louisiana's problems were of the same kind as those of the other Southern states, except that they were more acute. School officials and teachers were inadequate both in number and in training, and the public resented taxation for school support. At best, public education was a gesture. Of the 253,000 school-age children in the state, only 23,000 were enrolled in the schools when State Superintendent T. W. Conway made his report in 1870. Of the fine freedmen's school system that General Banks had built, only 230 schools were left, and only 524 teachers were available and working at this time. Corruption haunted the system, and W. G. Brown, a Negro who became state superintendent after Conway, called this matter to the attention of the people of the state in 1871. Backed by what he called "indisputable proof," Brown reported that school officials had embezzled $2,005 during that year.[56] The mixed school system was allowed to become a constant source of irritation. It was used as an excuse for not paying taxes in support of schools. Dr. Barnas Sears, agent of the Peabody Fund, had denied aid to the state because officials of the fund did not believe the schools to be fully supported and sanctioned by the people of the state. Progressively, during the days that followed, the people attributed every problem of the schools to the policy of mixing white and Negro pupils. Conservatives used this psychological state as a leverage to get the policy undone.

The well-to-do opposed paying taxes for the support of schools in Virginia; therefore, the schools opened faster than financial support grew. They stayed open only because private support came in to supplement meager public funds. The Negroes took more advantage of these opportunities than did whites. They attended schools in larger numbers. Reports from Prince Edward County in 1871, for instance, announced that every colored school was crowded and growing in enrollment all the time. Similar reports came from other parts of the state.[57] Because of the work of the educators of the freedmen's school system, teachers for the Negro schools were more adequate in number and training than those for whites. There were no normal schools for training white teachers in the state. There were two for Negroes: one at Hampton and one at Richmond.

Under the new law specified by her constitutional convention of 1868, Texas organized a definite public school system in 1871. J. C. DeGrees was made state superintendent. His first report spoke of strong opposition and much prejudice, some of which was shown through occasional intimidation of teachers and overt acts of violence. Much of the antagonism was due to the fact that many Texans considered the schools too expensive. They felt that money was being spent needlessly. However, new laws came to the system's rescue, reducing the number of school districts and decreasing the number of officials employed to administer them. The *Houston Weekly Telegraph,* usually vocal on school matters, expressed great satisfaction with the fact that the number of school districts had fallen from 35 to 12. The paper claimed that the change was for the better in that it would save much expense and husband the school fund then being so rapidly depleted.[58] DeGrees' administration felt the effect of the *Telegraph*'s crusade against "high" school expenses and its implication that even fewer school officials were needed. He expressed a willingness to present public proof that the Texas system, in proportion to children taught, was cheaper in its operation and higher in its standards than the school systems of other states.[59]

Like the state superintendent of Arkansas, DeGrees sought to capitalize on the freedmen's school system already operating in the state. In his first report, he called attention to the overcrowding of colored schools caused by the Negro's enthusiasm. Where it was impossible to lease buildings, he reported, the Negroes offered their churches and, in many instances, put up school buildings with their own funds. The biggest problem he experienced with the Negro schools was securing teachers. "Few persons have the nerve," he recorded, "to meet the continual insults, the social ostracism, the threats of injury, and all the annoyances to which the teachers of colored schools are subjected." [60] The *Telegraph* reacted harshly to the superintendent's report on the colored schools, not because of the accounts of violence it contained, but because the editor felt that the colored children were being given the greater share of the school fund.[61]

And so it was that by the last quarter of the nineteenth century, without the force of direct purpose, the Southern states had experienced the establishment of a system of free public schools for all their children. In its attempt to regain its traditional control over the Negroes, Southern white society had ventured beyond the limits of tolerance granted by Congress and thereby had provoked Congressional reprisals advantageous to the former slaves. With the numerical weight of their newly found citizenship so vital at the polls, Negroes had been able to accumulate sufficient representation at the various constitutional conventions to make their bid for a free public school system effective.

III · THE GREAT DETOUR: A TRANSITION TO NEGRO EDUCATION

The interplay of purposeful and unintentional functions, a process that has been so creative in the history of the South, is not always direct in its course. There are times when the evolutionary process that the interplay defines, as Teilhard de Chardin suggested,* turns back upon itself and reverses its field.

This is what began to take place in the early 1870's — a system of free public schools was being established in the various Southern states. Conditions were being readied for the development of a great detour in the hidden passage through which the Negroes had been advancing toward equal educational and social opportunities. Like all the other major changes in the relations between the races in the South, the detour was to result from a political and legal conflict that would lead eventually to a new pattern of interracial accommodation. But this time the process was to operate against the Negroes, as if history were slowing down things — giving itself time to think. The detour would overthrow the balance enforced by congressional Reconstruction, introduce a policy of racial segregation, and prompt the formation of an educational system aimed at perpetuating the segregated order. It would become the most important change in the entire history of the Negro American.

It is useful to look at the conflict that set the process in action. The opposition of Southern whites to the political and social equality of the freedmen was not crushed under the weight of con-

---

* This evolutionary conception has been used as a focal point in Teilhard de Chardin, *The Phenomenon of Man* (New York: Harper and Row, 1959).

gressional Reconstruction. Disapproval of Negro rights as provided by the amendments and the acts persisted in the minds of many whites, continuing to smolder underneath a surface of apparent calm. The more sensitive element of the white population continued to feel that Southern rule had actually passed into the hands of Negroes and their Northern supporters. Many complaints along these lines were lodged with the joint committee appointed by Congress for the purpose of inquiring into the condition of affairs in the Southern states. Criticizing the theory expressed in such grievances, the committee reminded Congress of the danger. "The complaint," it reported, "goes to the foundation of reconstruction and republican government. It is that the minority, differing in opinion from the majority, are not permitted, on questions affecting the majority, to govern according to their own will." [1]

Signs of even greater discontent were reflected in the minority report by Francis P. Blair, Jr., — a document that emphasized the charge that Negroes were unholy tools of Northern adventurers.[2] Judge R. P. Carpenter of South Carolina, testifying concerning the intelligence of Negroes, rigorously advised: "The colored population upon the seacoast and upon the rivers, in point of intelligence, is just slightly removed from the animal creation as it is conceivable for man to be. . . . They talk a very outlandish idiom, utterly unknown to me. They are very ignorant, and still have very strong passions, and these bad men lead them just as a man would lead or drive sheep." General John B. Gordon of Georgia presented similar testimony. In concluding his minority report on this issue, Blair warned: "These statements might seem like exaggerations, but when the gross ignorance and superstition of Negroes of the extreme South are understood, they will be fully appreciated." This really was a Southern white view, held in defense of Southern white traditions. It would later become active in the formation of an ideological system that was to purge the public conscience, at least in part, of any sense of wrongdoing where overt opposition to the reconstructed government was concerned; and it would make many believe that the restoration of white conservative control, by fair means or foul, was an act of virtue.

In fact, overt opposition to the reconstructed government was already in existence, underneath the organization that Congress had imposed upon the South. Since the various constitutional amendments and congressional acts prohibited organized government from limiting the political and social privileges of Negroes, the limitation was rigorously imposed by voluntary associations that constituted the South's ever-present "underground." Chief among these was the Ku Klux Klan, a secret order organized in 1865 by a group of white men at Pulaski, Tennessee. Through strange garb and mysterious ways, the Klan attempted to play upon the fears and superstitions of Negroes. It succeeded in becoming one of the most dreaded agencies of "popular justice" and extralegalized violence in the South.

Although the Klan was supposedly dissolved in 1869, its program became a model for other such societies whose methods were quite comparable. Each established itself as "judge and jury" by incorporating ideologies that were generally acceptable to the informal South. All of them professed to acknowledge the supremacy of God, claimed for themselves the mission of defending the Union and the Constitution, and declared a dedication to the supremacy of the white race.[3] Their members made special attempts to display supernatural powers. Some of the Klan, for example, carried skeleton hands concealed by the gown sleeve. A frequent trick was for a ghostly looking horseman to stop by a Negro's cabin at night and ask for a bucket of water. The horseman, as if consumed by a raging thirst, would grasp the bucket and press it to his lips, holding it there until every drop was poured into an oil-treated sack concealed beneath his white robe. Returning the empty bucket to his amazed host, the horseman would say, "That's good. It is the first drink of water I have had since I was killed at Shiloh."[4] It was during frightening moments like these that so-called "uppity" Negroes were counseled as to their future behavior or threatened concerning some past misdeed.

Such underground activities were skillfully designed to eliminate the Negro from politics through intimidation and force.[5] They did not stop with threats, nor were they solely attributable to the Klan. On February 14, 1866, General Clinton B. Fisk wrote General Howard: "A freedman was attacked in his cabin and shot. He and his wife ran to the woods, with bullets flying thick and fast around them from five or six revolvers, the woman escaping with her life by tearing off her chemise while running, thereby presenting a darker-colored mark." [6]

The Klan inhibited both freedmen and whites from voting the Republican ticket. A witness, speaking of the Klan's activities in Louisiana, reported that before and on the day of election, principal roads in parishes leading to the different voting places were patrolled by armed men of the Klan who were there for the purpose of intercepting Republicans going to vote. In many instances, the report continued, plantations where freedmen were employed were guarded by armed men to prevent the freedmen from going to the polls. [7] General Howard reported like instances of intimidation in Arkansas, Virginia, Georgia, and other Southern states. Concerning Virginia, the General said, "The secret organizations, known as the Ku Klux Klan, have made their appearances in various localities, visiting the houses of colored men at night, in some cases placing ropes around their necks and threatening to hang them on account of their political opinions." [8]

The findings of General Howard's report were certainly validated by the South's lynching record for the period from 1871 to 1873, which James Elbert Cutler revealed almost a quarter of a century later. There were thirty-two Negroes lynched during this period, and twenty-eight of these were in Southern states. This figure included ten who were lynched by the Klan in the state of South Carolina. [9]

Established government was too weak to cope with these instances of organized intimidation. As General Alfred H. Terry reported for Alabama in 1870, life and property in many localities were insecure. Crimes were frequent, and the civil authorities were utterly powerless to prevent or punish those who broke the law. General Alvin Gillem of Mississippi reported that the great defect in the administration of justice was not in the courts, since once offenders were taken into custody punishment usually followed. The difficulty was in identifying and arresting criminals. Crimes were usually committed at night and under the cover of a disguise. [10]

THE CHANGING TIDE OF POLITICS

As the tide of undercover violence rose in the South, the Negro's future in the realm of national politics gradually deteriorated. Problems of greater national scope plagued the Republican administration, claimed its major attention, and pressured it into leaving the South free to handle the Negro question in its own way.

The panic of 1873 took place just before the first Congress of Grant's second administration went into session. When Congress met in December 1873, it was flooded with petitions for financial relief. In April 1874 the House passed an inflation bill providing for an increase in the issue of greenbacks. Whether or not this measure would have brought economic relief to the country is unimportant. Of more significance is the fact that Grant's veto of this bill increased national opposition to the Republicans.

Heaped upon this setback was a series of scandals within Grant's administration. The fraud and graft revealed in the autumn of 1874 further weakened Republican influence. In the meantime the influence of Southern Democrats was increasing both at home and in the North. General amnesty had been extended to all Southern states except Mississippi, Louisiana, South Carolina, and Florida. All except these had gained Home Rule and had elected Democratic governments.

Other incidents claimed the undivided attention of the Republicans. Special interest groups began to express themselves, aiding in the development of a new sense of nationalism. The Granger Movement, begun by Oliver H. Kelley as an association of mutual aid in 1867, was rapidly expanding. The railroad interests were growing stronger. Track mileage increased from 30,000 to 52,000 between 1860 and 1870, bringing thousands of homestead acres within easy reach of hungry markets. Eastern factory workers, seeking higher wages because of climbing prices, stimulated a rapid increase in labor organizations. These various interest groups became conscious political bodies, seeking to influence both Republicans and Democrats in their favor.

Meanwhile, the image of "Democrat" was changing in the national mind. It virtually shifted from that of "traitor" to that of "patriot." This, together with increased competition between the parties, caused both the Republicans and Democrats to seek the support of the Southern people. During the campaign of 1876, both parties offered inducements to those who demanded an end to Federal interference in Southern politics. In his speech accepting the Presidential nomination, Rutherford B. Hayes sided with the idea of giving Southern people complete protection in the "free enjoyment of their rights." He had already endorsed a laissez-faire policy toward the South in a letter to Guy M. Bryan of Texas.[11] Through the platform of his party he was even further committed to this policy. Encouraged by a favorable reaction to these moves, Hayes made a tour of the South in September 1877, attempting to secure Southern pledges to observe the war amendments. This action was anticlimactic. The President had already committed himself to Southern appeasement beyond the limits of return. He had summoned the rival candidates for governor of South Carolina, Daniel H. Chamberlain and Wade Hampton, to the White House and had secured from Hampton, although not from Chamberlain, a promise to recognize the rights of Negroes and an assurance that peace would be maintained in the state. On the strength of these promises he had removed from the state capitol the troops that had been supporting Chamberlain. A similar step had been taken in New Orleans, where Negro-supported Governor Stephen B. Packard had been held in office over the Democratic Nicholls. Troops were moved in favor of Nicholls when the "pretending" governor promised to respect the amendments and to provide a system of public education supported by equal taxation and available with equal advantages without regard for race or color.

Out of these developments in national and local politics came the famous Compromise of 1877 which restored the South to parity with other sections and freed it from Northern intervention in Southern race relations.[12] By this time it was clear that despite losing the war, the South had won the peace. During the two decades that followed, conservatives, Southern radicals, and liberals vied with each other for regional support. This competition required that each make some effort to win the Negro vote, and this condition kept the scale of race relations balanced at the point to which segregation had developed during the Reconstruction.[13] But the trend away from Republicanism continued with even greater vigor in the South. One by one the Southern political groups whose competition had been able to maintain a balance in race relations lost their influence, and the will to subjugate the Negro gradually came out into the open and eventually found its way into the legal and formalized social structure of the nation.

THE CHAIN OF LEGAL CONTAINMENT

Added to this abandonment of the Negroes by the Federal government was the institution of a process of legal attrition that was to leave the race at a status position just above slavery and far short of full citizenship. The congressional power behind the Negro's civil liberties was to be nullified; the liberties guaranteed him by the Fourteenth Amendment were to be eroded; and his entire life was to be curtailed by a system of segregation sanctioned by legal authority. The process began with a series of civil rights decisions rendered by the Supreme Court of the United States from 1873 to 1898. First, the citizenship of the Negro was redefined as a result of the decision handed down in the *Slaughter House Cases* of 1873.[14] In these cases, Justice Samuel F. Miller and a majority of the Court rendered the privileges and immunities clauses of the Fourteenth Amendment almost meaningless by holding that it was never the purpose of the Amendment to federalize the privileges and immunities of state citizenship and to transfer their custody to the Federal courts.[15] The Court set a precedent in this decision, coining a judicial theory that separated citizenship in the Federal government from that within a particular state.[16] Privileges of state citizenship, the court reasoned, rested for their security and protection "where they heretofore rested" and were not embraced by the Fourteenth Amendment.

Following this dualistic concept, subsequent court decisions exposed Negroes to the discriminatory will of private individuals who

66

were not acting as agents of the state. This trend as expressed on the national level is best indicated by such cases as *U.S. v. Reese, U.S. v. Cruikshank,* and *Hall v. DeCuir.* On March 27, 1876, the Court ruled in the Reese case that municipal election inspectors in Kentucky could not be indicted for refusing to receive and count a vote cast by William Garner, a citizen of African descent. The Court held that Congress had not prescribed by "appropriate legislation" punishment for the said offense. "To limit the statute in the manner now asked for," stated Chief Justice Morrison B. Waite, "would be to make a new law, not to enforce an old one." [17] Reflecting clearly the *Slaughter House* ruling, the Court, deciding in the case of *U.S. v. Cruikshank,*[18] also refused to punish private persons who had broken up a Negro meeting. According to the highest tribunal, interference by private individuals could not be a crime when such a meeting was held for some purposes connected with national citizenship. The assembly had convened to discuss local Louisiana elections, not national elections. Two years later, the Supreme Court, in the case of *Hall v. DeCuir,*[19] ruled in favor of segregation in interstate commerce. Its ruling was based upon the theory that the failure of Congress to prohibit such distinction actually granted the plaintiff, John G. Benson, the liberty to adopt "reasonable" rules and regulations for the disposition of passengers on his boat. Therefore the statute of 1869 prohibiting segregation was ruled unconstitutional.

The Supreme Court's decisions in the *Civil Rights Cases* of 1883 struck down all the legal defenses that had been available to Negroes in their fight against discrimination. These decisions completely nullified those provisions of the civil rights acts which prohibited discrimination in places of public accommodation and which had imposed penalties directly against persons guilty of such discriminations regardless of whether the state was in any way involved.[20] The acts were declared unconstitutional because, in the opinion of the Court, they were not authorized by the Thirteenth and Fourteenth Amendments. The former amendment, the Court held, dealt only with slavery, whereas the acts constituted corrective legislation. Evidence that the Court, in deciding these cases, had abandoned Negroes to the will of their white adversaries is apparent in this statement from Justice Joseph P. Bradley's opinion: "When a man has emerged from slavery and by the aid of beneficent legislation has shaken off the inseparable concomitant of that state, there must be some state in the progress of his elevation when he takes the rank of a mere citizen, and ceases to be the special favorite of the laws, and when his rights as a citizen or a man are to be protected in the ordinary modes by which other men's rights are protected." [21] Following the trend of previous decisions, the Court made it clear in this case that the Fourteenth Amendment afforded protection only against state action. Thus the protection of the Negro's civil rights against infringement by individuals was left to the states.

The judicial attrition of the Negro's civil liberties continued unabated on a national as well as regional basis at the state and local levels. As early as 1874, there were indications that the various lower courts would not look with disdain upon the segregation of Negroes and the systematic dilution of their liberties which had already begun. The Supreme Court of Illinois ruled that the directors of a school district could not set up a special school for four Negro children and thereby separate them from the other children. However, in making this ruling for the court, Justice Alfred M. Craig obviously avoided the segregation question and seemed to have considered the economics of the separation more important. "Had the district contained colored children sufficient for one school, and white children for another," he added, "and had the directors, in good faith, provided a separate room for each, where the facilities for instruction were entirely equal, that would have presented a question not raised by this record, and upon which we express no opinion." [22] During the same year, the Supreme Court of California had an opportunity to meet the segregation issue more squarely. In the case of *Ward v. Flood*,[23] the Court ruled in favor of segregated schools on the grounds that the separation does not deprive Negro children of their constitutional rights. In giving the opinion of the Court, Justice William T. Wallace made this clarification: "In order to prevent possible misapprehension, however, we think proper to add that in our opinion, and as a result of the views here announced, the exclusion of colored children from schools where white children attend as pupils, cannot be supported, except under conditions appearing in the present case; that is except where separate schools are actually maintained for the education of colored children, and that unless such separate schools be in fact maintained, all children in the school district whether white or colored, have an equal right to become pupils and at any common school organized under the laws of the state." As time passed the general pattern became set that court rulings against the separation of white and Negro pupils in the public schools be based specifically upon the absence of state statutes authorizing such separation.[24]

The path of legal attrition was not always straight. The due process and equal protection clauses did operate to some extent as a shield against racial discrimination. The case of *Yick Wo v. Hopkins*[25] is certainly evidence of this. The Supreme Court in this case ruled that a board could not discriminate against a person because of color. In rendering this decision, Justice Matthews concluded: "The discrimination is therefore illegal, and the public administration which enforces it is a violation of the Fourteenth Amendment of the Constitution." Six years before, the Court had respected the due process and equal protection clauses in the case of *Strauder v. West Virginia*.[26] It had early held that the exclusion of Negroes from a grand or petit jury in a case involving a Negro defendant, whether by state or administrative action, was a denial of equal protection. But there was really little relief for Negroes here. The statute providing for removal to the Federal courts by a defendant "who is denied or cannot enforce in the judicial tribunals of the state" his right to equal treatment was gradually restricted to cases where discrimination violated a state statute. It held, too, that a statute is not invalid merely because it vests unlimited discretion in the jury commissioners or discriminates against Negroes on some other ground than race.[27] Despite the *Yick Wo* and *Strauder* rulings, the Negro's pursuit of equal protection was to be a long and arduous task.

Attrition continued in the field of public accommodations where, particularly after the *Civil Rights Cases* of 1883, there developed a gradual tendency for the courts to rule in favor of the policy of racial segregation. Peter Joseph won his case against the proprietor of the Academy of Music in New Orleans, where he had been denied the privilege of using the first-class ticket he had purchased.[28] However, the courts consistently ruled in favor of segregation thereafter, requiring only that the accommodations be equal in quality and convenience for both races alike.[29]

The freedom to discriminate against Negroes finally worked its way into the state statutes. Its main passageway was probably afforded by the Supreme Court's decision in the case of *Plessy v. Ferguson*.[30] The Court ruled in this case that an act requiring that white and colored persons be furnished with separate accommodations on railway trains did not violate the Thirteenth Amendment. It also ruled that a state statute requiring railway companies to make the separation and providing for the punishment of a passenger who insisted upon using accommodations other than those provided for his race did not violate the Fourteenth Amendment. Indicating a willingness to leave matters of social equality to the people themselves, the Court stated: "If the civil and political rights of both races be equal one cannot be inferior to the other civilly or politically. If one race be inferior to the other socially, the Constitution of the United States cannot put them on the same plane." But Justice John M. Harlan felt otherwise. In his dissenting opinion, he said:

> I am of the opinion that the statute of Louisiana is inconsistent with the personal liberty of citizens, white and black, in the State, and hostile to both the spirit and letter of the Constitution of the United States. If laws of like character should be enacted in the several states of the Union, the effect would be in the highest degree mischievous. Slavery, as an institution tolerated by law, would, it is true, have disappeared from our country, but there would remain a power in the states, by sinister legislation, to interfere with the full enjoyment of the blessings of freedom, to regulate civil rights, common to all citizens, upon the basis of race, and to place in a condition of legal inferiority a large body of American citizens, now constituting a part of the political community, called the "people of the United States."

The Court's decision in this and other cases had actually formed a legal blueprint according to which a system of black and white castes in the nation was to be assured.

The chain of legal containment lengthened to bind other areas of the Negroes' rights. State by state there came into existence laws and constitutional provisions designed to curtail the race's political effectiveness. Some of these laws were created to keep the Negro vote under white scrutiny and direct supervision; others were made to curtail it and render it null and void. On March 4, 1891, the Arkansas legislature passed a law providing for the alternate admission of whites and Negroes to certain voting precincts when citizens of these races appeared to cast their ballot. In precincts in which more than one hundred votes were cast at the election preceding the one being held, and where the voters consisted of persons belonging to different races, the judges of the election and the sheriff in attendance were required to admit persons to the voting place in such a manner as to permit voters of the white and Negro races to cast their ballots alternately. The Georgia registration law of 1884 required separate lists for white and Negro voters. These lists, showing clearly the race of each voter, were filed with county registrars. Laws like these, although they allowed Negroes to exercise their franchise, actually made it easy to keep track of how large the threat of the Negro vote might be.

More direct steps were taken by the Southern states in the interest of nullifying the Negro vote. The Mississippi constitution of 1890 imposed a uniform poll tax (a lien only upon taxable property) on every male inhabitant of the state between the ages of twenty-one and sixty years, and instituted the requirement that every voter must read or explain any section of the constitution about which he was asked. The South Carolina constitution of 1895 imposed a literacy test or the payment of taxes on property having at least a $300 valuation. In 1883 the Georgia Supreme Court decided that a legislative act requiring voters to cast their ballot in their own districts was not in conflict with the Georgia constitutional provision granting eligibility to vote on the basis of residence — where a citizen had lived one year in the state and six months in the county in which he offered to vote. The Louisiana constitution of 1898 followed Mississippi in requiring "literacy" as a qualifying basis for voting, but it exempted the grandchildren of those entitled to vote before 1867.[31]

The "primary" method of disfranchisement was begun as early

as 1895. In April of that year the Texas legislature passed a law requiring political parties to hold primary elections. By this law Texas recognized these parties as a functional segment of the state's governmental machinery. Six years later the state required voters to hold a poll tax receipt in order to vote. But if the receipt were lost, one was entitled to vote only upon making an affidavit before an authorized officer to the effect that such a receipt had been lost. The Terrell Election Act of 1905 made the Democratic primary the state's most effective device for disfranchising the Negro. It required any party which polled 100,000 or more votes in the previous general election to nominate its candidates by primary election.[32] Since the party operated as a club or a society definitely closed to Negroes, Negroes were prohibited from participating in a nomination which was tantamount to an election. Other states followed these varied examples until, by 1910, every former Confederate state had "legally" disfranchised the South's Negro population.

The final links in the chain of containment were forged through a series of statutes, ordinances, and customs enacted to control the most personal aspects of the lives of Negroes. This action was basic. It laid the foundation for a biracial society, separating whites and Negroes into distinct castes. Provision was made for the separation of the races on all public occasions where people gather; intermarriage involving whites and Negroes was prohibited; and a special place in the economic order was assigned to Negro workers.

Although sporadic attempts to separate the races in public gatherings had been made by the Southern states prior to the *Civil Rights Cases,* no definite system of segregation was instituted at that time. In 1890, however, the Mississippi legislature passed a law providing for the separation of white and African races while passengers on railway carriers. All railway companies carrying passengers in that state were compelled to provide "equal" but separate and "sufficient" accommodations for white and African races by supplying two or more passenger coaches for each passenger train. In case the company carried one car, that car had to be partitioned by wood to accommodate white passengers at one end and Negro passengers at the other. Similar provisions were legally required in the case of waiting rooms at depots. Conductors and train officials were given the authority and responsibility to enforce this law. Comparable laws were enacted by Georgia and Louisiana during this year; Arkansas followed the next year; and North Carolina passed such legislation in 1899.

Almost simultaneously, legislation separating the races invaded the theaters, saloons, and eating places. A Louisiana statute of 1908 required separate saloons for white and colored persons, but the following year the separation was made even more complete by Court interpretation. The Supreme Court held that the sale of liquor to white and colored persons could not be conducted in the same building, and that the statute was not obeyed by providing separate bars in the same building.

In addition to separating the races in voluntary association, state statutes required the segregation of the physically ill, the criminal, and even the insane. In 1890 Georgia passed a law prohibiting the chaining together of white and Negro prisoners at any time, and in 1908, the races were separated in their work at state prison farms. Arkansas and North Carolina enacted similar legislation, and Mississippi extended it to the physically ill. The state passed a law in 1892 that required white and colored races to be kept in separate hospitals. The opening of the twentieth century saw some states make racial separation a birth and a death matter. The Mississippi legislature permitted the Ladies Auxiliary Cemetery Association, a white organization, to remove the remains of a Negro state official to a Negro cemetery. New Orleans added insult to injury by requiring white and Negro prostitutes to live in separate districts, although this law was held invalid in 1917.

In a desperate attempt to prevent the races from mixing their blood, each Southern state enacted rigid laws against personal association and intermarriage. South Carolina's constitution of 1895 declared the marriage of a white person with a Negro or a person having one eighth or more Negro blood unlawful and void. Mississippi not only prohibited such marriages but also provided for a $500 fine to be imposed upon anyone found guilty of printing, publishing, or circulating printed or written matter urging or suggesting social equality or intermarriage between whites and Negroes. By 1900 the South had erected a blanket ban against interracial marriages involving blacks and whites.

The walls of caste were raised higher and higher by law and custom. Within the first decade of the twentieth century the Southern states further elaborated their laws requiring separation of the races in various forms of transportation. Between 1911 and 1914 many Southern states passed ordinances segregating residential areas, and the custom of selling agricultural lands to Negroes only where specific areas were involved became a fixed part of the Southern norm.[33] The crop lien laws, passed in 1865, were still operational at the turn of the century. They lingered to legalize the continual dependency of sharecropper upon planter. As sharecropping became the basic labor pattern of Southern agriculture, many Negroes and poor whites were pressed into this service.[34] As the "Negro's place" in the South was further defined, it became quite evident that the two races were destined to live in two separate worlds for many years to come.

THE RISING TIDE OF "NEGRO EDUCATION"

Under the impact of new constitutional interpretations and limiting statutory laws, racial segregation became institutionalized and provided a special mold according to which education for Negroes was to be shaped for almost one hundred years. The biracial society in the South limited the education of Negroes to a special kind considered suitable for their status; it anchored the support of Negro schools more in the willingness of white citizens to provide for them than in the ability of the states to support them; and, most important of all, it directed the development of Negro children out of the mainstream of American culture into the bayous. If there is any period that can be said to mark the beginning of what is commonly called Negro education, this is it.

The period began with the serious barriers to the education of Negroes that the whites had restored, and it became quite apparent that these barriers had to be removed if the Negroes were to receive any education at public expense. There were still whites who opposed any kind of education for the freedmen. Some feared that education would bring more interference from the Federal government. Others felt that it would make Negroes unfit for the place to which Southern society had assigned them. And there were many who contended that since Negroes paid few taxes to make education available to them at public expense would mean exploiting whites for the benefit of the blacks.[35] Also, the attitudes of Southern paternalism had melted away. Most whites had begun to view the Negro as a stranger to whom they had scant obligations. George W. Cable, writing in 1885 concerning Southern sentiments along these lines, reminded the nation that foremost among all Southern beliefs was the idea that the Negro was by necessity an outsider; that the South had to anchor its laws, conscience, and conduct in the conviction that the "man of African tincture was, by nature and unalterably, an alien." [36]

Inherent in the very nature of this form of opposition to the Negroes and their education, however, were subtle hints as to how the opposition could be softened and how something could be salvaged for the freedmen. There was the hint that any movement to educate the Negro had to consider the Southern view. It had to place the blame for Southern disorganization at his door; it had to place the obligation to change upon his shoulders; and it had to prove that a particular kind of education could be of decided advantage to both races, especially the whites.

The last quarter of the nineteenth century saw Southern and Northern leaders picking up these hints and advocating views that complied with these limitations. Joseph Hodgson, superintendent of public instruction in Alabama, took the lead in his speech before the National Education Association at its annual meeting in Boston in 1872. After citing the "alarming" percentage of illiteracy found in the population of the Gulf Coast states, the superintendent warned the association that governmental control would move mainly to the hands of an untutored electorate that was dominantly colored if steps were not taken to extend education to both groups.[37] Five years later, *The Nation* extended this view by basing the entire solution of the race problem on the "education of Negroes for intelligent use of the ballot." It decried the tendency of Negroes to vote commonly on political questions, and attributed such collective behavior to mass ignorance rather than common aspirations.[38] The persistence of such views eventually bore fruit, and many who had most bitterly opposed the education of Negroes admitted that there was possibly some wisdom in a policy of training the freedmen for their "place in the lower sphere of life."

If there was any further doubt in the minds of Southern educators concerning the advisability of extending education to the Negroes by way of a special route, it was severely eroded by the influence of General S. C. Armstrong, an officer of Negro troops during the Civil War who had founded the Hampton Normal and Agricultural Institute for Negro youths in 1868 under the auspices of the American Missionary Association. Accepting the Southern system of segregation and its concept of the natural difference of whites and blacks, General Armstrong outlined the South's chief educational obligation in a speech before the National Educational Association in 1872. He appealed for training schools to meet the overwhelming demands for Negro teachers that private and public sources of education had already created. He based the advisability of meeting such a need on several grounds — all of which were acceptable to the South: He contended that the South could not, in its present economic condition, provide these teachers without admitting the Negro to her white schools of high grade. The right point of cooperation between Northern aid and Southern needs, he felt, was in the normal schools. That this education should be special, he based on a concept of racial difference. Speaking of the Negro, General Armstrong argued that he is "capable of acquiring knowledge to any degree, and, to a certain age, at least, with about the same facility as white children; but lacks the power to assimilate and digest it. The Negro matures sooner than the white, but does not have his steady development of mental strength up to advanced years. He is a child of the tropics, and the differentiation of races goes deeper than the skin." General Armstrong cited a great and growing demand for Negro teachers and reminded the association that these teachers were not only best able to elevate their own race but were far less "obnoxious" to Southern men than white teachers.[39]

76

Less than two decades later, a definite ideology of special education for Negroes began to challenge the liberal method that Northern missionaries had established throughout the South. Once again the South found its chief ideologist in General Armstrong. By 1890 his theory of Negro education had matured and was beginning to attract disciples for the movement he had started at Hampton. He told the First Mohonk Conference, in its session at Ulster County, New York, that he was sure the moral uplift of Negroes could be achieved through labor. He presented industrial education as the character-building force capable of elevating Negroes to a level of acceptance by the South and the nation. He identified hard work as a Christian virtue "next to the grace of God." He told the conference, "hard work, in its largest sense, is the most vital thing in Christian civilization. . . . Of the Negro I think this labor doctrine is true." [40] In his thinking, Negroes had been forced to work all their lives. This developed in them a distaste for labor. They had to be given an idea of the dignity of labor. This, he thought, could be done through the "industrial system," which would open wide to Negroes various opportunities in the agricultural, mechanical, and household industries. Not only would the opportunities render Negroes self-supporting, the general contended, but they would make them valuable, thereby giving the South a labor force of great potential wealth. Speaking of the result of the Hampton system, he said, "An able-bodied student represents a capital of perhaps a thousand dollars. We propose to treble that. When they earn a trade, they are worth three-fold more in the labor market." [41]

Reactions to the Armstrong philosophy of Negro education were mixed. Some educators rejected the idea altogether, taking a rather firm stand in the opposite direction. Others accepted the theory of industrial education but made it only second to important considerations of a more liberal and classical education. On the whole, however, educators of both races and from all regions concurred in the feeling that Negroes should be trained in a manner consistent with their position in American life and that this should be mainly industrial in nature.

Among those who rejected the idea was William T. Harris, United States Commissioner of Education. In his appearance before the

77

First Mohonk Conference, he made a special plea for normal schools in which Negro teachers could be trained, but he differed seriously with Armstrong as to what this training should be. "Education, intellectual and moral," he told the conference, "is the only means yet discovered that is always sure to help people to help themselves." Claiming industrial education to be merely economical in nature, the commissioner urged that "intellectual education" could prevent Negroes from reverting to their "former lower stage of spiritual life." [42] Since segregation had robbed them of the more uplifting contacts with whites, this type of education, Harris believed, could go some distance toward making up the difference.

By 1895 Harris had become even more attached to this idea. In an address before the students of Atlanta University, he warmly commended the work of higher education for Negroes as carried on at that institution. Without depreciating the importance of elementary and industrial training for the masses of Negroes, he advised the students that nothing is more "practical" than getting an insight into Western civilization. Showing remarkable insight concerning the course of subsequent events, he added this prophetic note:

> As our civilization is largely derived from the Greeks and Romans, and as Negroes of America are to share it with the Anglo-Saxons, it is very important that the bright minds among them would get acquainted with it, as others have done, through the study of Latin and Greek. This is the more necessary, since, with the advance of civilization and the development of machinery, the proportion of manual laborers in every community is steadily diminishing, while the proportion of the directors of labor and other brain workers is correspondingly increasing.[43]

There was further opposition to the idea of industrial education. It came from those educators who felt that industry was the one aspect of American life with which Negroes were probably more familiar than whites. Such a view was expressed by Judge A. W. Tourgee in his response to General Armstrong's appeal at the Mohonk conference. Since many of the educators at the conference had referred to the Negro's industrial inefficiency, the judge expressed surprise that no one had made reference to the industrial excellence of the race. "I have always been less impressed," he confessed, "with the industrial needs of the colored man than his industrial achievements." [44] Professor William E. Hutchins of Biddle University shared this view. Although he accepted the idea of "industrial education," he felt that there were obvious reasons why the emphasis should be on the "education" rather than the "industrial." To carry this point, he said, "If there is an industry in the South, the Negroes have it. What they want is education. What can you teach colored women about washing clothes?" [45]

But General Armstrong, the chief ideologist of the industrial education, very readily found a most efficient apostle. His doctrine was to be spread to all corners of the nation by Booker Taliaferro Washington, who in the early days after the Civil War had managed to find some rudiments of education in a night school at Malden, West Virginia, and had entered Hampton in 1872. After studying at this institution until 1875 and later at the Wayland Seminary in Washington, D.C., the young student was called back to Hampton by General Armstrong to act as his secretary. The part Hampton played in shaping his educational philosophy must have been decisive, for Washington wrote this concerning his tenure there: "The great and prevailing idea that seemed to take possession of every one was to prepare himself to lift up the people at his home. No one seemed to think of himself. And the officers and teachers, what a rare set of human beings they were! They worked for the students night and day, in and out of season. They seemed happy only when they were helping the students in some manner." [46]

Washington's conversion to the Armstrong philosophy must have been exceptional, for early in 1881 the general selected him, on the application of the citizens of Tuskegee, Alabama, to start in that town a Negro normal school for which the Alabama legislature had just granted a charter, in addition to an annual appropriation of $2,000 for teachers' salaries. The school was to be modeled on the plan of Hampton. [47] In this way began one of the most illustrious careers in the history of American education. Thus, too, began one of the most unique educational experiments in the history of man's long quest for control over himself.

In a dilapidated shanty near the Negro Methodist church — together with the church itself as an assembly room — Booker T. Washington began the long trek toward making thirty Negro pupils self-supporting industrious citizens of the South. This beginning was unruffled by its primitive setting. Education, as he had learned from General Armstrong, had to be related to the common needs of life. Consequently, Washington struggled to make the school a real part of the community in which it was located. He won this struggle.[48] His graduates were trained farmers and mechanics as well as trained teachers. However, the influence of Washington's ideas upon Negro education can be said to have begun to spread in the Midwest rather than in his home region.

In the summer of 1884, in Madison, Wisconsin, Washington, like General Armstrong before him, spoke before the National Education Association, facing the broad question of race relations and outlining the structure of his program dealing with the race problem. This program, as he sketched it at Madison and executed it at Tuskegee, was grounded in two basic convictions: first, that the two races had to live together; second, that they could coexist symbiotically. He believed that the Negro's home was permanently in the South and that the interest of one race was inextricably tied to the other. He contended that both races were engaged in a struggle to adjust themselves to the new conditions produced by the war and that anything done for Negroes would be of no real value to them if it did not benefit the whites who surrounded them. This confidence he placed in the symbiotic — in the tendency for racial groups to be useful to and dependent upon each other — was not really whistling in the dark. It was born of Washington's fundamental belief in the inevitability of human progress. "Progress is the law of God," he said. "One might as well try to stop the progress of a mighty railroad train by throwing his body across the track as to try to arrest the ceaseless advance of humanity." [49]

This faith manifested at Madison was, eleven years later, to make Booker T. Washington the most dominant figure in the field of Negro education. Speaking before the Atlanta Exposition in 1895, in the same year and city in which W. T. Harris had so convincingly extolled the virtues of classical education, Washington laid out the ground rules on the basis of which blacks and whites could make peace with each other in the South. The rules specified that Negroes abandon their interest in starting at the top of Southern society, that they put forth their best efforts to exploit the opportunities they had always encountered at the bottom where they lived. As if apologizing for the Negro's failure to do this in the past, Washington said, "Ignorant and inexperienced, it is not strange that in the first years of our new life we began at the top instead of the bottom; that a seat in Congress or the state legislature was more sought than real estate or industrial skill; that the political convention or stump speaking had more attractions than starting a dairy farm or being a truck driver." In the place of this strategy which had always elicited conflict and hard feeling between the two races, Washington suggested that each race start where it was. In a cry that sounded around the world, he advised: "Cast down your bucket where you are." To Negroes, he appealed that they "cast down in agriculture, mechanics, commerce, domestic service, and in the professions." He appealed to whites to "cast down upon the eight millions of Negroes" who could, once again, form the South's basic labor supply. With these appeals, he gave each race reason to have confidence in the other. He assured whites that the most intelligent of the Negro race had understood that agitation of the question of social equality was "the extremist folly" and that progress in the enjoyment of all the privileges that could come to Negroes had to be the result of severe and constant struggle rather than of "artificial forcing." He assured Negroes that "No race that has anything to contribute to the markets of the world is long in any degree ostracized. It is important and right that all privileges of the law be ours, but it is vastly more important that we be prepared for the exercise of these privileges. The opportunity to earn a dollar in the factory just now is worth infinitely more than the opportunity to spend a dollar in an opera house." [50]

Washington put his educational philosophy to work through the great Tuskegee "experiment." One of his basic aims was to train Negroes to do better what they had always done. Consequently, his early efforts at Tuskegee involved studying the conditions under which the colored people of the county and its surrounding areas lived. Several of these conditions shaped the curriculum of the

Institute. One certainly was the landlessness of the masses of Negroes who lived within the shadows of Tuskegee together with the evils of sharecropping that permeated the Negro family life, leaving it morally weakened and economically insecure.[51] Another was the aimless mobility of the colored population. The curriculum had to accommodate this problem. As Washington put it: "Something must be done to stem the swelling tide which each year sweeps thousands of black men and women and children from the sunlit monotony of the plantation to the sunless iniquity of the slums; from a drudging that is not quite cheerless to competition that is altogether merciless." [52] Agriculture, therefore, became a chief course in the Institute's curriculum. The school's mission was largely that of supplying well-equipped teachers for the various schools, but it was intended that the teachers be able and eager to teach gardening and carpentry as well as grammar and arithmetic.[53]

Washington found it necessary to break down the students' prejudices against this type of education. To many of them education was something quite different from what they met at Tuskegee: It was an escape from the world of work they had always known rather than a dedication to a different kind of work in the same old world. They interpreted education as an instrument designed to set them apart from the rest of the community rather than an influence designed to make them work closely with their people. Washington's desire that they prepare themselves to go back to the rural districts from which they had come was disturbing to many. His insistence that they do some work while studying at Tuskegee was irritating to some of the parents. Many requested that their children be taught "book learning" but not be required to work.[54]

Most of these prejudices were eliminated through Washington's close contacts with students of the Institute. These contacts began with the school's inception. After giving an entrance examination in arithmetic, grammar, and history to the first thirty pupils enrolled there, he lined up the entire group for the first of the school's daily inspections. He called attention to missing buttons, grease spots, dirty collars, and other failures to meet the standard of neatness and cleanliness upon which he insisted.[55]

What he considered the real meaning of education was discussed in his Sunday evening talks before the students. In these discussions, frequent emphasis was placed on the dignity of labor, the essential affinity of mental and physical activity, and how happiness comes from the common things of life.[56]

The most effective method of converting students to his view was probably that of integrating theory and practice. The student body was divided into day students and night students. The latter worked, in the industries mostly, at common labor all day and attended school at night. Through their labor they could pay their current board bills and eventually save enough to cover their expenses for attending day school later. Day students, therefore, were either former night students or those whose parents could afford to pay a considerable part of their expenses.[57] Nevertheless, each student was required to do some type of work. The student was more directly exposed to the work idea through his course of study. The Tuskegee method specifically involved the infusion of vocational training into the so-called academic courses. In mathematics a student of carpentry would be asked to determine which common length of board would suffice for a given job with a minimum of waste. A girl learning dressmaking would be required to state the smallest number of yards of cloth required to make dresses of several sizes. And a boy in agriculture would be required to know the selling price of his bale of cotton at the prevailing price per pound. Of this method Washington would say, "An ounce of application is worth a ton of abstraction." [58]

Among the many impressions which Booker T. Washington made upon the course of education for Negroes in the South, two stand out above the rest. First, his educational philosophy and practice allayed the fears of Southern whites concerning the Negro and won the support of whites of both regions for the public education movement. Because of the large number of Negroes in the various states of the South, whites of the region felt insecure in an atmosphere where blacks were struggling for political control, social equality, and mixed schools. Washington assuaged these fears by accepting an educational test as a requirement for voting and implying that the ballot could be reserved for a few "intelligent" Negroes. He accepted segregation as a system with which Negroes could expect to live for many years, and he showed evidence of structuring an educational plan that was an adjustment to it rather than a source of conflict with it. The separate or mixed school question he readily dismissed as a problem carrying its own solution. Responding to a railroad official who raised this question with him in Colorado, Washington said:

> As a rule, colored people in the Northern states are opposed to any plans for separate schools, and I think their feelings in the matter deserve consideration. The real objection to separate schools, from their point of view, is that they do not like to feel that they are compelled to go to one school rather than the other. It seems as if it was taking away part of their freedom. This feeling is likely to be all the stronger where the matter is made a subject of public agitation. On the other hand, my experience is that if this matter is left to the discretion of the school officials, it usually settles itself. As the colored people usually live together, there will naturally be schools in which colored students are in the majority. In that case, the process of separation takes place naturally and without the necessity of changing the Constitution. If you make it a constitutional question, the colored people are going to be opposed to it. If you leave it simply an administrative question, which it really is, the matter will very likely settle itself.[59]

The whites who lived near Tuskegee and observed the effect of Washington's handiwork gradually fell under the spell of the educator's convincing plan. They first observed with mistrusting curiosity. They later condoned and even praised the fruits of his efforts. And, still later, they gave some of their funds in order that the work might move more rapidly toward what they had been led to believe it could become. Public school superintendents, finding this kind of tolerance with regard to the education of Negroes, revitalized their efforts to build schools for Negroes at public expense. As Northern philanthropists came to know Washington, they looked to him as a counselor for their interest in the development of Southern education. His influence led John D. Rockefeller to establish the General Education Board in 1902, stimulated the establishment of the Anna T. Jeanes Fund, and played a large part in the creation of the Phelps-Stokes Fund and the Rosenwald rural-school program.

Not only did these funds assist the Tuskegee extension program, but they also affected practically every branch of Negro education in the South.[60]

The second and greatest Washington influence, however, probably rested with the weight he gave the "special education" movement. He left little doubt in the minds of a large number of educators and philanthropists that Negroes required a particular kind of education for their particular condition. He seemed to have looked forward to a completely biracial society of benevolent coexistence with whites. He chose to educate Negroes within the framework of a racial division of labor that had always existed in the South. Although he did not advocate industrial education for every Negro to the exclusion of the professions and other branches of learning, he did imply that the sole excuse for these latter branches was in the existence of the segregated communities where Negroes were forced to live.[61] His emphasis upon the "industrial" hit the Negro radical leaders with an exaggerated force. With the radical interests championed by W. E. B. Du Bois, there was a running verbal battle between Washington and the "classical" education leaders for a long period of time. In the end, both the industrial schools like Hampton and Tuskegee and the liberal arts schools like Atlanta and Fisk were engaged in the task of "Negro education." The two types of schools educated Negro youths for different classes within the same caste system.

THE STRAW IN THE WIND

As the idea of special education for Negroes developed in the minds of Southern and Northern educators, the economic base for the support of Negro schools shifted from the apportionment provided by law to the amount of the tax fund that school officials saw fit to allocate. The shift was as gradual as the events that caused it. It came as a wind carrying a straw — as a hint of discrimination without conscience.

During the initial stages of the public education movement and before the idea of special education had claimed public attention, little difference existed in the financial support given the Negro and white schools. Of the 146,737 children attending the public schools of North Carolina in 1873, 38 percent were Negro. The state spent $139,433.66 for the operation of its public schools that year and one-third of this was assigned to schools for Negro children.[62] Relatively little racial discrimination had developed in the allocation of school funds as late as 1889. Negro and white schools in the various Southern states were open approximately the same number of days each year, and their teachers received approximately the same monthly salary. The greatest difference in the average length of the school term was three days in favor of white children in North Carolina, and the greatest difference in salary was $12 per month in favor of the salary of white teachers in that state. In fact, the salaries of Negro teachers were higher than those paid white teachers in Kentucky and Louisiana during this time.[63]

As the years passed, however, the strain of taxes became so great that public officials began to search for devices by which they could take from Negroes the equal share of the state funds they had hitherto enjoyed — either to divert a large portion of the money to the support of white schools or to reduce school taxes in general. A convenient opportunity for discrimination was found in the legislation adopted by most Southern states that permitted local boards and school officials to use their own discretion in the distribution of school funds.[64] The Mississippi law of March 5, 1875, is an example of this. It provided for separate schools for the two races and the stipulation that teachers be paid according to the class of certificate which they had been issued. Since these certificates were secured through examinations given by county superintendents, it was possible for all teachers' salaries to be controlled by the officials who graded the examination papers.[65]

The general political conditions of the times created even greater opportunities, which had crucial impact. The "separate but equal" concept, which had become the basic theme in the South, came to deprive the Negro school of even the equality that this legal doctrine had originally implied. This was a vague concept, subject to many different interpretations — none of which involved objective criteria. What was considered equal by one race was not necessarily

86

considered equal by the other. It all depended upon the race for which the equality was being defined. Legal disfranchisement was equally damaging. Negroes were robbed of the basic tools by which they could keep their schools strong. Without full political participation, they could not offer themselves for the offices through which school systems were run or school funds were appropriated, nor could they vote for those who could be candidates. If they did not like the way things were going, they could do relatively nothing about it within the framework of the law. Their most effective source of relief had to operate within the framework of sycophancy. Negroes had to court the favor of influential whites by advocating the kind of education whites wanted Negroes to have or by bootlegging the kind Negroes felt their children must have.

A convenient excuse for discrimination in the allocation of the funds to schools for the respective races was the concept that the type of education that Negroes needed was less complex and less expensive than that needed by whites.[66] Temptation was therefore sharpened by circumstance, and the structure of "Negro education" became consistent with its function. As a result, near the close of the nineteenth century, the development of Negro public schools began to slow down and taper off. The average length of the term grew slowly; teachers' salaries increased little; and the per capita expenditure for the education of Negro children fell consistently behind that for whites. The average length of term of the white schools of Alabama increased gradually from 81 days in 1876 to 108 in 1905, while the term of the Negro schools in the same period increased only from 77 days to 92. The average monthly salary of white teachers increased from $23 to $40, while that of the Negro teachers remained virtually constant during this time.[67] The per capita school expenditure for whites and Negroes in North Carolina in 1876 was $.95 and $1 respectively, but by 1905 it had increased to $1.91 for whites, remaining at $.95 for Negroes.[68] The per capita expenditure for the respective races in Tennessee during this period changed from $1.40 and $1 to $1.75 and $1.[69] These racial differences were merely straws in an evil wind that was to reach gale force less than a quarter of a century later.

The wind was evil mainly because it significantly restricted the development of Negro children, confining their aspirations and achievements to the limits of their own world of color. Their school community was color-bound. White and Negro pupils were taught in separate buildings, and the buildings, of course, were located in separate neighborhoods. If the children were to get new ideas, they were to get them through innovations that originated within the respective races. The industrial curriculum to which many Negro children were exposed, supposedly designed to meet their needs, reflected the life that accompanied their status at that time. They had always farmed. The curriculum aimed to make them better farmers. Negro women had a virtual monopoly on laundering, and Negro men had largely worked as mechanics. The industrial curriculum was designed to change this only in so far that Negroes were trained to perform these services better. A measure of the wisdom of this type of educational philosophy was to come later. It was to come in the attitude of management toward the use of Negro labor at the level of skill on which this type of training placed them. Nonindustrial training did occur at all levels, but most of this served either to prepare Negro teachers for Negro schools or to prepare Negro professionals for service in the Negro community. Through this system of "Negro education," serious blockages occurred in the diffusion of the general culture to members of the race. Therefore, the need for cultural assimilation which had inspired the movement to educate the freedmen was forgotten. The assimilation of Negroes was blocked by the very institution that had been designed to foster it. This was the Great Detour.

IV · DECISIONS AT
CAPON SPRINGS

The idea of a special kind of education for Negroes, championed by a few individual educators from the North and South, eventually spread to become the basic ideology of the Negro school system. Northern and Southern leaders, realizing that an equalitarian approach to the development of educational opportunities for the Negro American was not acceptable to white Southerners, joined forces to save for the former slaves what could be salvaged. At the close of the nineteenth century an organization that came to be known as the Conference for Education in the South, and which was to meet annually seventeen consecutive times in all, came into being under their leadership. In creating this organization they accepted the caste system imposed by the South and built within it an educational structure of their own.

This method of interracial accommodation, which is what the great detour really was, continued to develop and to produce the kind of leadership that was essential for the establishment of the method as an intentional and acceptable function of Southern society. This method was a compromise — a route over which the Negro's developing educational opportunities could be carefully directed by a dedicated leadership. Since the South would not accept any other kind of Negro education, especially education aimed at developing the race for general participation in Southern society, leaders of the great detour struck a compromise with the South and settled for a special kind of education that would prepare Negroes for the caste position prescribed for them by white Southerners. As it turned out, the leaders were men with common educational ideals who were capable of identifying the main problems of Negro education and building an organization designed to overcome such problems. The ideas generated by the Conference for Education, beginning in the minds of so few and spreading to involve so many, gave a new impetus to universal education in the former Confederacy and laid the foundation for Negro education as we have come to know it.

CONCEIVING AN EDUCATIONAL COMPROMISE

As the minds of Northern and Southern leaders had met to effect the political Compromise of 1877, so did they meet to effect the educational compromise that crystallized two decades later when an Episcopal clergyman from Massachusetts met a former Confederate soldier from West Virginia. The clergyman was Dr. Edward Abbott of Cambridge, who had become dedicated to public service in the field of education through attending the Mohonk Conference on Indian Affairs and International Arbitration in 1890. The soldier was Captain William H. Sale, who operated a resort hotel at Capon Springs, West Virginia. Eight years later, while making an extended tour through the South, observing schools and learning of their needs, Dr. Abbott stopped at Capon Springs and proposed to Captain Sale that the latter convene a conference on Southern education at his hotel. His proposal was prompted by the success of the conferences at Lake Mohonk. Sale liked the idea and authorized Dr. Abbott to form a committee to select the persons to be invited and to arrange the program.[1]

On the advice of his committee, Dr. Abbott arranged a program to explore two basic questions concerning public education in the South: how far could the public school system in the South be improved and made effective, and how far was it feasible to introduce industrial education? Following the singing of "Nearer, My God, to Thee" and a prayer offered by Bishop Thomas Dudley of Kentucky, the First Capon Springs Conference for Education in the South opened on June 29, 1898 and began seeking solutions for the many educational problems that were plaguing the South. Northern and Southern leaders, in what they thought to be one final and

benevolent effort to achieve interracial peace, began to establish
a common ground on which they could build a new kind of education for Negroes.

The very nature of the conference personnel made the situation
ripe for compromise. Among the founders were educators who,
though representing diverse regions, were acceptable to both the
North and the South. All of them had won the confidence of white
Southerners through the work they had done with the Negro schools
which they headed. They included Hollis Frissell, white, president
of Hampton Institute; and the Reverend A. B. Hunter, also white,
president of St. Augustine's College at Raleigh, North Carolina.
(St. Augustine's had already won some acclaim for having trained
teachers for the state's understaffed Negro schools.) Also present
were the heads of other institutions whose programs were consistent
with the prevailing Southern philosophy about training Negro
teachers and leaders. Among them were Dr. D. J. Satterfield of
Scotia Seminary at Concord, North Carolina; Professor Charles
F. Meserve of Shaw University at Raleigh; Dr. Julius D. Dreher
of Roanoke College in Virginia; President Wilbur F. Thirkfield of
Gammon Theological Seminary at Atlanta; and the Reverend
George F. Fairchild of Berea College in Kentucky. In all, thirty-
six persons attended the first conference — among them fourteen
ministers of seven denominations and nine presidents of separate
colleges for both races in the South. Coming from thirteen different
states, including the District of Columbia these men represented
rather exactly the kind of leaders with whom white Southerners
felt they could do business.

The conferees were divided little, if at all, on those educational
issues that favored the Southern racial ideology.[2] They met on
common ground concerning the Negro and grew even closer together in their racial concepts as their organized association with
each other continued. At the very beginning they launched upon
a sincere search for racial issues that were even more common to
them, and they emerged from their first engagement with several
common convictions. Since they had largely been concerned with
the education of Negroes, their discussions dealt mainly with this
problem. Despite past controversies involving such matters, their

deliberations paved the way for their arrival at a common view that the South had not been so bad for the Negro and that Negro education had not been so bad for the South.

Frissell, attempting to summarize the situation, set the compromise in motion by insisting that whites and Negroes could live together in the South and by contending that slavery even proved that peaceful relations could be beneficial to both races. "There are those," he told the conference, "who are bold enough to believe that Christianity has revealed some truths which ancients did not know, that the world has made some progress . . . that there is no reason in the nature of things why different races of different colors should not dwell together in peace. I believe that in the South today, in spite of difficulties that prevail, that condition of affairs is working out. We are all agreed that slavery was a curse. . . . Yet, when Indian and Negro are placed side by side in schoolroom and workshop at Hampton, it is very clear that slavery was a much better training school than was the reservation." In describing further the work at Hampton, he called attention to the fact that the Institute's method of teaching Negroes encouraged them to build their own homes, to cultivate their own land, and to escape the clutches of the crop-lien system. Speaking of this system as a counterpart of slavery, he hastened to add that the South's greatest need was to bring the white man as well as the black man out from under this condition.

The Reverend D. J. Satterfield, in a later speech before the conference, reemphasized the mutual aid that this new movement offered both races by defining the mission of the conference as that of cooperating with the friends of education to the end of making public schools work in the South. "I look upon the latter," he added, "as the only hope, the only law for lifting the masses, and our influence and efforts cannot be given too freely to the task of molding a public sentiment in favor of building up the best possible type of common school education." In speaking of cooperation among schools, the Reverend A. B. Hunter sealed the union between Northern and Southern members of the conference by advising the group that their purpose was to combine something of the democratic spirit of a New England education with the "gentle manners and highborn ways of the South."

Speakers at later conferences continued to emphasize this common interest in education and the mutual benefit that could accrue to both whites and Negroes as a result of it. J. L. M. Curry pleased the Southerners greatly when he told the second conference: "I shall not stultify myself by any fresh argument in favor of Negro education, but I must be pardoned for emphasizing the fact that there is greater need for the education of other races. The white people are to be the leaders, to take the initiative, to have the direct control in all matters pertaining to civilization and the highest interest of our beloved land. History demonstrates that the Caucasian will rule." He hastened to add, however, that this white supremacy should mean friendship rather than hostility toward the Negro.[3]

William H. Baldwin, Jr., who was later to become a powerful factor in both the work of the conference and that of Tuskegee, shared Curry's view and added to it a brutal definition of the Negro's role in a society of white supremacy. When speaking of education for citizenship, he reported to the second conference: "In the Negro is the opportunity for the South." [4]

By the close of the nineteenth century, Northern educators had made a crucial decision. They had decided to sell the idea of Negro education to white Southerners by sacrificing the principle of racial equality. They had decided, too, that the best way to assure the sale was to emphasize its value to the purchaser. At the close of the third conference at Capon Springs, it was agreed by all members that the best way to provide training for Negroes was first to provide adequate schools and training for the neglected whites. Separate schools, there must be, they decided, but the schools would have to be provided for in one body of laws, and the system supported by taxes paid by all the people.[5] This organization of educators, therefore, gambled on the assumption that their stand in favor of white supremacy would remove the last barrier to universal education in the South and would salvage for Negroes whatever vestiges of freedom the movement of Southern restoration had left.

93

Not all the Southerners accepted this point of view, however. Many of them, still haunted by bitter memories of radical Reconstruction, feared that the Southern educational movement was another Northern attempt to force social equality upon the South. But wherever leaders of the new movement encountered this fear, they always countered it with the assurance that the plan sought to preserve rather than destroy Southern ways. When a reporter asked Walter Hines Page, a founder of the Southern Education Board, if there was not a "nigger in the woodpile," his reply was: "You will find when the woodpile is turned over not a nigger, but an uneducated white boy. He is the fellow we are after. We want to train both the white boy and the black boy, but we must train the white boy first, because we cannot do anything for the Negro boy until his white friend is convinced of his responsibility to him." [6] The Governor of Georgia was reported to have responded to the new educational effort by saying, "We can attend to the education of the darkey in the South without the aid of these Yankees and give them the education that they most need. I do not believe in the higher education of the darkey. He must be taught the trades. When he is taught the fine arts, he is educated above his caste, and it makes him unhappy." [7] Leaders of the movement again responded to criticism with words arranged to be reassuring to the South, but they spoke them with Southern voices. The *Review of Reviews* attempted to imply general Southern acceptance when it said concerning the fourth convocation:

> While most newspapers have shown an intelligent understanding and appreciation of the purposes of the educational Conference held at Winston-Salem in April, the impression has to some extent been created that it was made up in the main of a company of visitors from the North whose particular interest South of the Mason and Dixon Line lay in the higher education for the Negro race. The great majority of the members of the Conference were, in fact, Southern educators, most of them concerned with the instruction of white pupils.[8]

Through the invitation of the *New York Herald,* governors of several Southern states were asked to express their views on the movement. Governor Charles B. Aycock of North Carolina responded

94

through a letter to the paper, saying: "The Fourth Annual Conference for Education in the South will be of great benefit. We know more of the Northern view and the visitors know more of us. We do not, probably, entirely agree, but we respect more than ever the opinions of each other." [9]

Though trading was slow, there gradually appeared evidence that the South was buying the educational product which the North was exporting. The Right Reverend C. K. Nelson, Bishop of Georgia, on noticing the change, told the conference of 1899, "we rejoice rightly over the disappearance of sectional lines, and that the great question of moral and social deviation accompanying education has come to be universally regarded as paramount to all other considerations." [10] That the educational ideals pursued by the conference had at least become a part of the South's thinking was made apparent in the expressions of Governor A. J. Montague of Virginia before the sixth conference at Richmond. In his address of welcome, the governor accepted the concept of universal education for the South. "The education of our people," he said, "is the supreme task of statesmanship, as it is the supreme need of the masses of the people. Political despotism carries with it academic despotism." [11] As the Southern Education Board, the executive branch of the conference, progressed in its influence, the movement grew until it finally became one of the most powerful organizations in the South. By the opening of the new century, therefore, the North had once more invaded the South, but this time, on more friendly terms.

After winning the support of the Southern people, members of the Conference for Education in the South turned their attention to conditions relating specifically to the schools. First to claim their attention was the lack of standardization that characterized the schools with which they were to work. Some of the difficulties growing out of these conditions naturally pertained to the Negroes themselves. The Negro's position in Southern society had given a peculiar shape to his aspirations, often stimulating an ambition that exceeded his reach. As a result of their experiences following emancipation, many Negroes had been led to believe that education and politics were the chief means by which they could gain respect in the new order. As their opportunity for political participation melted away under the heat of disfranchisement, their confidence in education as a social ladder grew stronger. Books, grades, and degrees became the real symbols of an educated person, and knowledge, all too often, was pushed into the background. The tradition of superficiality in matters of education — having college degrees without corresponding qualifications — was planted deeply in their subculture. The new educators who came South had the big job of uprooting this tradition in order to realize their objectives. Since the Negro's hopes had been raised beyond the opportunities that white Southerners were willing to give him, leaders of the conference felt that he was inclind to neglect fundamentals for values which at that time were highly superficial. It was against this type of racial psychology that Booker T. Washington both spoke and acted, and there is little wonder that this educator's ideals echoed through the conference halls over and over again.

Leaders of the new educational movement saw this inconsistency between hope and opportunity as it openly operated in the various Negro schools. They knew that a series of Negro institutions called "colleges" had been established throughout the South as a result of the freedmen's school movement. They also knew that many of these institutions had apparently been engaged in a mad scramble to determine which one could give the greatest variety of college degrees to the greatest assortment of "Negro leaders." A. B. Hunter had complained against this indiscriminate conferring of degrees in a speech before the first conference. In criticizing this superfluity of honors, he said, "We have Bachelors of Arts and Bachelors of Science and Doctors of Philosophy, not to mention Doctors of Divinity galore." He reported an instance in which a Negro "university" received a charter from a state legislature and elected an all-Negro board of trustees, which, shortly after its organization, conferred the degree of Doctor of Divinity upon its President and the Doctor of Philosophy upon his brother. "All over our American land," Hunter lamented, "we are circulating counterfeit and debased coins. Is it not time," he asked, that "we should agree upon some common course of study?" [12] Speaking further on this matter of "counterfeit" education, the Reverend G. S. Dickerman of New

Haven told the second conference: "Another serious mischief of such schools is that they bring the public schools in discredit. The simple-minded parents are likely to think it an especially fine thing to send their aspiring boys and girls to the 'Institute' or 'college' or perhaps the 'university' while they were not more than eight or ten years old." [13]

This anxiety concerning standards in the Negro higher educational institutions was apparently appropriate. Although these institutions were established as colleges, most of them were mainly elementary schools with some high school students and only a few students matriculating on what could be called a college level. Although clusters of these schools were supported by denominational and charitable funds, each sought to operate as a separate and sovereign unit, unmindful of the work of sister institutions. A student who became *persona non grata* because of financial or disciplinary tangles in one institution very freely transferred to another, often without the tarnish of a previous record.

And there was yet another facet to the problem of standards. The spirit of the times made it open season on Northern philanthropy. Every possible scheme for educating Negroes found its way North to elicit the good graces of the benevolent societies. George F. Fairchild of Berea College led the attack against the "many solicitations that were being made by unscrupulous persons who sought the favor of Northern charities." So strongly did he protest against this type of indiscriminate campaigning that he proposed making a list of those institutions that were worthy of charitable support. "Such a list," he advised, "must be comparatively small, and be made with regard to (1) age and equipment, (2) efficiency of administration, and (3) location." [14] When carried to its fullest implication, this proposal meant an end to the indiscriminate establishing of Negro colleges, an increased dedication to the improvement of those that had already been established, and some kind of blockage of the growing tradition of adulterating academic standards.

Similar difficulties involving standards were recognized in the public schools. Although each Southern state had established a system of free public schools, there was little uniformity among them. This lack of uniformity hampered the work of the conference even

97

into the twentieth century. Charles W. Dabney, Director of the Bureau of Investigation and Information for the Southern Education Board, complained about this to the sixth conference at Richmond in 1903. "The work of the investigation has been extremely difficult," he said, "there is not, as a matter of fact, a complete system of public schools in any Southern state. No state has a thorough system of reporting upon the schools, with the result that the official reports are inadequate and lack uniformity." [15] There were specific conditions that encouraged this disorder. The various states continued to strain under the weight of their respective tax loads without pooling their experiences as to the best method of meeting the tax problem. Although their aims were rather common, their educational standards were as varied as their names. School terms differed considerably; the school curriculum was almost unique with each state; and criteria for selecting teachers had little in common except political expediency. The Fairchild proposal was not broad enough to encompass the jealousies that developed between private and public institutions. Since the conference manifested an interest in both, these jealousies grew more acute as both types of schools jockeyed for a more favorable position. The purification of standards and the coordination of school systems, therefore, was judged by conference leaders as one of the big problems that had to be solved if education in the South was to be improved. Although the motives of these educators were benevolent, even as far as Negro education was concerned, time was to determine whether their work in the South would purify or adulterate standards; centralize or decentralize the various kinds of schools.

Another set of problems that conference leaders recognized was related to the school curriculum. Although all agreed that the education offered Negroes should be different from that offered whites, they had to make important decisions as to how different it should be. Their decisions reflected two ideas that had already taken shape in their minds: the mental ability of the Negro race and the Negro school as an educational agency.

Because of their experiences with the Negro students and their schools, the educators agreed during the early phases of their work that the Negro's capacity for higher education had been demonstrated. They took some pride in the fact that many Southern whites had gained equal confidence in the Negro's ability. In a statement illustrating this faith, D. J. Satterfield informed the conference: "The County examiners often tell us that they have no better qualified teachers to examine than our Scotia students." [16] Thirkfield of Atlanta University also took the position that Negroes were generally able to acquire higher education. He warned those inclined to doubt his claim that judgment on this question could not be based upon mental capacity as it is expressed through the participation of the individual in his environment and civilization. Implying that limited participation had inhibited the full development of the Negro's potential, he reminded the conference that people had "learned to distinguish between the intellectual capacity, with which God has endowed every race, and the mental and moral acquirements, which are the outcome of civilization and environment." [17]

But these few swallows failed to make a summer. As time passed the expressed confidence that the educators had in the Negro's mental capacity became limited to the ideals of special education around which they were planning to build his future. Accepting the biracial society already established in the South, the leaders agreed that institutions of higher learning were essential to the development of leadership for the race. There was the feeling that Negroes did not have access to mass systems of cultural diffusion — libraries, the press, and learned classes — as did whites. They were shut off from higher fellowship in the civil, political, and religious life of the white man and were even shut up in their own schools and churches. It was necessary, the educators agreed, that they train their own leadership. With wealth, political power, and civic affairs in the hands of those who proposed to keep Negroes a subject people, many conference leaders felt that the future of the Negro masses was hopeless without educated leaders. It was decided, therefore, that certain Negro colleges would be made strong for the purpose of training ministers, physicians, and lawyers. These institutions would be assigned the task of developing a strong professional class that

99

would be responsible for raising the moral and physical standards of the race generally.* It should be said for the honesty of these educational planners that they did not seek to sell the Negro people short on purpose. They merely tried to fit training to needs — individual needs. It was this motivation that led President Horace Bumstead of Atlanta University to say, "We have too long made the mistake of regarding the race as a homogeneous mass instead of recognizing the diversity of its different classes." [18] With respect to individual differences, therefore, the new educators who had come South emerged from their early deliberations with the common agreement that the Negro college was to be preserved for the mentally elite of the race; that all could be elevated this way. As Bumstead put it, "The masses may not be able to go to college, but they may send their representative to college, and when he comes home they be wise by proxy." [19]

But the problem of educating the Negro masses still remained. What kind of education should be provided for them? Industrial education emerged as an emphatic answer. This answer was almost foreordained, for the leadership of the conference was composed of men who had long been converted to this educational ideology. Robert Ogden, who became a strong leader of the conference after attending the second convocation, had had a part in the industrial education idea from the beginning. He and General Armstrong were warm personal friends. It was in the parlor of Ogden's Brooklyn residence in 1866 or 1867 that a few men had met to consider Armstrong's plan for an industrial institute for emancipated slaves. Hampton was born from this meeting, and Ogden was associated with the Institute for forty-five years, serving as a trustee, as a financial supporter, and finally as the president of its board.[20] William Henry Baldwin, Jr., who also became a leader of the conference, was likewise oriented toward industrial education. He went South as a businessman conscious of the value of Negro labor. He considered this labor necessary to the efficient operation of his railroad, for he needed thousands of Negro workers — but needed

---

* It should be notel that nowhere in their plans was there any intention that this class would develop the force to destroy the system of interracial accommodation that gave it birth.

them trained. He was convinced that the prosperity of the South, as well as his railroad, depended on the productive ability of the population, and he felt that the source of this ability was and always would be the Negro. Baldwin was even more closely tied than Ogden to the concept of industrial education. At the request of Booker T. Washington, he gained firsthand familiarity with Tuskegee Institute and later became one of its trustees.[21]

The conferences were also influenced by other devotees of industrial education. One of these was Captain Charles F. Vawter, who joined the Southern education movement at its third conference and remained to win status as one of its main supporters. It was certainly he who presented the first dramatic appeal for the devotion of some interest to the education of the whites. His interest in industrial education had been of long standing. Having developed a strong appreciation for labor and discipline as a result of his farm and war experiences, he had given up his professorships at Emory and Henry Colleges to become superintendent of the Miller Manual Labor School, established for orphans at Albemarle County, Virginia, in 1878. Here he had realized his desired opportunity to develop a school that would train mind and hand together. Although it emphasized the needs of the white race, his speech before the third conference was weighted heavily to incline those mainly interested in the education of Negroes toward sharing his view.[22]

Through the influence of personalities like these the various conferences made three distinct decisions with regard to industrial education for Negroes. It was agreed at the first conference that the conditions under which the masses of Negroes lived made industrial education an essential part of their school curriculum. Slavery, it was believed, had shaped within their minds some undesirable attitudes that this type of education could remove. This condition of servitude had made them believe that work was for the bondman and leisure for the free. Whites, the educators thought, shared this attitude. Also, it was believed that this negative attitude had been reinforced under the influence of Northern teachers who, it was alleged, led the Negroes to hope that through books they could enjoy the fruits of a literary education like white men. Therefore, there was a consensus expressed at the second conference that the

Negro had been educated away from his natural environment and that his education should concern those fields available to him. This was a key decision, for it marked the formulation of the concept of "Negro education."

Another strategic decision along this line, developed during the third conference, was the acceptance of the idea that the Negro's industrial education had to be directed toward increasing the labor value of his race. This meant that in the minds of all Southern people, the Negro would be recognized in exact proportion to his economic value. Inspired by this concept, Baldwin cried out in his advice to the Negro: "Face the music, avoid social questions; leave politics alone; continue to be patient; live moral lives; live simply; learn to work and to work intelligently; . . . learn that it is a mistake to be educated out of your environment." [23] These ideals very quickly became a part of the ideology of common schools. Industrial departments sprang up wherever there were Negro schools large enough to have a plot of land for a farm or a small room for a shop and kitchen. These little departments were used to draw more money from the purses of charitable organizations than any other element of the Negro school program except the singing of Negro spirituals. Although they may not have intended it, the architects of this program designed a structure of education that encouraged the very academic adulteration against which they had spoken so vehemently in earlier conferences. All that was needed to complete the job was a crew of construction engineers properly trained to put up the building.

But as they scrutinized the South's Negro teaching force, they found it lacking in several particulars. From the point of view of qualifications, they found "teachers without pedagogy." This problem, too, had a history — a history that helped shape the attitudes toward it. When the first schools for the contrabands were opened, they were largely staffed by New England missionaries who, having much religious zeal and a firm liberal arts training, proceeded to teach the Negro children and even adults as they had been taught. Curricula and method were New England in nature. But the newer group of educators who had come South and instituted the conference method of dealing with educational problems envisaged a more "practical" education for Negroes and considered the older method inadequate in the light of the circumstances under which the race had to live. They knew that the freedmen's schools had grown much more rapidly than the supply of teachers, and they recalled too many instances in which the qualifications of those who taught were limited to the ability to read and demonstrate the bare rudiments of learning. As individuals, some of these new educators had been involved in efforts to remedy the problem. Frissell, speaking of his experiences along these lines, reminded the conference as early as its first meeting that during the period from 1869 to 1881 Northern charity had established Negro schools like Hampton, Tillotson College, Atlanta University, Berea College, Fisk, and Tuskegee for the purpose of training "young men and women who should make the common schools not only centers of intellectual training, but of morality, thrift, agriculture, and home life also." [24] Hampton graduates, he added, had made some decided progress along these lines. The problem as he saw it was the small number of such teachers available to the large number of schools that needed them. In his report to the third conference, the Reverend G. S. Dickerman emphasized the same need. "In most regions of the South," he contended, "no one is competent to teach. Superintendents report this as their biggest problem." [25]

The teacher situation posed yet another problem for the educational planners. Politics had invaded the realm of teacher selections. In some instances, superintendents, because of either indifference or graft, took the responsibility of teacher selection too lightly. D. J. Satterfield, who had worked closely with the local school boards of North Carolina, reported such an instance. He had visited a room where Negro teachers were being examined. The examiner there had arranged the room and had given out a printed list of questions, leaving the group unattended as soon as this was done. Showing his suspicions of this procedure, Satterfield remarked: "I shall not pretend to assign a motive for such unbounded confidence. I shall only say that nothing could be more of a farce than that examination." [26] Teachers and superintendents in four or five different states reported to Dickerman that appointments to teach were often sold for cash, awarded for political services, or bestowed for even more objectionable ends.[27] Some superintendents accounted for this laxity on the grounds that Negro teachers were so scarce that they had to take what they could get by any method that worked. Others dismissed the whole question by accusing conference leaders of expecting too much of Negroes or of measuring members of the race by "white standards." But these excuses and accusations were not acceptable to the conference. Its leaders believed that people could not be elevated any higher than the prevailing expectations for them. They decided that in matters like these the denominational schools had a special mission, that they were the chief hope at that time, and that there was a bitter need for additional institutions to share the burden. The future of Negro education in the South was properly seen as directly related to the training of teachers.

ORGANIZING FOR COOPERATIVE ACTION

The leaders of the new educational movement defined problems and developed a course of action almost simultaneously. They were not long in recognizing that all the difficulties experienced by Southern schools, by Negro schools in particular, resulted from a lack of coordination in the total educational effort. Therefore, beginning with their early convocations, they started to design schemes that promised to bring all the schools of the South under central control. This was the control of a "minister without portfolio." The conference was vested with no legal authority by any Southern state, and yet it wielded an influence as if it were so vested. Its leaders made their impact upon the total educational system of the South through indirect methods. They first created a means by which they could keep their ears close to the ground — could observe firsthand what was happening. Later, they developed almost absolute control over those charitable funds that tended to flow southward for educational purposes, and they institutionalized their efforts by creating a permanent team whose responsibilities were basically to represent them in the field and execute their policies.

When the Second Conference for Education in the South convened at the Capon Springs Hotel on June 20, 1899, a clear definition of its policies was stated, and an organization to implement this definition was created. The leadership of those whose educational ideas had begun to dominate the conference was given official sanction. J. L. M. Curry, agent of the Peabody and Slater boards, sat as president; Robert C. Ogden, businessman from New York, presided as vice-president; and the Reverend A. B. Hunter of St. Augustine's College served as secretary-treasurer. A committee, specifically oppointed to formulate conference objectives, presented and secured the adoption of the following resolutions:[28]

1. That the Executive Committee be authorized . . . to employ an agent of this Conference, who will work under the direction of Dr. Curry, its President, whose chief duty will be to study conditions in detail, and to ascertain such facts with respect to Southern education, both public and private, as will make more clear what methods and agencies are to be encouraged and what to be avoided or reformed, and will secure better harmony and more efficient concentration of effort in all educational work carried on in the South. Such agent will report to the Executive Committee from time to time, and the Committee will make annual reports to the Conference.

2. That the Conference recognizes the discernment and wisdom of the pleas that have been made in its sessions for the encouragement of secondary schools in the South as a necessary line between the common schools and the colleges, and that it recommends the subject as one urgently appealing on the one hand to counties and particular localities, and on the other hand to framers of the educational system and policies of the states.

3. That in the development of industrial education upon the lines now well established by noteworthy models, the Conference recognizes a basis for hearty and united cooperation on the part of all friends of Southern education, and further recognizes a hopeful means toward the better working out of existing social, economic, and racial problems. . . .

4. That the Conference gives grateful endorsement to the wise and helpful administration of the Slater and Peabody Funds; that it pays tribute to the rare comprehension and high devotion with which Dr. Curry performs the duties and exercises the discretion

devolving upon him under those trusts; that it appreciates the urgency of the need for a general committee of direction, in harmony or in conjunction with the management of those funds, to guard against the hazard, and in some cases, harmful use of money contributed at the North for Negro education; and further that we commend the work of teachers' institutes at the South as promoted by Dr. Curry, and appeal for the improvement by all possible means of the lot of the young women teachers of the common schools.

The conference further extended its organization toward the implementation of its objectives by making the Reverend G. S. Dickerman its field agent.[29] It also appointed a committee for the purpose of inquiring into the fraudulent solicitation of funds that had been going on in the interest of Negro education. This committee reported at the third conference, charging that these solicitations were undermining public confidence and recommending that a special committee be created to serve as a bureau of information on the subject. The bureau was to investigate all schools claiming to educate Negroes. Included in the recommendation was the suggestion that the public be notified of the conference action along this line and that all persons be asked to consult this bureau before giving aid to unknown parties.

By the opening of the current century, the organization of the conference as the dominant educational force in the South was complete. In its convocation of April 1901, the fourth conference accepted a resolution to appoint an executive board of seven, who would be fully authorized and empowered to conduct a campaign for free schools for all the people by supplying literature to the press, by participating in educational meetings, and by general correspondence. The resolution also provided that the board conduct a bureau of information and advice on legislation and school organization, that it raise and disburse funds to employ a secretary or agent, and that it do whatever was necessary to carry out effectively those essential measures.[30] Through a series of planning meetings called by Ogden, the board went into operation at its initial session in New York on Monday, November 4, 1901. Consistent with the conference resolution that gave it birth, the board agreed that its functions were twofold: to create public opinion in behalf of public schools and to handle gifts from private persons, boards, and foundations to promote public education. When it became incorporated and elected its own trustees, these functions were divided. It finally took the name "Southern Education Board" and kept for its own work the first of the above functions. The latter function, that of handling gifts and grants, was delegated to its trustees, who later became known as the General Education Board.[31]

In keeping with its newly chosen functions, the Southern Education Board, less than three months after its organization, established the bureau prescribed by the conference resolution. Dr. Charles W. Dabney, then a professor at the University of Tennessee, where the bureau was later housed, was made director. Assisting him were P. P. Claxton, Joseph D. Eggleston, Jr., George S. Dickerman, Wickliffe Rose, Lillian Johnson, and Edgar Gardner Murphy. Dabney's report to the fifth conference revealed that the bureau was engaged in the investigation of the actual conditions of the public, normal, industrial, and other schools and was active in the dissemination of information on such school matters as organization and legislation. The work of the bureau was begun with a systematic study of rural schools, emphasizing the condition of their buildings, equipment, teachers, supervision, finances, enrollment, and attendance. Its work was extended to the social problems of Southern people as a whole. Statistics were compiled as to the illiteracy and economic welfare of both races, and facts were systematized to make possible comparisons between counties and even between states.[32] Through its fact-finding functions, the bureau became the nation's most dependable source of information about Southern education.

In this way the Conference for Education in the South became the most influential educational force in the history of the region. It spanned the entire policy-making realm of Southern education. Philanthropists consulted its boards before making contributions to Southern schools. Public school officials sought counsel from its agents on such matters as selecting teachers, building schools, or arranging curricula; and legislatures were even more greatly inclined to appropriate funds for educational purposes on the basis of its recommendations.

ASSESSING THE EFFECTS
OF ORGANIZING EFFORTS

Although the conference leaders knew that educational changes were not easy to stimulate in the South at that time, they began their work fully confident that, with organized and persistent effort, significant alterations could be made. This faith grew as they gained a greater understanding of the situation through the work of their agents and as they saw their ways spread to engulf local and public officials who, at first, were hesitant to copy them. By 1920 the leaders of the original movement were able to retire to the background of the Southern educational picture and say of their work: "Well done."

A strong confidence in the possibility of change had been inspired by facts cited during the early Capon Springs meetings. J. L. M. Curry, summarizing the educational progress in the South after the war and at a time when interest in education was least expected, drew this encouraging conclusion before the members of the second conference:

> Though there was no system of universal education even for whites in the South, systems for both races were established in the course of a few years. This was done though population was sparse, roads were bad, schoolhouses did not exist, no acquaintance with public machinery existed, good teachers were not available, and the people were too impoverished for taxation. . . . In spite of all hopelessness, there were a few who believed that the salvation of the South and the recovery of its lost prestige depended on universal education.[33]

S. E. Breed added to the inspiration when he drew vivid pictures of the contributions of industrial education to the development of Negro women. An experiment in the industrial method, operating at night and with adults in Norfolk, Virginia, had demonstrated that mothers could be stimulated to send their children to school, that families could be encouraged to move from the slums of crowded cities to the small farms that surrounded them, and that mothers could form sewing circles and provide clothing so that children could attend school.[34] Bishop Nelson of Georgia also added to conference enthusiasm by his report on the general educational progress of the South: "The masses are taking more interest in the subject of education; more schoolhouses are being built every year; the teachers are equipping themselves more perfectly; and larger appropriations and longer terms have been provided of late." [35] It was against this type of inspirational background that members of the conference on education formulated a strong faith in the idea that the South could be influenced to change its ways in matters of education.

Gradually, and after well-organized efforts, educational progress lost some of its haphazard quality and became general. Such a picture could be pieced together by conference leaders from the reports of their agents in the field. Dickerman reported to the fourth conference that the counsel and friendly assistance of intelligent whites in various areas of the South were invaluable in the development of educational facilities for the colored people: In Wilcox County, Alabama, where more than three-fourths of the people were Negroes, schools were established under the care of churches, and each had the constant protection of wealthy and influential citizens who contributed generously for the purchase of the land and the erection of the buildings.[36] Charles D. McIver, district director of the Southern Education Board, in his report on the work in North Carolina, told the fifth conference that the teaching profession had never been so well united upon the point of meeting the educational needs as at that time, nor had its opinions ever before commanded the general respect of all classes as at the time of his observations.[37] Robert Frazier, also an agent, reported that the program of the Virginia agents, in which the aim was to set up demonstration schools at strategic centers, was making observable progress. Several communities were already earnestly at work establishing manual training schools through local effort.[38] Of Alabama, Joseph B. Graham reported that, by comparison with their past history, the people of the state entered the twentieth century in fairly good condition. He told the sixth conference, "More than one-half of the entire income of the State has been set aside as a trust fund for the education of the youth of the State, and the Legislature is instructed to make additional appropriations when revenues and collections shall justify it." [39]

But if the educators who aimed to change the South had had any hope that their objectives had already been accomplished, Dabney's report to the sixth conference in 1903 crushed it. He told them that there was not a complete system of public schools in any Southern state and described the educational depths from which the South had to be raised by summarizing the illiteracy picture and its relation to the free ballot. He reported that approximately fifteen percent of the native white population ten years of age and over in Tennessee, Virginia, North Carolina, South Carolina, and Georgia were unable to read or write in 1900. Of the males of voting age, over one fifth could neither read their ballots nor write their names. Almost half of the colored males of this age were equally as illiterate. Although conditions were better in the cities, Dabney still considered the problem to be grave. Reports like these gave conference leaders a more realistic attitude toward their task and caused them to direct their organizational structure more specifically toward the educational difficulties from which the South suffered.

But the dedicated effort began to show an effect as a larger number of influential Southerners saw changes in the South, copied the ways of the conference movement, and became identified with the program. One influential person who joined the movement was Michael Hoke Smith, once publisher of the *Atlanta Journal* and later Governor of Georgia. Smith showed a decided interest in the movement when he reported to the fifth conference on the steps Georgia had taken toward the solution of her own educational problems. While indicating that over $1,000,000 had been spent by the South in educating Negroes, he implied that there was a continued Southern dedication to that kind of educational progress. "As intelligent and Christian character pervades the men and women of our Section," he declared, "they will become unanimous in favor of educating the mind and heart of the Negro children as well as the heart and mind of the white children." Edwin A. Alderman, president of Tulane University, made a similar declaration of purpose. The South, in his thinking, had reached three fundamental conclusions: First, a civilization could no more grow and become great in poverty than a man could grow and work in hunger. Second, public education was an investment, not an expenditure, and therefore common schools for both races had to be universally established to enrich the productive and moral power of the community. Third, the South realized, as it never had before, the spiritual and political value of childhood. President David F. Houston of Texas A. and M. College sounded a similar note of dedication on the part of the Lone Star state. He described how the state at that time was spending 4½ million dollars from the general revenue and local taxation for education and how it had established educational institutions that included a university, an agricultural and mechanical college, three normal schools for whites and one for Negroes.[40]

Not only did the conference win favor with influential Southerners, but it also stimulated organized educational efforts in local areas. The various district conferences that the Southern Education Board sponsored were widely attended by the people in the areas in which they were held. One of the first, held at Greensboro, North Carolina, was attended by superintendents and school officials representing twenty counties, in addition to the presidents of public and private colleges. These meetings set up local self-help procedures in which the people of the various counties voted taxes to support and improve the schools for all the people. Each district raising revenue by this method received a matching grant up to $4,000 from the General Education Board. This amount was paid to the districts through the various state departments of education. Through movements of this type, vigorous campaigns were launched to secure the consolidation of school districts and the provision of tax revenues. Other patterns of self-help were inspired by these local conferences. Students of the State Normal and Industrial College of North Carolina organized a Women's Association for the Betterment of Public School Houses. They endeavored to influence the alumnae of the institution as well as public-spirited women of every locality to join in the effort. Local associations were formed with every schoolhouse as a center. Through these organizations, buildings were better kept and grounds were beautified. A local conference, held at

Raleigh through the influence of Governor Charles B. Aycock, was attended largely by teachers and officials of both public and private schools. It made a strong declaration against illiteracy and in favor of rural schools. It inaugurated a campaign to consolidate weak school districts, to improve public school buildings, and to adopt local taxation to supplement the state school tax.

Signs of progressive local action were reported for other areas of the South. Hollis B. Frissell gave an account of what he enthusiastically called "the work of the evangelization in Virginia." Governor Montague had met with his committee at its first meeting in Richmond and had expressed "his entire willingness to cooperate in the work." He had taken a courageous stand for public education, had expressed a sincere hope that the public schools would be made free of politics, and had uttered a strong appeal for the introduction of industrial education into "every school of the Commonwealth." [41] Forty-seven delegates, representing all the educational interests of Louisiana, met at Baton Rouge. A central educational committee formed by this local conference issued a declaration to the people, setting forth the "great problem of democracy involved." The declaration was printed and distributed to newspapers and citizens. A committee on local campaigns was organized to aggregate financial support through local taxation and to perform public services like those undertaken by the many conferences organized on a state level in so many other areas. Before the first decade of the new century had passed, Texas had joined the local conference fold. Its work, organized along the lines of the general Southern conferences, was reported by Clarence Ousley of the *Fort Worth Record* to the Conference for Education in the South at its twelfth annual meeting in Atlanta. Its achievements shared equal honors with other local conferences but went ahead of them in some instances. [42]

That Negro schools were included in these local actions was evidence of a decided change in the attitude of whites toward these schools. In one county in Virginia, it was reported, the per capita expenditure for the Negro schools exceeded that of the white by one fifth, although it was felt that the difference was considerably due to the increased cost of separate schools.

Educational progress up to this time had been so effective that Dr. Walter H. Page included the following commendation in the resolutions he offered the fifth conference: "Since the free education of all people is the foundation of democracy and the highest function of an enlightened commonwealth, this Conference applauds the patriotic position taken by those Governors and other public servants who have made it the foremost policy of their administration, and it applauds also the newspaper press and the pulpit that emphasize it as the basis of good citizenship." [43] This was a commendation well earned by both South and North, for it appeared that two geographical sections with divergent ideals on most important matters had been able to subordinate their differences in the interest of human welfare.

Did this marriage between North and South really matter? Did the social and political structure of the South alter its course because dedicated men had labored to this end? Answers to these questions were supplied by the various conferences themselves. Although some changes in the public attitude concerning Negro education began to appear after the first group of educational missionaries assembled at Capon Springs, it was not until the ninth conference convened at Lexington, Kentucky, on May 2, 1906, that the real impact of the Southern educational movement was felt. At this meeting of hundreds of school officials from all over the South, leaders of the new educational movement were given a good opportunity to assess the results of their work. They could see the progress they had finally made toward the solution of their problems.

The impact had been fundamental in nature. It had changed the public attitude toward education and had made Southern people more willing to accept self-imposed taxation for the purpose of financing education for their children. The change had been diffused. It had affected practically every Southern state. The Kentucky General Assembly of 1906 appropriated $50,000 to establish two state normal colleges. Its aim was to adequately staff its common schools. It appropriated funds to defray the expenses of the superintendents so that they might supervise the schools of the state more satisfactorily. Twenty counties raised the salaries of these public school officials during the year. As a summary of the entire financial picture, it was reported that the per capita expenditure for education in the state had increased from $2.60 in 1903 to $3.25 in 1905.[44]

The people of Tennessee appeared equally inclined to support their schools. Twenty-five counties in the state levied taxes for education as high as 40 cents per $100 valuation in 1902, but by 1906 fifty-seven counties carried an educational tax burden at least that heavy. The schools received $1,883,744 from tax sources in 1902 and $3,101,847 in 1905. Almost one million dollars was spent for buildings that year, and the salaries of rural school teachers in the state increased 20 percent in three years.

The Virginia constitution of 1902 provided for additional local taxation to support public schools. The General Assembly appropriated $200,000 per year to pay primary and grammar school teachers, and it appropriated approximately $50,000 annually to supplement local funds in the establishment of state-approved high schools. School funds raised from taxation, therefore, increased by $69,000 between 1903 and 1904 and by $161,000 between 1904 and 1905. The Legislature of North Carolina provided a loan fund for local school districts to use in erecting new schools. In 1905, fifty-three school districts in the state voted a special tax for the support of public schools. During the following year, 133 districts accepted this tax obligation. The loan fund was important in building and improving school structures, and the value of school property more than doubled in six years. The year 1905 was considered by school officials of South Carolina to have been "the most remarkable in the educational history of the State." A bigger tax obligation was voted than ever before, and income for schools reached its highest peak. As a result more school buildings were erected and repaired.

Progress in the deep South was almost equally as impressive. The campaign for local taxation made rapid progress in Georgia. Four counties and 100 school districts voted a local school tax in 1905, making the erection of 280 new school buildings possible. The Alabama legislature made increased appropriations for schools in 1901, and the people showed a decided willingness to tax themselves for school purposes. By 1906, thirty-seven counties, including 2,368 school districts had voted a local tax. Arkansas experienced a great educational awakening during this period. The Arkansas Press Association, the Arkansas Bar Association, and several other societies made the topic of educational improvement within the state the basis for deliberation at their annual meetings. Educational mass meetings were held in various parts of the state, and the press gave wide coverage to the movement. The state legislature adopted a proposed constitutional amendment that increased taxation for school purposes, and many school buildings were erected and repaired as a result. Louisiana increased appropriations for schools from $922,304 in 1904 to $1,223,954 in 1905, but the amount spent for Negro education increased from $409,637 to $661,768 during the same period. Mississippi also fell under the spell of the South's educational renaissance. By 1907 the state had set up machinery by which school taxes could be levied, and elaborate plans for school improvements were made.

When more adequate school funds had begun to flow into the public treasury of these states, various phases of the educational system began to experience significant changes. Weaker schools were consolidated to make stronger ones. County superintendents were employed on a full-time basis, and more adequate funds for supervision were provided. Rural schools were more carefully supervised. Twenty-two counties in Kentucky increased the salaries of their superintendents. Thirty-two Virginia counties employed full-time superintendents in 1905, although not one county had given them full-time employment before that time.

Plans for teacher improvement were laid in practically every Southern state. Teachers organized associations and attended summer institutes in large numbers in order to foster their professional development. Of the 7,662 teachers in Arkansas in 1905, 5,783 attended institutes in June of that year. In order to ensure the selection of better teachers, county examiners exercised greater care in giving and scoring examinations. But there was a reward for the added effort required of those who followed the teaching profession. Each state increased the salaries of its teachers by sizable amounts. Tennessee increased her salaries by as much as 20 percent.

There were also improvements in curriculum. More funds were

appropriated for libraries; more libraries were established; and more books were added to those already in existence. The schools were even more properly graded. Types of work, grade by grade, became more similar when compared state by state. Children were encouraged to study by various types of programs. The Agricultural Society of Georgia gave $500 prizes to students of various school districts for the best corn or cotton yield on $\frac{1}{16}$ acre. For all these "blessings," thanks were due to the Southern Education Board.

Although Negroes were rarely consulted on the plans that created so many changes, they shared some benefits. As funds increased for white schools, racial differentials in expenditure became smaller. In a few states the school terms for the two races were made equal. In most states they remained unequal but were lengthened in each case. Manual arts, domestic science, and other forms of industrial education were taught in both white and Negro schools, but the Negro teacher was expected to follow this type of curriculum more assiduously. Her students were thought to need the training more. As time passed, this type of education became almost solely a Negro-school interest. Some normal schools for Negroes were established out of the newly acquired public funds, and many such schools already established were strengthened.

The Southern Education Board, at its meeting of May 29, 1914, resolved to close its work and transfer its functions to the General Education Board from which it had drawn its economic sustenance. Thus came to an end the key force in the South's educational renaissance. The war to make the South accept its educational responsibilities to the Negro had been won. But the peace that followed had made education universal for the whites and special for the blacks. The Negro's aim for equality of educational opportunity in the South, like his aims for political and social equality, had been sacrificed in the interests of peace.

V · DEEDS OF PHILANTHROPY

Despite the effectiveness of the massive program launched by the Conference for Education in the South, there still remained a major problem — particularly as related to the Negro schools. The program had been projected far beyond the range of funds then available to the conference. The organization's influence, though significant, was not strong enough to open the public purse to the extent necessary to meet the needs of all the schools. Consequently, another source of financial support had to be found if the program was to move forward.

This support was found. It came, in surprising strength, not so much out of the Southern paternalism and *noblesse oblige* to which C. Vann Woodward attributed the philanthropic movement,[1] but mainly from the basic historical process that made it necessary. Even as the great detour was being shaped, financial support for it was being developed. The booming period of industrial expansion that caused the national government to abandon the Negroes to the will of Southern people operated, as if by benevolent design, to create an industrial class whose philanthropy the leaders of the conference would be able to stimulate.

By the close of the nineteenth century an economic revolution had begun in the United States. The large populations that had shifted westward after the Homestead Act of 1862 and the pacification of the Indians were bound into a single economy by the cementing force of railroad extension. The urbanization process, which had started on the Atlantic seaboard, flowed westward to spur the development of gateway cities along the inland waterways until, interspersed with small regional communities, our inland empire had matured. Opening up incredible resources and vast markets for manufactured goods, these opportunities challenged the imagination and ingenuity of a select group of men who built the large fortunes that were to support the Southern educational renaissance and the Negro American's great detour.

Therefore, when the special educational program was completely designed and ready to go into production, industrial America had already produced the philanthropists who could afford to finance it. Andrew Carnegie, whose philanthropy was to provide library services for many Negro communities in the South, had made his start during this period. Having come to this country from Scotland in 1848, he had a million-dollar steel plant in operation by 1875 and was well on his way toward building the fortune that would make his philanthropy possible. John D. Rockefeller, a twenty-year-old bookkeeper had resigned his $50 a month job in the summer of 1859 to take his first steps toward becoming America's foremost industrial pioneer and most generous philanthropist. Seven years later "his Cleveland refinery had begun to expand with almost explosive force," [2] and the young industrialist had started the career that would make him the oil magnate of all the world, savior of a goodly portion of the South's free public school system, and patron saint of the Negro college.

George F. Peabody had already applied his ingenuity to the development of America's industrial class with astounding results. Moving with his impoverished parents from his native South to Brooklyn, New York, after the Civil War, Peabody had climbed from errand boy in a mercantile house to partner in an investment business. By 1867 he had built a vast fortune, created an intricate network of relationships with large industrial firms, and established a special fund for the advancement of education in the South. John F. Slater, whose uncle may well be considered "the father of American manufactures," came into the inheritance of his textile properties about the time that Carnegie was building his first steel plant. Less than one decade later Slater was to create a fund for industrial education among the freedmen of the South. Julius Rosenwald, although of a slightly later period of American industrialization, is also one of this group. The fortune that fed his wide philanthropy apparently started with his modest investments in Sears, Roebuck and Company during 1895.

Of equal significance is the fact that those who were to trigger the great philanthropic movement were also products of these times and, though to a lesser degree, members of this developing industrial class. While Rockefeller was on the rise, Robert C. Ogden, who was to guide his philanthropy in Negro education and to become the diplomat of the great detour, was establishing himself as an important retail merchant through a partnership with John Wanamaker. William Henry Baldwin, also to be a source of influence among the potential philanthropists, was building a strategic career with the Union Pacific Railroad and the Southern Railway Company.

There is no need to expand this list of American industrial pioneers or to describe their entrepreneurial exploits in greater detail: The story has been adequately told elsewhere.[3] It must be emphasized, however, that they constituted an industrial class whose business methods were not wholly acceptable to the American public. Influenced by the Social Darwinists, and particularly by the philosophy of Herbert Spencer, these men shaped an ideology of rugged individualism to justify the methods that made their achievements possible. But big business was not to remain a class virtue, nor poverty a personal vice. The great combines so hurriedly erected as weapons against competition were opposed by the development of conflict between the propertied and nonpropertied classes. The ideas of Henry D. Lloyd contributed heavily to the development of this conflict. Through articles published in the *Atlantic Monthly* during 1881, he pictured the Standard Oil Company, for example, as an unscrupulous monopoly and aroused the country against the industrial class and its business methods.[4] The Sherman Antitrust Act of 1890 threw a halter about the necks of the unbridled industrialists, and by 1898 the labor movement had developed to the point where organized workers had begun to challenge seriously management's exclusive control over labor policy. As the new century opened, the die had been cast. Industrial conflict had threatened industrial peace, and the image of the new industrial class had been seriously tarnished.

To a class so plagued by threats of public rebellion against its private ways, the South offered a convenient avenue of relief. Its readiness for industrial exploitation had already been heralded by Charles Nordhoff, who, after a trip through the region in the spring and summer of 1875, had written exuberantly: "I was deeply impressed with the natural wealth, mostly undeveloped, of the states I saw." [5] Southern workers were still not strongly organized; industrial peace prevailed in the region; and the growing population offered a good source of cheap labor. With its tax base still impaired, the South became a good outlet for charitable expressions that could possibly repair the image of the industrial class then being shattered by rising class conflict in Northern cities. It presented industrialists with a good opportunity to regain public acceptance while remaining true to their class ideology of rugged individualism. Through charitable contributions to the South's institutional life, they could help the Southern people help themselves, increase labor value where wage scales were kept lower by custom, and open greater consumer markets for the many manufactured products then being created through their industrial leadership. Most attractive of all must have been the appealing recognition that the region's educational leadership had passed to those who identified with the industrial class — to a breed of men who not only spoke the language of this class but also shared its basic aspirations. Therefore when Ogden and his associates really opened their campaign to secure funds for the support of Southern education, they found ready converts in men who, in addition to having the money to give, were badly in need of an opportunity to show their humanitarianism and to preserve the dignity of their class.

SPECIAL FUNDS FOR SPECIAL EDUCATION

The type of humanitarianism that Northern industrialists had seen fit to direct southward was to assure the preservation of educational opportunities for Negro Americans, but only within the limitations of the great detour. Unlike the benevolent and religious societies that sponsored the freedmen's school movement, the various funds established by the industrial philanthropists were not used to launch a crusade of racial equality. Remaining personally aloof from the racial conflict that was still active in the South, the industrialists accepted the great detour as the best policy for the region and so prescribed as the conditions of their gifts that the region's peace not be disturbed. Of course Rockefeller and some other potential donors visited the fourth conference in Winston-Salem, North Carolina, when Ogden ran his special train South to open the campaign; but this made no difference in their humanitarian intentions. The financial giants did not change the direction of Negro education their advisers had previously set.

The Peabody Fund, having been established first, had set the tone of noninvolvement in racial matters. It had aimed to keep the peace while holding fast to the racial *status quo*. It was to assist "in some significant way" those states that had suffered the ravages of Civil War. It did not aim to help the Negroes particularly, although the latitude of its provisions made such help permissible.

This permissive quality was clearly evident in the letter that Robert C. Winthrop read to the fifteen trustees he invited to assemble at Washington, D.C., at the request of the donor. In his letter, Mr. Peabody told the trustees: "I will give you . . . the sum of one million dollars to be by you used and applied in your discretion for the promotion and encouragement of intellectual, moral, and industrial education among the young of the more destitute portions of the Southern and Southwestern states of our Union; my purpose being that the benefit intended shall be distributed among the entire population without other distinction than needs and opportunities of usefulness to them." [6] These discretionary powers were augmented in a second meeting of the trustees. It was then made clear that the benefits of the fund should be confined to common schools of the South, but it was emphasized that such measures should be adopted as could give educational advantages to the greatest number of children. This was to be done through assistance in the establishment of a permanent system of public education, in the granting of scholarships to students who were studying to be teachers, and in the promotion of that education which "sought to apply science to the industrial pursuits of man."

The elasticity of these provisions gave the trustees of the funds a chance to aid Negro education within the framework of Southern approval — within the framework of the special-education concept. They could make racial distinctions if they thought the differential treatment would provide the greatest chance for usefulness. Since their actions were expected to provide the greatest good for the greatest number, much latitude was left for diplomatic strategy in the very touchy area of race relations. Therefore, the trustees, taking advantage of the freedom inherent in their trust, directed their efforts toward the job of providing separate schools for the races. They felt, and probably honestly so, that the disputes surrounding those schools that did not follow a policy of separating the races rendered such institutions unstable and likewise inefficient in their use of the fund. Consequently, they established the policy of withholding aid from those states that had not provided for racially separate schools, and they worked only with other funds and movements that tended to recognize separate schools as a desirable way to educate the races.

Soon after the Southern Education Board was organized, a more powerful fund, offering also many discretionary powers, was created for the general support of Southern education. Ogden's influence with the Rockefeller interests brought its reward when, between 1902 and 1909, the philanthropist placed $53,000,000 with the General Education Board and accompanied the gift with suggestions that some of it could be used to meet special needs of Southern education. With these two boards combined through an interlocking directorate, the financial strength necessary for carrying on the new educational movement in the South was virtually assured. Like the Peabody Fund, the Rockefeller provisions were sufficiently unstructured to allow the Negro schools to share in the fund's blessings as conditions dictated.

In fact, the conditions that would involve all the funds in the problems of Negro education, though at the special level, were already fully evident in the South.

When the funds began their work in the region, school facilities for Negro children in both rural and urban areas were pitiably inadequate. Urban schools were noticeably deficient and conditions in rural schools were appalling. Financial security was a luxury that not even the schools for white children enjoyed, and support far short of this level would have been considered adequate by many who still aspired to give the Negro children an opportunity to get an education.

Although the Southern Education Board had succeeded in creating public toleration of the schools and had influenced some degree of public support for them, the trickle of money from the public treasury had been too small to build new schools or even to keep older ones in sustained operation. Those buildings that had been erected were too few and poor. As a result, classes were held in churches, lodge halls, and even in abandoned huts. These buildings were often in ill repair, with leaking roofs and gaping walls. There was little in the way of furniture — a few blackboards, but no desks or other equipment. If there were benches at all, they failed to fit the children. Even such schools as these were few and far between. Rural children who were lucky walked miles over bad roads to recite their lessons in chilly rooms. Most of them, however, did not attend school at all. They could have walked miles without finding one to attend.

There were many instances in which serious training was lacking in such schools as were available. The curriculum often bore no relation to rural living, and the institutions made little or no impact upon the lives of those who lived near them. For many who aspired, education was too short. In all the South, as late as 1910, there was not a single eighth-grade rural Negro public school. No Negro public school, rural or urban, was approved for two years of high school work. The schools, such as they were, operated for an average of four months out of each year. They were run by teachers whose average training was that of an eighth-grade student and whose annual salary in many states was less than $150 on the average.[7]

Colleges for Negroes were almost equally as deprived. The support given by the denominational societies had begun to melt away. The educational aspirations that the Northern missionaries inspired caused the establishment of too many "colleges," and the enthusiasm had resulted in the creation of an educational base too broad to be supported by the subsequent flow of funds into the Negro educational movement. Equipment, woefully inadequate from the start, had therefore worn out by the turn of the century as a result of the pressure of numbers, the weight of persistent use, and the infrequency of replacement and repair. Many of the teachers in these colleges were also inadequately trained, and there was little hope that the public schools would be better staffed by the graduates who managed to complete courses prescribed by these institutions.

Recognizing early that support for the improvement of the Negro schools could not be expected from the various Southern states, John F. Slater, the textile manufacturer of Norwich, Connecticut, established his fund for such support in 1882. Stimulated also by the apparent success of the Peabody Fund, this philanthropist gave one million dollars "for uplifting the lately emancipated population of Southern states." [8] That this was also a provision for a special kind of education for the race was very clearly indicated in a report of the fund's trustees nine years after its establishment. The trustees contended that the religious groups responsible for establishing many schools for Negroes after the Civil War had made the blunder of liberally dubbing the schools "colleges" and "universities" and had adopted inapplicable and unattainable courses of study. They complained that methods and courses, borrowed from advanced civilizations, were applied without reference to race, age, pursuits, environments, and capacities.[9] Methods of the Slater Fund, the trustees implied, would be more realistic and in keeping with the Negro's special conditions. As time passed, therefore, those who managed the fund became more dedicated to this principle of "realism." Two objectives took precedence above the rest: to provide more normal and industrial work in Negro schools and colleges and to establish Negro county training schools throughout the South.

The Slater Fund was later joined in its aims by another rural school movement which, in this instance, was motivated by the problem of neglected school supervision. Although some progress had been made in the field of rural school supervision in the South, the first decade of the twentieth century found these schools virtually unnoticed by public officials. There were too many of them for one county superintendent to visit. Since most of the Negroes lived in the rural areas and since there was not too much interest in their education anyway, schools for their children naturally suffered most from official neglect. In the interest of relieving this suffering and making these schools more useful to the people who depended upon them, Dr. Hollis Frissell of Hampton and Dr. Booker T. Washington of Tuskegee approached Miss Anna T. Jeanes, a Quaker philanthropist of Philadelphia. They sought financial assistance in the development of rural school programs that had been started by their respective institutions.

The two educators had ample reason to believe that the Quaker woman would respond favorably to their request. The Friends had maintained a traditional interest in the education of Negroes — an interest that went back before the Civil War. Too, Miss Jeanes had shown deep concern for American charitable and educational institutions and had given liberally to their support. She had made her first gift to Negro education in 1905 under the encouragement of Mr. Peabody, who was treasurer of the General Education Board at that time. She had sent a check for $200,000 to the board, designating that the money be spent under the direction of Frissell and Washington in a program of assisting Negro rural schools.

Apparently, Miss Jeanes liked the work of both Hampton and Tuskegee and showed an even greater interest in the rural schools and communities that surrounded them. She gave Frissell a check for $10,000, which was used for the salaries of teachers in extension work, and gave a like amount to Washington, who used it in building rural schoolhouses in the communities that surrounded Tuskegee. Not long before her death, however, the Quaker philanthropist donated one million dollars to the rural school effort. She requested that the two educators administer the fund and expend it for the purpose of assisting the "rural schools of the Southern U.S. Community," where lived the great mass of Negroes to whom these schools were alone available.[10] The fund's deed of trust was drawn on April 22, 1907, and incorporation occurred seven months later. And so was born the Rural School Fund which later played such a significant role in the development of educational opportunities for rural Negroes.

However, like those that had preceded it on the Southern educational scene, the Rural School Fund carried its own inclination toward the job of nourishing the special education concept. In 1908 the board of trustees formulated a three-step policy in keeping with this idea: (1) that the general educational situation be studied carefully, (2) that any work undertaken should be with the entire approval and cooperation of the local school officials, and (3) that so far as possible the fund should be used to help provide opportunities for effective training for rural life among Southern Negroes.[11] One year later, the trustees created an organization that would stabilize the execution of these policies. At a meeting of its executive committee on July 1, 1909, Booker T. Washington, the chairman, suggested the possibility of gathering facts in order to ascertain whether the Negro was getting his share of the funds appropriated for his education and of publishing them "in some kindly way to induce the school authorities to be fairer in the distribution of funds." He also made two other suggestions: 1) that Dr. James Hardy Dillard of Tulane University, who had been selected as president of the fund, be given an assistant whose duty would be to go among the people and to urge them to raise money for their own schools, and 2) that a suitable Southern white man be employed to devote himself to influencing public sentiment in favor of Negro education. With B. C. Caldwell appointed as field agent for the fund, these suggestions went into operation December 16, 1909,[12] and the Jeanes Rural School Fund was thereby placed firmly under white control.

Greater and probably more extensive aid in the education of Negroes was given later by the merchant philanthropist, Julius Rosenwald. His interest in the general welfare of the race was broader in scope than that of any individual donor. As early as 1910 he began to play an important part in the betterment of the conditions under which Negroes lived in the United States. He became a trustee of Tuskegee Institute, maintained sympathetic contact with Booker T. Washington, and aided the Institute and its program materially by making gifts in behalf of the rural school movement. Funds provided by this philanthropist made possible the erection of sixteen YMCA buildings and one YWCA for Negroes. They stimulated other gifts to similar projects in many cities of both North and South, and supported a large Negro housing project in Chicago.[13]

It was not until 1917, however, that Mr. Rosenwald brought into existence a foundation that was destined to attract more money to the cause of Negro education than any single philanthropic enterprise up to this time. On October 30 of that year, the Julius Rosenwald Fund was incorporated as a nonprofit enterprise under the laws of the State of Illinois. Although its broad chartered purpose was stated as providing for "the well-being of mankind," the fund aimed, more specifically, to stimulate more equitable opportunities for Negroes in a democracy that had fallen short of its promises. It did not aim to do the whole job but to get both Negroes and whites accustomed to doing it themselves. Backed by approximately forty million dollars, which the cash value of the fund exceeded at one time, Mr. Rosenwald and the directors of his trust directed their attention first toward building rural schools, later toward the support of high schools and colleges, and finally toward the provisions of fellowships to enable Negroes and whites of unusual promise to advance their careers.[14] No foundation ever cast a more benevolent shadow across the path of the Negro school.

By the third decade of the twentieth century, a complete financial structure for educating Negroes along special lines had been laid. Adequate support for building those rural schools that aimed at training young Negroes for a better rural life had been assured. More uniform standards and closer supervision of these schools had been provided, and the South's fears that these changes would lead to social equality between the races had been reduced by placing supervision of the work ultimately in the hands of the white school officials. The private Negro colleges that had received the blessings of the Southern Education Board, but whose future was still uncertain, had been given greater economic security and had even learned that this security increased in proportion to the emphasis they placed upon industrial education. Although its more permanent endowment was still to come, the Hampton-Tuskegee pattern had become set as the ideal type for the Negro school, giving shape to the physical, administrative, and instructional growth of the entire Negro educational complex. Nothing reflects this inclination more clearly than the way in which these various funds were spent.

FINANCING THE SPECIAL EDUCATIONAL PROGRAM

Consistent with their respective purposes, the various funds persistently supported those special activities of Negro schools that had been specified as essential to and compatible with white Southern purpose. There was the immediate problem of keeping the schools in action. The Peabody Fund was the first to attack this. During the first year of its activity, the board of trustees made arrangements in North Carolina and Georgia for the expenditure of $4,000 in support of schools "for colored children." The aid given was significantly conducive to the maintenance of schools that would have closed prematurely. It not only retained the teachers for another year but extended the terms to nine months. The Negro schools of Virginia were similarly aided the following year. In 1870, the fund completely supported all the primary-school pupils in Mobile, Alabama. During the same year the schools of Huntsville, Alabama, were given $2,000 in support of 2,000 pupils, among whom were 1,200 Negro children. In his annual report to the trustees on February 15, 1870, the general agent of the fund announced that $16,000 had been designated for Negro education during that year.[15]

By the following year a definite scale of assistance to public schools of different sizes was made known to the public. In the explanation accompanying the scale, the Peabody trustees made a distinction between grants to white schools and to Negro schools. Negro schools were to receive aid at a rate based upon two thirds of the scale. The general agent justified this policy on the grounds that "it costs less to maintain schools for the colored children than for the white." The fund gave $3,100 to Richmond for local school assistance. But $800 went to the aid of a Negro normal school; $1,500 to promote public schools for both races; and the remaining $800 to the white normal school of that city. The Negro school of each ward of Norfolk, Virginia, was granted $500 by the fund, although maintenance had already been provided by a city ordinance.

A school for whites with 150 pupils and one for Negroes with 200 were maintained in Branford, South Carolina, through grants of $50 and $100 respectively. And the Negro school of Montecello, Florida, was given a grant of $200, although there were 100 pupils under two teachers in the school.[16] It appears that grants were made more regularly according to need than according to the scale the trustees had worked out. Nevertheless, the trustees of the Peabody Fund directed their activities among Negro schools in keeping with the separate school sentiment.

During the 1880s, the fund shifted its interest from the problem of maintaining schools to that of developing teachers. However, its biracial policy was continued. It assisted Negro teacher-training activities in the Negro normal school at Lynchburg, Virginia, where more than two hundred students were enrolled, and it provided scholarships for students in the teacher-training program of several Negro colleges. Through a Peabody grant, South Carolina supported ten students at Hampton Institute that year, and similar grants made it possible for the State of Georgia to give Negro students $1,000 scholarships through Atlanta University. The Peabody Normal School of Louisiana was granted $1,300, but twelve institutes for Negro teachers were held in Tennessee during the year. When the public school system of the South appeared to be assured, the fund turned its major attention to the establishment of normal schools. In 1911, the support of the various state agents whom it had maintained was taken over by the General Education Board. And in 1914, when a final distribution of the Peabody Fund was made, its last direct activity in the field of Negro education occurred. It assigned $350,000 to the Slater Fund because the latter was devoted solely to the support of schools for Negroes.[17] In this way, the influence of George F. Peabody continued to work as a focal part of the financial resources that were being created in the interest of Negro schools.

The trust could not have been passed to a more dedicated force. Whereas the Peabody Fund assisted the Negro school program incidental to its support of the public schools in general, the Slater Fund, from its very beginning, moved boldly into the matter of creating special educational opportunities for the Negro race. Its role in the complex problem of aiding Negro schools pointed more in the direction of providing the race with opportunities for training on the higher level. The fund supported colleges in order that they might develop teachers for the complement of county training schools which it was seeking to build. More specifically, it first provided substantial support for the Negro colleges that denominational groups had established, and it later financed the building of secondary schools at strategic points in the rural South.

The implementation of Mr. Slater's benevolent objective of "uplifting the lately emancipated population of the Southern states" was made possible by a corps of dedicated men who successively accepted the responsibility of directing the work of the fund. They were Southern men like Dr. Atticus Green Haygood of Atlanta, Georgia, who was elected the first director of the fund in 1882; Dr. J. L. M. Curry of Alabama, who became the second agent of the fund; and Dr. James Hardy Dillard, president of the Jeanes Fund and father of the county training-school idea. It was this idea that became the Slater Fund's shining example of philanthropy in public education.

Through the leadership of various members of the board of trustees, the Slater Fund first turned its attention toward the task of aiding worthy Negro colleges whose survival depended upon additional aid. Dr. Curry succeeded in convincing the trustees that they should select for support a few institutions which "would seem to justify special cultivation." Because of the brilliant example that Hampton and Tuskegee had set in the field of industrial education, these institutions received the largest gifts from the fund.[18] But other Negro colleges also claimed the fund's attention. In observing the work of colleges like Spelman, Claflin, and Tougaloo, the trustees saw a blessing that was touching too few. They recognized that these institutions were serving only 45,000 Negroes. Their facilities had to be increased and their coverage widened, the trustees felt, if millions of Negroes were to be uplifted by their own schools. During the first year of operation, therefore, the Slater Fund contributed over $16,000 to twelve of these colleges. By 1901, appropriations had increased approximately three times that amount for eight colleges.[19] Over half of the appropriations, however, were assigned to Hampton and Tuskegee.

Less than five years later, a definite policy was crystallized. Contributions to Negro colleges were made mainly through the process of paying the salaries of those employed in the fields of teacher training and industrial education. During the school year 1905–06, the fund contributed $40,000 to eighteen Negro colleges scattered throughout the South. The money was spent primarily for the establishment and maintenance of industrial departments. This was true even for colleges originally founded as liberal arts institutions. Shaw University, originally established to train ministers, teachers, and later doctors, spent over half of its $2,500 appropriation to pay the salaries of teachers of cooking and sewing, although a budget of $1,200 was provided for teachers of the normal department. Tougaloo University, a similar institution, spent all of its $3,600 appropriation for teachers in its industrial department. Claflin University used $3,900 of its $5,000 appropriation to support teachers of industrial courses. This institution was attempting to teach courses in blacksmithing, carpentry, printing, tailoring, machine shop, bricklaying, and painting. Straight University of New Orleans spent two thirds of its budget of $1,500 for the support of industrial education, and Paine College used its $150 grant to pay a teacher of carpentry.[20] For twenty-nine years the Slater Fund confined its work to colleges, making it possible for these institutions to maintain a foundation upon which a system of secondary education for Negroes could be built.

In 1911, believing this foundation to have been fairly well laid, trustees of the Slater Fund began to encourage the development of a system of county training schools throughout the South. The purpose was "to provide high school training, and to offer simple courses, as far as possible, in teacher-training and the basic industries of the community." It was hoped that grants made for this purpose would hasten the inclination of public authorities to provide educational facilities for Negroes in rural areas and would raise educational standards for the race as soon as possible. Consequently, the fund made offers to assist in the establishment of county training schools under these conditions: that the school property would belong to the public, that salaries of not less than $750 would be appropriated from public funds, and that the teaching would extend through the eighth year, with the intention of adding two years as soon as it was possible to make such an extension. This "bribe-money" policy operated on a diminishing scale and was to be discontinued after the schools had become well organized and after the responsibility for their support had been accepted by the public school board. A grant of $500 per year was made to each school during the first three years; $250 annually for the next two; and $100 for equipment needed after the expiration of the five years.[21]

The county training school movement became a reality during the school year 1911–12, when Dr. Dillard, B. C. Caldwell, and A. M. Strange worked out a plan whereby the Kentwood Agricultural and Industrial High School of Louisiana was changed to the Tangipahoa Parish Training School for Colored Children. Training schools were also organized in Arkansas, Mississippi, and Texas during that year. In each instance the Slater Fund made a grant according to its policy, and the county officials of the respective states made the schools a part of the public educational system.

This movement not only encouraged public support of Negro secondary schools but also primed a greater flow of funds from other philanthropic sources. In the fourth year after the plan was in operation, the Peabody Fund gave $21,000 to the movement, and the General Education Board gave $52,000. The total appropriation for the purpose aggregated $108,000.[22] It was not too long after the movement started that the county training school became a permanent part of the South's public school system. County by county these schools were established through the cooperation of school boards, superintendents, state agents, and the various philanthropic funds. The General Education Board made a special contribution for securing needed industrial equipment, workshops, and teachers' homes. On the whole, these secondary schools increased from 4 in the first year to 107 in the school year 1919–1920.[23] In less than three decades after the movement started, there were 380 county training schools in the South. The Slater Fund had spent over $350,000 to bring about this change in Negro education. Whereas there had been no rural high schools at all for Negroes, now secondary education with a mainly industrial flavor had very readily become available — through the benevolence of philanthropy and the final acceptance of some degree of public responsibility.

Other funds complemented Mr. Slater's brilliant effort. Soon after the Jeanes Fund was established, the dream of Miss Anna T. Jeanes to do something for the Negro "cabin" school began to come true. Influential men of common ideals came together to put the program in operation. Among those who formed the fund's first board of trustees were former President William Howard Taft, Andrew Carnegie, George Foster Peabody, Robert C. Ogden, Hollis B. Frissell, James H. Dillard, Samuel C. Mitchell, Booker T. Washington, Robert R. Moton, and Robert L. Smith. The interest of President Taft added significantly to a group of men who had already won considerable national respect through their work in education and industry.

With Dr. Dillard as president and director of the fund, the trustees commenced at once on a plan that involved close cooperation with other existing funds and agencies interested in Negro education.

The plan that was later to become the Jeanes action-pattern was placed in the hands of the trustees by Miss Virginia E. Randolph, a Negro teacher who was working assiduously with a Negro school in Henrico County, Virginia, when the Rural School Fund was created. The schools of this county were under the supervision of Jackson Davis, and it was through him that the industrious work and aspirations of this dedicated woman were noted. On his many visits to her school, Davis noted the orderliness of her surroundings — how she kept the floor scrubbed, windows washed, and yard clean. He also noticed her work in the common industrial arts — how she taught the students to prepare hot lunches and to acquire the simple rudiments of clean living. Inspired by his respect for her work, Miss Randolph asked permission to visit some of the teachers of other schools and help them improve their schoolhouses and to start industrial training. Many letters concerning Miss Randolph's proposal passed between Davis and Dr. Dillard until in October 1908 the first Jeanes teacher was appointed. By decision of the fund's president and with the approval of its board of trustees, Miss Randolph was to become the forerunner of a veritable army of such teachers who were to come upon the Southern educational scene in the following years.

As a result of the instructions that were given Miss Randolph, the pattern she established was to be woven acceptably into the public education structure.[24] The work she undertook, as well as that of all who came after her, was to be determined by the wishes of her superintendent, the needs of her local situation, and the special qualities of her personality. She was to be a helper primarily rather than a supervisor, and it was required that she be recognized as a regular employee of the local school system, responsible to the local superintendent and his school board.

When superintendents of other counties observed the work that Miss Randolph was doing, they asked Dr. Dillard for similar teachers. The salaries of these teachers were provided by the Jeanes Fund, which made it possible for the work to spread through Virginia and into North Carolina. In less than three years after the program began, 129 Jeanes teachers were being supported by the fund at a cost of $44,250. Impressed by this beginning, other financial sources began to lend a helping hand. The various counties provided funds for the work, but the demands for this new kind of rural teacher far exceeded the supply. In 1911–1912, however, the Phelps-Stokes Fund gave significant aid, and two years later, the General Education Board made its first donation to the movement. By 1918–1919, the sum donated by the board amounted to $20,000. Two years later it had grown to $80,000.

Furthermore, other forms of cooperation were taking shape, which made it possible for this school program with the humble beginning to become organized into a unified, integrated movement throughout the rural South. Once again, the Southern Education Board, the General Education Board, and the Peabody Fund joined together to sponsor a white agent who would travel the state in the interest of better schools for Negro children. Jackson Davis succeeded in getting these groups to back the work in this field throughout Virginia, and the General Education Board, on the strength of his fine administration, extended the work to other states. Through the departments of education of the various states, the board provided the salaries and expenses of these agents, but the states themselves appointed the agents and assigned them to work with the Negro public schools. These rural workers, virtually assistant superintendents, were accepted and put to work by Alabama, Arkansas, Georgia, Kentucky, North and South Carolina, Tennessee, Texas, and, of course, Virginia. Between 1915 and 1920, expenditures for their services amounted to $246,500.

To both Negroes and whites, this was a new and somewhat strange method of education. And from this strangeness came many obstacles that the Jeanes teachers had to overcome. There were times when the trouble originated with a recalcitrant school principal whose objections were overruled by enthusiastic parents. Occasionally it was parents who opposed the program, objecting to the introduction of industrial features into the public school. Now and then the obstacle was not people but the terrain and weather. The roads were often impassable, making movement between schools most difficult. Where distances permitted and no means of transportation were available, Jeanes workers found it necessary to walk from school to school, carrying with them food and often, too, materials for industrial work. Until the coming of the automobile, a horse and buggy supplied by the generosity of some interested school patron was the teacher's most dependable means of transportation.[25] Work was also hampered by the inadequacy of many teachers whose schools the Jeanes worker visited. In fact her work unwittingly served to make these inadequacies more apparent. It was at this point — to meet the urgent need for better teachers — that the county training schools established by the Slater Fund became a functional part of the program. Through these institutions, the Jeanes teachers, and special superintendents, public education for Negroes in the rural South took on an organized and more integrated pattern. Much of the lack of coordination from which the schools suffered was overcome.

What public officials lacked in their ability or willingness to supervise and nourish rural schools for Negroes, the state agent and Jeanes teacher supplied. The latter, almost alone, served well as a coordinator. Each Jeanes teacher, working with her school, became the point around which the functions of rural schools pivoted. The program was broader than the school, although the school was its core. It was concerned with public relations in that it sought to cultivate community interest in school welfare. It involved general community improvement, attacking the problems that usually haunted rural people. And it incorporated changes in the curriculum, seeking to integrate what children learned in books with what they encountered in their everyday environment.

Jeanes teachers often labored in their respective counties in an effort to stimulate interest and encourage cooperation in building more and better schools. They occasionally attended Sunday services at the local churches for the purpose of speaking to the congregation on matters relating to the school. These teachers organized improvement leagues and mothers' clubs as a means of cultivating a constant flow of school patronage. They sponsored concerts and entertainments in order to raise funds. Frequently they helped teachers plan school commencement exercises in order both to end the session effectively and to rally public interest and support to the school. They cultivated methods of "handling" those white citizens who were hostile or indifferent in their feeling about the Negro schools. Through their diplomacy, therefore, many who would have been formidable foes often became staunch allies.

Their program of community improvement centered around the home. Wherever possible the Jeanes teacher attempted to stimulate the development of a school garden and to teach the children to grow or make at home many of the products their parents had been straining to buy from stores. The school garden and its products demonstrated how models could be shaped at school to guide the student's domestic life at home. Garden products grown by students of agriculture were canned and preserved by those studying domestic arts. Under the supervision of the Jeanes teachers, much new equipment for the school was made by the students rather than bought. Pupils of manual arts learned to change apple boxes into furniture and pickle jars into attractive vases.

Carrying out this type of program was not easy. Aside from the many obstacles inherent in the novelty of the scheme, there were other more difficult barriers that were inherent in the crop-lien regulations of the plantation system under which most Negroes lived at that time. Now and then a landlord opposed a garden or livestock project for children of his tenants, either preferring to run the cotton rows up to their back steps or to utilize their spare labor in pursuits more "profitable" to him. Since he represented an important part of the community's power structure and could add either friction or lubricant to this kind of program, diplomacy often dictated that the Jeanes teacher retreat at a time when her emotions commanded attack. Nevertheless, the influence of these teachers did grow and spread through Southern rural communities. Jeanes supervisors, as they were commonly called, made the people more dissatisfied with their lot, but not so much that they became too discouraged to do something about it themselves.

Not all the Jeanes teachers' work was on the educational fringe. Some of it dealt with the very heart of the instructional program. In their duties as supervisors they helped the teachers develop their lesson plans. Skill in this field naturally increased for both teacher and supervisor as the work of the summer institutes and normal schools began to bear fruit. In later years after the program of the Negro Rural School Fund fully matured, projects of a more daring nature were undertaken by some of the Jeanes workers. A "curriculum integration" program was put into operation in some of the Southern states. The traditional textbook was dropped and new courses more closely related to rural life were instituted. This is an example in point: if a community project was being developed around poultry, all subjects in the school would carry this emphasis. New words that the children learned to spell and use included the various breeds of chickens and the diseases that often threatened them. Arithmetic was taught in terms of the relations of feed to animal body weight, and geography consisted of the local environment and how it related to this type of animal husbandry.

This program did not fully develop until a host of rural agents began working in the communities under other auspices. As if to serve some divine purpose, these agencies were taking shape at the same time that the various benevolent funds were being organized. Dr. Seaman A. Knapp, at this time, began to make some progress in his attempt to convince the American government of the necessity of a farm demonstration program. In the fight against the boll weevil, Congress finally succumbed to his persistent efforts and appropriated $40,000 for farm demonstration work similar to that which he had been doing in Louisiana and Texas. In 1906 the first farm agent under Federal support was placed in Texas and soon after in Oklahoma and Mississippi. As the movement expanded to include other states, Senators A. F. Lever of South Carolina and Hoke Smith of Georgia succeeded in getting the Smith-Lever Act passed, and farm demonstration work became tied into agricultural experimentation through the various land-grant colleges. When home demonstration agents were added, the Agricultural Extension Bureau of the United States Department of Agriculture provided professional helpers for practically every farm, home, and community in rural America. By 1917 the Smith-Hughes movement had been enacted into Federal law. Vocational education of less than college grade in agriculture, home economics, and trades and industry was made available to girls and boys in all rural states.[26] In addition to the state agents, county superintendents, and Jeanes supervisors, the Negro rural communities of the South had access to the farm agent, vocational agricultural teacher, and the teacher of trades and industry. Some Southern states, seeking to utilize the services of all these agents, developed what became known as a "Coordinated Community Program." Community problems were attacked through the unified and combined efforts of all these various agents. Although it was not a complete success, many Negro rural communities experienced significant improvements from this coordinated effort.

THE INFLUENCE OF THE ROSENWALD FUND

The work of the Rosenwald Fund, however, permeated the educational experiences of the Negro more deeply than that of any other fund. It inspired the construction of Negro schools where none had ever been before, facilitated the development of more specialized industrial high schools for Negroes, sponsored libraries and provided reading materials where books had been rare objects, and financed the development not only of Negro teachers but of doctors and other professionals as well. The corresponding assistance to Negro schools that it stimulated from other sources ranked the Rosenwald Fund as the most influential philanthropic force that came to the aid of Negroes at that time.

The fund's first and greatest undertaking was its constructive cooperation with Southern states and local school districts in building schoolhouses for Negroes. This was started at Tuskegee by Mr. Rosenwald through the encouragement of Booker T. Washington. The philanthropist agreed to contribute to the building of any schoolhouse for Negroes in the vicinity of Tuskegee, provided that it were made a unit of the public school system and that the Negroes of the community gave evidence of their desire for schooling by supplying money and labor in support of the enterprise. The first of what were to be called "Rosenwald schools" was built in Macon County, Alabama, a few miles from Tuskegee in 1913. It cost $942. Negroes raised $150 to purchase the land and gave labor estimated at a cost of $132. White citizens contributed $360, and Mr. Rosenwald gave the remaining $300. State and county authorities agreed to maintain the school as a part of the public school system. This school building program lasted from 1913 to 1932,[27] and during this period, 5,357 public schools, shops and teachers' homes were built in 883 counties of fifteen Southern states.

Even more ambitious school-building programs were undertaken later in the fund's history. Impressed by the comprehensive plan of P. F. Williams, which called for one high school and a pattern of consolidated three-teacher school plants with eight grades and an eight-month term for Negro children of rural Mississippi, the Rosenwald Fund agreed to aid in the building of thirty-six schools, seven teacher's homes, and seven vocational buildings. Most of this program was completed within a year. The high school included in this pattern — the first in Mississippi — was finished in two months. The Rosenwald Fund made the initial gift for this school, but substantial assistance came from other sources. The General Education Board made a grant toward various parts of the school plan, including the construction of dormitories for boys and girls. The Slater Fund contributed to the county training school feature and industrial work. The Jeanes Fund aided in the employment of a trained county supervisor with headquarters at the high school. The state made contributions to the establishment of the school, and the state's vocational education department provided funds for the work in agriculture, trades, and home economics. Further aid was given by the General Education Board and the Julius Rosenwald Fund for a dining hall, library, and assembly hall. When the work was completed, this combined effort had produced an agricultural high school of fourteen buildings valued at $150,000 in the Delta region of Mississippi.[28] An additional limited building program was undertaken to provide facilities for the demonstration of better methods and standards for industrial training. This enterprise originated from the conviction that, as the South became further industrialized, Negroes could expect to advance in farming and trades only as they gained proper skills. Consequently, the fund appropriated $202,708 toward the building of five industrial high schools that provided instruction for boys in such industries as auto mechanics, printing, and the building trades, and for girls in cooking, dressmaking, millinery, and other branches of home economics.

The apparent lack of reading materials which Negro children suffered at school as well as at home, motivated the fund to begin work in the field of library services in 1925. Its program followed three basic lines of development: (1) the assembling and distribution of small sets of books to rural schools, (2) attempts to improve the library facilities of Negro colleges, and (3) cooperation in the establishment of county library systems. In carrying out the first line of development, the fund sought to make simply written books available to elementary pupils whose reading ability was limited but whose ages ranged from eight to twenty-one. Careful selection of various sets of books was made through the guidance of library experts, and changes were made from time to time as new and better books appeared. Even after the difficult problem of selecting appropriate reading materials was overcome, the fund still faced the problem of cost — how to secure these libraries for schools at prices they could afford to pay. The problem was solved by purchasing books in large quantities, obtaining them at half the normal cost. At first the several different types of libraries were for elementary Negro rural schools only, but in 1929 larger libraries for Negro high schools were added. The service was later extended to white schools that were similarly lacking in reading materials. They, however, paid the full cost for most sets. By 1948 the program of the Julius Rosenwald Fund in this field was complete and more than 12,000 library sets, containing more than half a million books, had been distributed to schools in all Southern states.

This newer program of the Julius Rosenwald Fund was equally as extensive in its scope as all the others. About sixty percent of the volumes distributed went to the numerous one- and two-room schools, and most of the remainder to towns and villages of less than 2,500 population. The books not only went where the people were but also where they were needed. In 1928 only two states — Kentucky and Tennessee — and some of the larger cities provided free textbooks for public school children. Many rural children could not afford to buy books. Consequently over half the rural Negro school population was without the simplest materials of instruction. For them the books of the little Rosenwald libraries were the only volumes of any sort available for use either in or out of school. Even where textbooks were furnished, these libraries usually represented the only supplementary reading materials in the community.

The development of libraries in Negro colleges was also stimulated by the Rosenwald program. Here the fund offered to contribute one third of the cost of well-selected books up to a maximum of $2,500, but the grant was made on three conditions: First, the colleges had to provide two thirds of the cost of the books that were to be selected from a list prepared by Miss Florence Curtis, director of the Hampton Library School — a selection that must include a goodly amount of children's literature for the use of prospective teachers; second, a suitable room or building, modern shelving and book stacks, library desks, tables and chairs had to be supplied; third, one or more trained librarians was to be placed in charge of the collection. This phase of the program ended in 1934 after total grants to forty-three Negro colleges in sixteen Southern states had reached $54,975.

But the work of the Julius Rosenwald Fund in the field of higher education included more than library services. When the fund was reorganized in 1928, efforts were made to enlarge the program in order to extend aid to Negro colleges. A special attempt was made to develop four "university centers" for the education of professional personnel and other Negro leaders. A total of $11½ million was contributed to university centers in Washington, Atlanta, Nashville, and New Orleans. The Washington center was dominated by Howard University. The Atlanta center was composed of a complex of colleges that included Atlanta University, Morehouse, Clark, and Spelman colleges, and Gammon Theological Seminary. The Nashville center included mainly Fisk University and the Meharry Medical College. Straight College and the old New Orleans University originally composed the New Orleans center. They eventually merged to form Dillard University, named in memory of the dedicated work of Dr. James Hardy Dillard.

Other Negro colleges, mainly those under private auspices, were aided by the fund. Grants were made to a number of them to maintain summer institutes for teachers, preachers, and agricultural workers. Nevertheless the Julius Rosenwald Fund never faltered in its effort to "maintain a few institutions of the very finest standard." Dillard University was given $60,000 toward financing a new administration and classroom building. This facility was occupied in the autumn of 1935 as Rosenwald Hall. The massive gleaming white structure standing majestically against a spacious green background along New Orleans' Gentilly Boulevard is a fitting symbol of Mr. Rosenwald's effective philanthropy. Similar symbols, though often less obvious, may be found at Howard, Fisk, and Atlanta universities.

By 1933 the trustees of the Rosenwald Fund began to express their philosophy of education in a way that was to influence the teachers in schools receiving the benefits of their philanthropy. The influence was directed toward both public schools and colleges. The trustees emphasized that the first and greatly needed reform among rural schools was to direct education toward the peculiar needs of country children. They contended that the kind of preparation children needed for rural living included the ability to read and to write clearly; some skill in the use of figures; a knowledge of farming, including some general understanding of biological processes and an appreciation of nature; manual dexterity, especially in the handling of wood, fabrics, and other utensils as related to simple mechanics; and a grasp of the fundamentals of sanitation or health. Believing that these objectives and the general progress of any people depended largely upon creative leadership, the fund established fellowships for able Negroes and Southern whites, giving them an opportunity to develop their talents along these lines. Through these grants many Negro teachers were able to acquire graduate degrees, both the master and doctorate, from practically every large institution of higher learning in the nation. As it became evident that no longer was it necessary to provide special opportunities for this neglected group, the fund resorted to efforts designed to incorporate all citizens into the general stream of American life. It shifted its emphasis to an active program in the field of race relations. And, at the close of its work in 1948, every facet of Negro life had been touched by the benevolence of Julius Rosenwald.

SHAPING THE SPECIAL EDUCATIONAL STRUCTURE

Thanks to the persistence and hard work of the new educators, the special educational movement that started at the close of the nineteenth century eventually bore fruit. The methods of the funds brought some measure of financial security to the schools they sought to save. It has been estimated that these various funds gave more than $134 million to Negro schools, and that $100 million more in matching funds came from the public treasury and interested private citizens.

During 1919 when the Slater Fund contributed $39,000 to the salaries of teachers employed in the county training schools it had helped to establish, the states spent $138,000 for buildings and improvements and $135,000 for salaries. Between 1908 and 1932 a total of $3,661,795 was spent for teachers' salaries in schools under the sponsorship of the Jeanes Fund. This fund provided $1,670,848 of this amount, but the remainder came from the public appropriations of the states and counties in which the schools were located. In 1928–1929, the Julius Rosenwald Fund gave $326,450 to aid in the construction of 326 schools for Negro children; Negro citizens contributed $306,909 more; white citizens gave $101,113; and $2,140,-386 came from public funds.[29]

This example is generally representative of the pump-priming power at which the funds aimed. Of the more than $28 million which was spent for the construction of rural schools for Negroes, the Rosenwald Fund contributed 16.5 percent; Negroes 19 percent; whites 4.5; and the public funds of the various counties and states 60 percent. By 1928, when the fund's school building program came to an end, the pumping job was complete. The average value of schools built for Negroes had increased from $2,100 in 1918 to $8,026 ten years later. The increase in real value was small, but it did indicate that the public had begun to accept more freely its responsibilities for supporting Negro schools.

This inclination for counties and states to respond to philanthropic deeds by contributing more heavily to the support of the Negro schools was enthusiastically noticed by educators throughout the South. John A. Abercrombie, superintendent of education in Alabama, wrote the Slater trustees as early as 1901: "The people of Alabama are fast taking hold of the idea that in the plans outlined and being worked out at Tuskegee and Montgomery will be found a solution of many difficult problems. There is no perceptible antagonism to the policy of the State fostering schools of this character of work being done in these institutions, and the influences which have been set in motion by them have created among the thinking people of the State an enthusiastic sentiment in their favor." Four years later, Joseph L. Shanklin, principal at Port Royal Agricultural School in Beaufort, South Carolina, expressed similar interests. He wrote the trustees: "The people show more interest in the school, and all the children are as eager to work as to study, both on the farm and in the house." [30] Remarks made by these educators were fairly representative of all who worked with Negro schools in the South. Hardly any institution had missed out on the blessings of the various funds, and every state responded to the benevolence at least to the extent of increasing its financial interest in Negro schools.

In addition, the various funds influenced Negro schools in the

South by expanding their physical structures to accommodate a greater number of pupils at both the lower and higher levels. The Julius Rosenwald Fund also facilitated this expansion for children in the rural elementary schools. In 1929 there were 3,052,523 Negro children of school age in fourteen Southern states. Approximately seventy percent of these were enrolled in school as compared with fifty-seven percent of the Negro population of school age in 1915. This change was made possible by the tremendous school building program sponsored by the fund. The 5,295 new school buildings added under the fund's influence accommodated an additional 650,000 pupils.[31]

The Slater Fund also contributed to the expansion. From 1914 to 1930 this fund established 384 county training schools in thirteen Southern states. Over half of them were located in Virginia, North and South Carolina, Alabama, and Georgia, where the larger portion of the Southern Negro population was concentrated. The rest were almost equally distributed throughout the other eight states.

This expansion had a twofold effect. It extended elementary and high school training to thousands of Negroes who had not been so fortunate before, and it relieved some colleges from having to provide high school facilities. As the county training school program matured, private and denominational colleges, feeling the relief, began retiring their high school departments year by year. In the main, Negro colleges were able to enroll the products of public high schools and the total enrollment of nine select Negro colleges increased over one hundred percent between 1922 and 1927.[32]

The Negro children who were drawn in greater numbers to the protection of school walls met a special kind of curriculum — a curriculum designed to prepare them more adequately for their special conditions. Their training in rural schools was mainly agricultural; their studies in the city public schools and even in the colleges were inclined more toward industrial arts. Hampton and Tuskegee had set the pattern. They had shown that Negro institutions of higher learning could not only win the respect of the South by their dedication to the manual arts but could use this dedication along with the splendid voices of their choral groups to elicit financial support for their programs. The pattern was copied by many other Negro colleges, and some of the imitators shared equally as well as the original designers. Out of the total course of events came the education of an entire people not for seamanship in the mainstream of American culture, but for survival in its eddy-waters.

VI · NEGRO EDUCATION
AS A WAY OF LIFE

By the close of the nineteenth century, the future of the Negro in American life had been settled for the next fifty years. It was clear that the black ballot would be virtually silent; that the two races would constitute distinct castes, neither crossing over into the domain reserved for the other; that white and black children would be trained in two different kinds of schools — indeed, in two distinct sociocultural worlds; and that whites and Negroes, though obligated to the same flag, would become two different kinds of peoples.

It must always be said that the settlement was not one of vengeance but one of compromise. Negroes had responded to their disfranchisement with verbal protests, but had accepted inferior educational and social opportunities as a consolation prize. They had agreed to gear their educational aims to standards defined in terms of their own limited life sphere rather than to aspire to become the white man's equal. Having lost their fight to become like all other Americans, they had settled for a chance to become different. In a successful attempt to save the Negro schools, Northern whites had designed educational opportunities for the Negro people which were directly in line with the conditions prescribed by the segregated order. These Northerners had gained substantial financial support from private philanthropy and had influenced the South to give public support to Negro schools under these compromise conditions.

It was this great detour that gave special education such a special place in the Negroes' long struggle to gain educational opportunities. Special education was more than a series of public schools and colleges. It was even more than the system of industrial education to which most of the public schools were turning at that time. It was a way of life to which Negroes were exposed for the purpose of perpetuating their caste condition, and the schools were to serve merely as the formal channel of this educative process.

Therefore, it was planned that the maintenance of Southern traditions as related to Negroes would come through a neat biracial arrangement of peoples and expectations. Negroes were to be kept socially isolated from whites by means of a rigid system of residential segregation; they were to be limited to special occupational pursuits by means of job restrictions; they were to be tailored in "Negro ways" through a rigid code of interracial etiquette; and they were to be reinforced in their obedience to caste rules through formal schooling. The point at which this biracial society began forming a way of life for Negroes, tailoring them into a particular social type, and utilizing the schools to serve the ends of segregation marks the real beginning of Negro education as a traditional American institution.

A PRIVATE WORLD OF COLOR AND
A LIMITED WORLD OF WORK

First, there was the creation of a new and very effective sociocultural setting through which the basic elements of Negro education could be informally transmitted and logically justified. This was a private world of color within which the life of every Negro was to be rigidly regulated and to whose limitations the Negro schools were to be firmly anchored. It was a world in which the races were to be symbiotically organized in all things economic but, as Booker T. Washington had proposed, kept as separate as the fingers on the hand in all things social.

The rise of this type of setting was a logical consequence of a Southern economy that had changed little in its use of Negro workers. The plantation economy had been dependent primarily upon cotton, sugar cane, rice, tobacco, and Negro labor. Wherever these crops had shifted, as when the cotton patches flowed west, a full complement of Negro labor had shifted with them. Not even freedom had been able to break this ecological affinity between the plantation and the Negroes. So firmly were the relationships rooted in the past that scarcely any change in the geographical distribution of the Negro population occurred between 1860 and 1910. Consequently the first decade of the current century found most Negroes concentrated in a very small area of the United States. Of the 9,827,763 Negroes in the entire nation at that time, 90 percent were living in the South. Over 60 percent of these were living in Georgia, Mississippi, Alabama, the Carolinas, and Louisiana. The census of 1910 showed the largest proportion to be located in an area composed of a band of counties extending from eastern Virginia and North Carolina, across Alabama, to the lower portions of the Mississippi River Valley.[1] Over half the population of these counties was Negro. This area formed the South's Black Belt and became the birthplace of the Negro subculture.

This Negro world was more than a mere geographical distribution of people. It was quickly shaped into a series of community structures whose respective populations were composed almost totally of Negroes. Paramount in the entire scheme were the small rural communities that exercised so much influence in shaping Southern Negroes into a particular kind of folk. Here one could find close-set rows of cabins on the edges of vast stretches of cotton fields.[2] Since the presence of a few whites in these settlements was not a violation of caste rules, the home of a white planter, overseer, or commissary owner often stood in the midst of a cluster of Negro cabins.[3]

Parts of the respective communities were bound together over a wide area by crooked little footpaths — threads of neighborliness.[4] The main paths and roadways led eventually to the white-washed church and the cabin school, which composed the focal points of rural community life. Some roadways stretched beyond, functionally uniting the neighborhoods with the villages they surrounded. Wagons, and eventually automobiles, carried families to town, where purchases were made from service institutions not available in the plantation settlement. Nevertheless many of the Negroes seldom got to town. Their supplies were purchased from the plantation com-

149

missary on credit and at rates that were almost certain to keep the purchaser in debt.

In similar fashion the small towns and cities of the South developed their Negro settlements too.[5] Like those of the rural area, these communities were composed totally of Negroes who, by tradition, were contained in a small amount of living space. Negro communities were basically peripheral, located on the edges of the larger villages. Seldom were white residential areas beyond them. Nevertheless they were separated from each other within the same corporate area by white neighborhoods whose paved streets, electric lights, running water, and sewerage connections seemed to run out before reaching the Negro homes.

As residential segregation spilled over into the larger cities of the South, Negroes began concentrating in relatively fixed positions near the central business districts of these cities, in areas that had already begun to deteriorate under the force of urban growth. For example, the free Negroes of Virginia who migrated to the cities of that state occupied huts along the docks and around the market-places since their presence was tolerated only in such areas. Sommerville, one of the first areas of Atlanta to be occupied by Negroes, was once a city dumping ground. Even where a highly diffused pattern of Negro settlement developed, as in Charleston, historic practices dictated the fact: Negro servants had been able to find living space in backyards of their wealthy employers. Beginning, therefore, under the effective control of a rigid code of racial segregation, Negro communities of the larger Southern cities developed into some of the most colorful areas of the urban South.[6] They became basically characterized by main streets that served as traditional symbols of all urban Negro communities and their ghetto-like qualities. There were Beal Street of Memphis, Rampart of New Orleans, Second and Leigh of Richmond, Dowling and Lyons of Houston, and Auburn Avenue of Atlanta. As early as 1900 the process of residential segregation had created a series of black islands in a great white urban sea.

Paralleling the Negro's private world of color was the limited world of work which constituted the basic economic dimension of his community life. This work-a-day world supplied him with job opportunities but only at the lower end of the occupational ladder. Whenever he worked at a higher level, it was mainly for the purpose of rendering some function to his own community and his own people.

The rigidity of the Southern policy of job restriction for Negroes may be seen in the proportion of workers who were employed in the various industries during the days when the special educational movement was being shaped. In 1890, six out of every ten in the Negro American labor force were engaged in agriculture. Three fourths of these were sharecroppers, holding the land by paying a share of their harvest as rent. Approximately three out of every ten were in some form of domestic and personal service, and the others were found working as laboreres in manufacturing and mechanical industries or serving as professionals in the segregated Negro community.[7]

Once again tradition had set the pattern of racial confinement. Agriculture continued to dominate the Negro's economic life because it offered him immediate employment. Immediately after emancipation, the cotton economy had provided him with a readily available and familiar means of earning a living in a free labor market. Nevertheless, there were particular changes which helped to foster more racial restrictions in the employment field. Many of the slaves who held high positions in the building trades prior to emancipation found it difficult to capitalize upon their experiences because of certain changes in building methods which the South experienced during its period of economic reconstruction. Plumbing, steam fitting, and electrical work became associated with these trades, and the training the former slaves had received did not encompass the skills required by this new kind of work.[8] Since emancipation meant the entrance of Negro workers into the free labor market, some hostility was naturally directed against them.[9] Urged to protect their interests, whites of the laboring class debarred most qualified Negro craftsmen from trade unions and refused to accept them as apprentices. Also the Southern image of work changed. The tendency to judge certain types of jobs as "nigger work" melted away under the shock of the economic revolution, and Negroes were eventually displaced in many of the jobs to which they had been assigned by tradition.

Since it was upon the agricultural industry of the South that the Negro's economic destiny most heavily depended, it was through it that his economic relations with whites were most dominantly shaped. Gripped as he was by the evils of the tenant system, the Negro farmer and his family experienced all the insecurities and depressions that regularly haunted those who fell victims of this type of land-tenure arrangement. The cropper who worked under the tenant system lived on a credit arangement that consisted of purchasing against his future harvest at a special store usually operated by his landlord. The average credit for him and his family was about $88 per year in the 1920s, and the interest rate was usually a flat 10 percent. Since the duration of the credit was only for a few months, the actual rate was approximately 37 percent. Commissary prices were often marked up considerably, and the interest plus the markup placed a severe strain upon the tenant family and virtually prohibited their rising above the sharecropper level. These arrangements often led to perpetual indebtedness and forced servitude.[10]

Enforcement of this state of perennial indebtedness rested with a constituted legal authority that accepted the protection of caste regulations as its moral obligation. As Ray Stannard Baker followed the "color line" through the South during the first decade of this century, he sketched this picture of the Negro sharecropper who struggled to escape the plight of peonage:[11]

> If he [sharecropper] attempts to leave, he is arrested and taken before a friendly justice of the peace and fined or threatened with imprisonment. If he is in debt, it sometimes happens that the landlord will have him arrested on the charge of stealing a bridle or a few potatoes . . . and he is brought into court. On appearing in court . . . the white man is there and offers as a special favor to take him back and let him work out the fine. . . . In this way, Negroes are kept in debt . . . year after year, they and their whole family.

Some statutes provided for the punishment of any laborer, renter, or sharecropper who would leave without the consent of his employer and before the expiration of his contract. These laws, however, were declared unconstitutional in the peonage cases of 1903 and by a Mississippi court in 1912.[12] Nevertheless these judicial decisions failed to give adequate protection to Negro farmers who sought to escape the tentacles of the cruel credit system. It was too easy for landlords to secure criminal convictions of Negroes on the slightest accusation of theft. Because of this fact many Negro croppers became imprisoned by the very land they tilled.

As the Negro's inferior position in the Southern social order crystallized in terms of residential segregation and job restrictions, certain sociological mechanisms designed to shape his mind went into operation. The caste system was brutal in its power to make every Negro think of himself as a "colored person." One mechanism through which this power operated effectively was social isolation, for through it the complete assimilation of the Negro race was blocked. Negro children tended to grow up almost completely within their restricted living space. The only sustained contacts they experienced across racial lines were those involving black and white children at play. But even here, maturity usually brought a clean break, causing those of each race to acquire a sharper image of their respective places than if the contacts had never been made. Since the main channels of personal communication with the larger society were closed to them, Negro children had no models except those of their own race. Teachers of the Negro schools most often originated in the same sociocultural setting as their pupils. Consequently, they tended to teach their pupils to grow up as they had done. Only occasionally did either teacher or pupil catch a glimpse beyond the horizon of his colored world and escape its tyranny. Nevertheless, the escape was often final. Few ever returned to pour nontypical traits into the closed world of the Negro community.

Social isolation also functioned at the adult level, for highly personal contacts between whites and Negroes at this level were kept to a bare minimum. Where these contacts did exist, they occurred underground in clandestine attachments or incidental to master-servant relations. Some cross-cultural exchange did occur this way, as when mulatto children inherited some of the prestige of their white parentage or when domestic servants acquired some of the more expensive tastes of their white employers. But the frustrations that often resulted from restrictions in the use of the ideas gained in this way rendered the goods seldom worth the cost.

There was still another mechanism operating to shape the Southern Negro into a particular folk type. This was a system of interracial etiquette that defined so clearly the Negro's inferior position in the general society. It was a series of codes of social usage required by custom and tradition in all contacts between the races.[13] The codes regulated ceremonial relations involving greetings, salutations, and conversations. They controlled contacts and situations in which reference was made to persons of either race; they directed conventions involving business relations in which economic obligations were at stake; and, in short, they shaped behavior patterns for most of the circumstances under which the two races met.

The caste badge was made prominent in all instances of greetings, salutations, and conversations. Negroes normally greeted white men with the title of "Mister." Occasionally, the title "Cap'n" or "Cap" was used where more persistent contact had bred some degree of familiarity. Familiarity also permitted them to address whites by their first name, as "Mr. John" or "Miss Mary." But in speaking of white women generally, Negroes were expected invariably to refer to them as "white ladies." On the other hand, white persons were not expected to address Negroes as "Mister," although "boy" was a good usage. Titles usually assigned to whites were seldom, if ever, assigned to Negroes. The title "Mrs." for Negro women was especially taboo. Newspapers referring to colored women of note would avoid using this title. Mrs. Booker T. Washington was referred to as "the widow of Booker T. Washington" or as a noted "negress." The lower-case *n* was usually used in reference to Negroes. There were times when the attainment and position of Negro men obviously required respect. Nevertheless, the ritual of greeting and reference firmly preserved the caste position of each race. Such

Negroes were addressed as "Parson," "Reverend," "Professor," or even "Doctor," but never "Mister."

Wherever members of the two races met in public places, fixed rituals went into operation. In hotels, offices, restaurants, or other public places reserved for whites, the Negro was expected to remove his hat whether others had done so or not. On the other hand, it was apparently not proper for a white man to remove his hat in either public or private places reserved for Negroes. Insurance and installment collectors who frequented Negro homes never violated this caste requirement. No matter how low his class, a white person was not expected to show this courtesy to Negroes. Bertram Doyle who depicted these requirements of interracial etiquette so well, added these cogent words: "Probably the only place where white men did remove their hats, though they were seldom there, was in the Negro church." [14]

Business relations between the races were never definite and contractual. They were so arranged that blacks had few demands that whites were obligated to meet. Trading arrangements involving credit were always settled on the basis of the white man's bookkeeping. If arguments about these obligations did arise, the Negro seldom won. Inherent in these relations, too, were arrangements between white employers and Negro workers. The arrangements made the Negro almost completely dependent upon the white man's mercy and most conclusively resigned to an inferior state.

Caste regulations constituted a most powerful force in the South's special educational program for Negroes. The methods of informal education inherent in the enforcement of these regulations *did* teach. They created within the minds of both whites and Negroes patterns of self-perception which were highly appropriate for the segregated order. As a natural outcome of the juxtaposition of two divergent ethnic groups, white and black people learned to distinguish themselves from each other as distinct kinds of persons, and both races eventually perceived the Negro as a contrasting conception.[15] Black and white were constantly presented as antipodes, negative and positive poles on a continuum of goodness. In the minds of whites, Negroes stood as the antithesis of the character and properties of white people. This psychology of self-debasement soon matured, and Negroes began to see themselves as whites did. Negro children learned to offend each other by calling each other "black." Negro business enterprises that did not seem to measure up to segregated standards were referred to as "nigger business" by Negroes themselves. Booker T. Washington, in speaking of his youth, recalled that it was assumed that everything white was good and everything black was bad.[16] Once the system of differential expectations was really set, the conduct of whites and Negroes came to be judged on different value scales, and there came into being a black and white code of morality.

It was logical that the greatest force in depressing the Negro's self-image should be found in the rural South, where so many Negroes lived under the constant threat of the tenant system. Here is where many of them tottered between dependency and utter despair, for there were times when the system kept both tenant and landlord poor. Statements made by sharecroppers of Macon County, Alabama, illustrate well the manner in which the character of the rural Negro eroded under the influence of the South's tenant system. When asked of his relationship with his landlord, one of the croppers reported, "I asked landlord to 'vance me er pair of overalls, he say he need overalls hisself." Another, unwittingly expressing the depressing effect of sharecropping upon human aspirations, summarized his hopes when he said, "Ain't make nothin', do'n spec nothin' 'till I die." And in obvious defeat, a cropper confessed, "Dis ole mule lak me — he ain't much good no more." [17]

The sharecropper's imprisonment was not confined to the land. It extended to an enslavement of his mind, for the system was a good teacher. It taught the cropper to mine the soil, use the fence rails for firewood, to make no repairs, to practice no economy of self-help through animal husbandry or family gardening.[18] With the cotton rows running to his cabin door, he could hardly have instituted this practice even if the system had not robbed him of the will.

Conditions like these — social isolation, occupational immobility, and the rigid enforcement of interracial etiquette — generated within Negroes the personality inclinations that now form the basis for the various negative stereotypes so often used against them. Negroes and whites became different because they were kept apart. White Southerners insisted that they be kept apart because they were different. Segregation begat segregation.

Nevertheless, this type of program of informal education did not influence all Negroes in the same way. Every Negro had some feeling of protest against the caste system, and each had some sort of conflict with the white world. But these represented various degrees of deviancy from the norm of caste acceptance and were met with sanctions consistent with the extent of rebellion. For most Negroes, no overt expression of rebellion came at all; in fact, some of these were aggressively cooperative in defending the prevailing customs. Whites thought of these as "safe" Negroes, the type who could be counted upon to employ their influence in the task of keeping other Negroes satisfied with the existing caste requirements. The "safe" Negroes developed their influence over the others of their race not because the others respected them but because they feared them. There developed also the "sycophant," the Negro who knew better but acted in his own personal interest. He worked with whites as Br'er Rabbit worked with Br'er Fox. He learned to gain community influence and to satisfy his own limited aspirations by flattering white people into serving his own ends. At the other end of the continuum developed the "uppity" Negro who, by training and ambition, mirrored a constant challenge to the caste line. He was often ignored by the Negro masses but was most usually feared by whites. The fear was logical, for the "uppity" Negro was eventually to become the white man's nemesis and the David who would eventually slay the South's Goliath.

A SCHOOL SYSTEM IN CAPTIVITY

Strategically located in the Negro's private world of color and skillfully designed to inculcate those values which would adequately adjust the Negro people to their caste conditions were the Negro schools, public and private. By the first decade of the twentieth century, these schools had found their way into the heart of the

Negro South. Despite some degree of public indifference and because of the generosity of philanthropic agencies, every Negro community of the rural or urban South could boast of some type of organized educational institution.

Setting the pace and characterizing the entire Negro educational structure at the public school level were the county training schools that were organized through the generosity of the John F. Slater Fund. Beginning with four of these schools in 1911, the Southern states, under the leadership and financial support of the fund, had developed 355 by 1928. By this time, 14,092 Negro children living in the various counties of the South were receiving secondary education from 2,379 teachers in these schools.[19] There was hardly a Southern Negro community in which a county training school was not operating when the 1933–1934 school year started.

Another look at the influence of John F. Slater will show that the trustees of the fund he established virtually captured the Negro public schools of the South. They facilitated the establishment of public high schools for Negro children by financially cooperating with all local agencies willing to share the initial expenditures and continue the support. They took the larger elementary schools of rural areas where the Negro population was dense and combined them in the largest consolidation movement the South had ever experienced. They designed a curriculum that placed emphasis on rural life and established "Smith-Hughes teachers"[20] as principals. Characteristically located in the open country of a Southern county whose population was predominantly Negro, the county training school developed a community-centered program aimed directly at the task of helping rural Negroes improve their living conditions within the framework of segregated living. No attack was made on the tenant system, but an occasional diplomatic move was made to secure the permission of a landlord to involve his tenants. Caste regulations were intentionally left undisturbed, and influential whites who had some fear that the program would threaten the *status quo* were encouraged to cooperate through an appeal to their self-interest. Local and philanthropic agents occasionally succeeded in getting them to believe that the school's program would make the Negroes more economically useful to them.

As the white South gained confidence in the movement, the schools moved firmly under the captivity of the segregated order.

Industrial education was the core of the county training school's program. Farmers were encouraged to buy equipment collectively; the schools served as custodians of this equipment, and the students used it in their studies. In 1929 farmers who came under the schools' influence were encouraged to drop cash crops like cotton and tobacco and to turn to food products like wheat, vegetables, and livestock.[21] The agents whom the various state departments of education had supplied for the Negro rural communities furnished the leadership in efforts designed to train the Negroes to live at home and like it. Following the methods that had been created earlier by the Jeanes teachers, these agricultural leaders taught the people to can fruits and vegetables, to butcher livestock, plant gardens, whitewash cabins, and even make household furniture out of discarded apple boxes and orange crates. Most of this was adult education, but some attempt was made to integrate it with the students' courses just as the Jeanes Plan had specified. Abstract mathematics was replaced by exercises in bookkeeping related to farming and farm products. World geography and history were replaced by a study of the local environment. So far as intentions were concerned, the pupils were to know a great deal about where they lived though little about the living conditions of other people.

Long before the county training schools were conceived, a thread of Negro colleges and universities was woven into the fabric of the South's Black Belt. These, too, were the product of philanthropic generosity and inevitably became captives of the South's program to educate Negroes for their caste assignments. Thirty of these institutions were established during the first decade after the Civil War, and others appeared gradually after that time until, by the middle of this century, 112 such institutions had been established for Negroes in the South.

Like the public schools, the colleges were strategically located. There was hardly a Negro community in the South that did not come under the influence of one or more of them. Organized originally for liberal arts purposes, the Negro college slowly instituted industrial education as one of its basic functions. Shops, kitchens, and sewing rooms were added as laboratories for the students, and some of the institutions that had been most dedicated to the liberal arts program advertised rather freely the emphasis they were professing to place upon the manual arts. Hampton and Tuskegee had set the pattern, and those colleges that showed the most vivid signs of following this pattern were given the greatest share of the money which had begun to flow South and into the Negro schools at the opening of our century. A system of Negro land-grant colleges grew out of some of the older normal schools, and teaching the manual arts became a public compulsion with this group.

The South's system of Negro education was completed by 1933. The Slater Fund and other philanthropic agencies like it had inspired the development of secondary schools for Negroes, and practically any Negro child in the South could get at least two years of high school training at public expense without walking too far for it. Higher education had been made available to the Negroes, and the "colored South" had begun to feel the effects of its influence. Although they did not attack the caste problem directly and with dedicated intentions, the private colleges, with their greater freedom, did venture in this direction. They worked to elevate the Negroes by pressing against the extreme end of the range of tolerance set by the agencies that gave them support and by the state officials who gave them their rating.

A SCHOOL SYSTEM IN UNCONSCIOUS REBELLION

Despite all the planning that had been put into the Negro educational movement, it was quite evident, even at the start, that some of its byproducts woud contradict its aims and rise to threaten the social system it was engineered to preserve. There were signs that neither the Restoration that followed the collapse of congressional Reconstruction nor the marriage between North and South that was consummated at Capon Springs would be able to survive the long pull of history. These signs appeared particularly in the public schools and colleges themselves. Apparently neither the schools nor the segregated communities were to serve the caste order without creating some dissatisfaction with it. Both were to vacillate between two different kinds of services to two different kinds of masters.

During the early days of the 1870s, when the South's public school movement was in its infancy, the signs of vacillation were subtle and obviously unconscious. Nevertheless, the seeds of growing dissatisfaction with caste were there, first planted by the public compulsion to make the curriculum of the Negro schools basically similar to that of other schools. Those who administered the public school system could not escape the magnetic pull toward the literary. Therefore, at the base of every Negro child's educational opportunity was a literary training that took precedence over the industrial. The classical academic tradition that Americans inherited from England proved to be extremely viable. It was considered to be the required foundation for all kinds of formal education. When the people thought of schools, whether for Negroes or for whites, literary subjects invariably came to their minds. Consequently, superintendents of the various systems looked for literary training in the teachers they sought to employ, and lamented the absence of this orientation in many who applied.

In 1870 the school examiners of Jones County, North Carolina, complained that both white and colored applicants for teaching certificates were so wanting in fitness that some regard for efficiency had to be sacrificed. Nevertheless, no certificate was issued to any applicant of either race until each had "passed" a tolerably fair examination in arithmetic.[22] Reporting later on the qualities that he looked for in teachers, Josiah H. Shinn, superintendent of public instruction for Arkansas, listed good scholarship as his first requirement. He expected his teachers of geography, for example, not only to treat the earth as a home for man but also to correlate the instruction with subject matter drawn from "the allied branches of botany, geology, and mineralogy."[23] In all the examinations given Negroes who sought to qualify for a teaching position, competency in English, mathematics, geography, and spelling was given close scrutiny. No test of the teacher's skill in industrial arts was ever recorded. This does not mean that caste regulations failed to function in the selection of Negro teachers, for seldom were the qualifications for teaching in the Negro schools as high as those required for teaching in the white schools. Neither does it mean that the curricula of the two school systems were absolutely the same. Caste limitations lowered the standards of the Negro schools, including schools for Negro teachers, but they failed to stem the imitative tide that was rising within the Negro community and causing Negroes to want the same curriculum as whites.

Throughout the South, as for the rest of the nation, the three R's, geography, and a bit of history composed the basic character of the region's graded school curriculum. The Negro school was no exception to this rule, and Negro children were constantly exposed to this kind of curriculum as they progressed to the higher branches, the normal school, and the college level. In an attempt to keep faith with the industrial education movement, some courses in the manual arts were offered, but these were basically supplementary, acting in no important sense as a focal point of the curriculum. By 1903 there were 13,797 Negro children receiving some kind of industrial training at the high school level in the South. Nevertheless, 8,055 of these were taking "classical, scientific, English, and business courses as the hard core of their curriculum." [24]

Different educational movements came later in an attempt to revive the industrial emphasis, but these were directed more toward the larger community than toward the school and its pupils. The Jeanes teachers made heroic attempts to get local teachers, particularly those in rural areas, to organize their courses of study around the everyday life and "practical" needs of the Negro communities in which the schools were located. Despite all their ingenuity and dedication, the more classical curriculum of even the rural schools remained unshaken, and the rural cabins from which the masses of Negroes were later to depart remained characteristically unpainted. The girls were exposed to some domestic science, and boys were given some carpentry, blacksmithing, and agronomy. However, this became merely window dressing, like singing Negro spirituals when white people came to visit the schools. It was merely a way of making favorable impressions upon some visiting school officials whose influence with philanthropic agencies could stimulate more money for the school.

Another force that inclined the colored schools away from the industrial and nearer the conventional curriculum was the Negro community in which each school was so tightly anchored. Since these communities constituted a separate part of a biracial society, the Negroes found it necessary to provide for themselves those institutions whose services were not available to them through the larger community complex. Therefore the importance which these institutions assumed in Negro community life spotlighted the need to make certain types of professional training available to the population. The Negro schools had to be staffed with teachers, and these teachers had to be trained. The summer institutes held for Negro teachers did not prove capable of meeting the demand. Gradually and with the help of philanthropic foundations the Negro colleges organized normal departments. By the 1920s practically all these colleges were in the business of training teachers.

The pulpits of churches had to be filled with intelligent leadership, for the Negro people, finding themselves surrounded by a hostile world, once again turned to a religious faith. Their churches multiplied rapidly and with the schools became the most powerful influence in Negro community life. The revival around the turn of the century was motivated not solely by emotional needs, although these needs still prevailed in all their dynamic force; it was also a result of the necessity to provide some source of mutual aid for the depressed Negro population. Not all the churches were involved, and most of those that were tended to center in the larger urban areas. But as early as 1897 Negro churches in nine Southern cities had accumulated 30,000 active members and $1,542,460 in real estate value. They had aggregated an annual income of $157,678 by that time and were putting forth some effort to protect the Negroes against their many deprivations. Twenty-seven of these churches were spending $8,907 annually for charitable purposes and had established mission units in the slums of these cities. Several were working with homes for the aged, orphanages, and other welfare institutions at that time, and some had even ventured to extend help to needy families through a system of home visits.[25]

Although it has been reported that the Negro church functioned in the interest of the caste system for many years,[26] there is no denying that it nourished some serious threats against the system. It cried out for and elicited a leadership whose training exceeded the limits of industrial education. Almost all the private colleges for Negroes had theological departments by 1890 and had produced 512 ministers who were trained in divinity before the close of the century. What the South did not know at that time was that out of one of these colleges would come the minister, Martin Luther King, whose leadership would spark a new kind of American revolution.

The demand for business enterprises within the Negro communities did not falter despite the unfortunate experiences which accumulated around the banks and fraternal orders that Negroes tried to operate. As time passed the need for these kinds of service institution grew larger, causing a rather complete set to come into existence. There first appeared eating, drinking, tonsorial, medical, recreational, and other places which offered services of a highly personal nature. They grew up along the main streets that pierced the Negro areas. They were seldom attractive or well run, but their monopolistic power to draw patronage encouraged the development of other kinds of institutions. Financial enterprises, insurance companies, and even newspaper establishments eventually won sufficient support to maintain a strong position in such Southern cities as Durham, Richmond, and Atlanta. Although these enterprises shared minutely in the Negro's total purchasing power, they were profitable enough to sustain a small proprietary class within the race. Gradually, physicians, dentists, preachers, teachers, and undertakers developed into a small professional class. These two classes — proprietary and professional — constituted the upper crust of a world that had turned black. It was the children of this class who were to demand higher and professional education; it was this class that was to gain power steadily and supply the force of discontent out of which the protest movements of later years were to grow.

Therefore, the many daily needs of the segregated Negro community justified giving young Negroes higher and professional training. Southern whites realized that if the segregated system was to work, the Negro schools, particularly the colleges, would have to teach courses in business, economics, journalism, medicine, teacher training, and theology. Some educators, both white and Negro, had anticipated this possibility when they contended, as did William T. Harris in 1890, that Negroes needed a more classical education, which would provide them with trained leadership.

Responding to this growing need with greater realism, the Negro colleges more speedily inclined their programs toward literary and professional fields. Hampton, Arkansas A. and M., Prairie View Normal and Industrial, and Alabama Agricultural and Mechanical College were founded especially for the purpose of giving industrial training. Along with eight other institutions that appeared in 1897, they helped to form a core around which the land-grant college system for Negroes was built. Nevertheless these agricultural and mechanical colleges very quickly became teacher-training institutions whose actual curricular emphasis was far more literary than industrial.

During the school year 1899–1900, Tuskegee offered six different curricula to 1,231 students. These curricula were liberal arts, industrial, agricultural, biblical, nursing, and musical. Courses composing these departments were taught by 80 teachers, but half of these instructors were assigned to literary courses. It was through these courses that Tuskegee hoped to correlate the literary and the industrial to furnish young men and women for leadership in the various phases of Negro community life. What Tuskegee had actually begun to do at that time, as later trends indicated, was to train teachers for the Negro public schools. Of the 321 students who were graduated from the Institute from 1885 to 1889, 255 were teaching at the close of the period.[27]

North Carolina's Agricultural and Mechanical College for the Colored Race showed a similar inclination toward the literary and teacher-training functions. During the 1903–1904 school year this institution taught four different curricula: agriculture and chemistry, mechanics, industrial, and liberal arts. These courses were taught to 163 students by seven teachers. Although only two of these teachers were instructing in the liberal arts department, this department, along with its teacher-training functions, seemed to have been the core of the college. The college graduated 72 students between 1899 and 1901, and two thirds of those graduates whose occupations were known to the officials of the school were engaged in teaching.[28]

Some of the Negro colleges got ahead in the literary field by accepting a teacher-training and liberal arts responsibility early. These are best represented by the many normal institutes established for Negro teachers by North Carolina and several other Southern states, and by the several liberal arts colleges that operated within the tradition of Talladega, Fisk, or the Atlanta University group. Beginning mainly as preparatory schools, these institutions were to evolve into four-year colleges, which would supply public school teachers, doctors, lawyers, businessmen, and even college teachers for the Negro society. While the theological departments of several of these colleges had turned toward the production of a formally trained Negro clergy by the opening of the twentieth century, Shaw University at Raleigh, Walden University at Nashville, and Howard University at Washington, D.C., had begun to produce a corps of doctors and nurses.

And so it happened that Negro education, instead of being specialized along industrial lines, became somewhat of a duplication of the education which was offered to white children. It was separate; it was judged in terms of the value scale held for Negroes; and it symbolized America's dual standard of academic competency. Nevertheless, it was to be the stuff out of which revolutions are made.

VII · THE FAILURE
OF AN EXPERIMENT

Through the program of Negro education that Northern and Southern educators had so carefully developed by the first decade of the current century, there was launched the most extensive experiment in interracial adjustment ever attempted. This new group of educators had committed themselves to the task of determining whether or not millions of Negro Americans could be trained to function effectively as a caste in a society that would otherwise be democratic, and whether or not they could be made to remain satisfied with their condition.*

As professedly implied in their promises to the Negroes, the white educators had aimed to create equal opportunities for upward mobility within the black caste. They had promised that their schools would be equal to those provided for whites, that a free ballot would be forthcoming for those who acquired literacy and the status of property owners, that occupational fitness and economic security would come to those who became industrially trained, and that the entire experimental exposure would produce a kind of moral and social stability with which Negro Americans could become socially acceptable as members of the larger society.

But there still existed the risk that the experiment would trigger traditional needs and inspire informal action contrary to its aims. Of course the promise of equal educational opportunities had been stitched into the fabric of the constitution of every state, and the Supreme Court had backed the constitutionality of this promise through its decision in *Plessey v. Ferguson.* The permissive quality

* The speeches made at the various conferences — the ideology of the great detour — definitely reflect these aims.

of this very decision, however, had unwittingly taken a goodly number of the Negro American's civil rights out of the realm of legal contract and placed them within the range of tolerance of American morals. Southern school officials had been given the liberty to do for the Negro schools that which they defined to be "right." The Negro schools had lost their protection under the law and had been placed, instead, under the shelter of a moral system that was weak. Racial discrimination was not only rendered possible but was even made publicly acceptable. The same fate awaited the educators' promise of the ballot for Negroes. Notwithstanding the Fifteenth Amendment, the discretion given the states in determining voter qualifications created abundant opportunities for Negro disfranchisement. No concept of equal employment opportunity had emerged from constitutional interpretation by that time. Consequently, the Negro's occupational mobility was made to hang not simply upon his industrial fitness but also upon his acceptability to white employers. So the entire system of opportunities for upward mobility within the black caste depended upon the extent to which the traditional needs of whites to discriminate against the Negroes would be revived. What could be the most troublesome problem of all was the inescapable possibility that the experiment would make the Negroes dissatisfied with their caste assignment rather than strengthen their satisfaction with it. There was always the question: How *Negro* can education be? There was always the ever-present risk that the Negro's need for racial equality would once again assert itself.

The experiment, therefore, consisted in the brutal exposure of the Negro's education to the acid test of time, whereby it would be determined whether or not the faith that the educators and the Negroes had had in the special education system had been well placed. Did an increasingly greater proportion of Negro Americans accept the facilities that were being organized especially for them? Did their educational level rise progressively under the system's influence? Were the facilities kept substantially equal to those provided for whites? Did industrial training make them more industrially fit, and were they allowed to climb the occupational ladder of the general national economy according to their fitness? Did literacy and property ownership win for them a free ballot, and did the general program result in their greater social stability? These are the questions that were later to elicit answers which could vindicate or condemn the judgment of educators who chose to educate the Negro American in this way. The vivid answers are found in the record that the Southern region compiled as it dealt with its Negro problem during the years that followed.

A FAITH STRONGLY HELD

The experiment had a good start. It began with the strong faith that Negroes placed in formal education and in the honest intentions of those who administered their schools. The seeds of their faith in formal education had long been planted. Ever since their earliest contact with the printed page, Southern Negroes had maintained an almost blind confidence in schooling. In many instances, their earliest interracial experiences had been the result of an involvement with the wealthiest and most cultured element of the white South. By the time of their emancipation, almost all of them had come to believe that those qualities of white people which they admired so much and tried so hard to emulate had resulted from formal education and that they, too, could acquire them if they once got the necessary schooling.

Many important people, Negro as well as white, had emphasized the necessity of some kind of special education for Negroes. Booker T. Washington's name had become a household word, and many Negroes had turned all matters pertaining to their welfare over to this brown diplomat of the South.[1] Their confidence was considerably strengthened one decade after the special education movement got under way when President Taft, responding to the forty-fifth anniversary of the founding of Fisk University, praised all efforts to organize education for Negroes around the industrial theme.[2] The various foundations had convinced the Negroes of the honesty of their intentions by pouring millions into the schools organized to educate Negro children. There were small, if noticeable, differences in the amount of money spent by the states to support white and

Negro schools when the races were separated, and Negroes had little reason to expect that these conditions would not remain.

With this kind of confidence in the educational program that the South had provided for their race, Negro parents of the region gradually began to send their children to school. Less than 10 percent of their children were attending school in 1870, but after three decades had passed almost one third of the 3,228,237 who were of school age were involved in the public school program. The number of Negro school-age children in the Southern states had increased to 3,403,237 by 1910; the percentage attending school had reached 45.4. The rate among white children was greater and also growing,

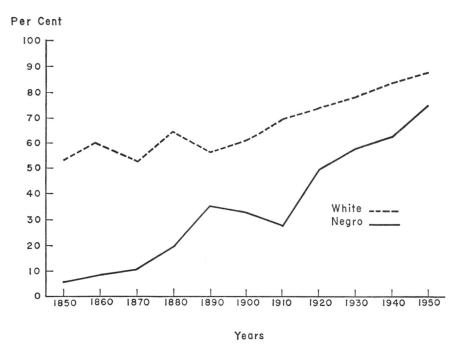

CHART 1. Percentage of white and Negro children, aged five through nineteen, who attended school in the Southern states, 1850–1950

Sources: Charles S. Johnson, *The Negro in American Civilization* (New York: Henry Holt and Company, 1930), p. 232; and Bureau of the Census, *Census of Population: 1950* (Washington, D.C.: Government Printing Office, 1952), vol. II.

but it did not indicate the same enthusiasm for public school attendance as the Negro rate, and its growth was significantly slower. When viewed over the first half of this century, and as shown in Chart 1, two facts of the Southern record remain unmistakably clear: Greater and greater proportions of the Negro children became involved in the public school program, and racial differences in the rate of school attendance gradually decreased.

The Negro's stride toward literacy under the influence of special education certainly vindicated his confidence in the program. According to Chart 2, less than half the South's Negro population ten years of age and over could read and write in 1890, but the literacy rate climbed rapidly after that time, and by 1930, slightly over four fifths of the Negroes were literate. On the average, the Southern

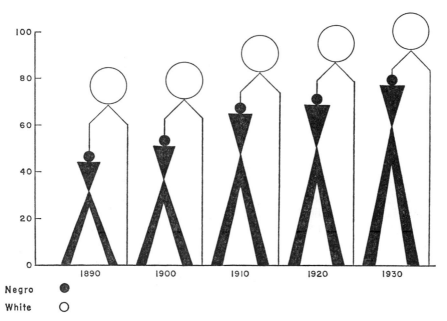

Negro ●
White ○

CHART 2. Literacy (percent) of whites and Negroes, twenty-five years of age and over, 1890–1930

Sources: Bureau of the Census, *Negro Population, 1790–1915* (Washington, D.C.: Government Printing Office, 1918), and *Negro Population, 1920–1932* (Washington, D.C.: Government Printing Office, 1932).

Negro's literacy increased 93.8 percent over the forty-year period. When compared with the 32 percent experienced by the region's total population during this time, the Negro's progress was phenomenal.

Credit for the vindication of this portion of the Negro's faith cannot be shared equally by the various states. Table 1 shows that

TABLE I. Literacy (percent) of total and Negro population, twenty-five years of age and over, in Southern states, 1890 and 1930

States	Total			Negro		
	1890	1930	Percent increase	1890	1930	Percent increase
Alabama	59.0	87.4	48.1	30.1	73.8	145.2
Arkansas	73.4	93.2	27.0	46.4	83.9	80.8
Florida	72.2	92.9	28.7	49.5	81.2	64.0
Georgia	60.2	90.6	50.5	32.7	80.1	145.0
Kentucky	78.4	93.4	19.1	44.1	84.6	91.8
Louisiana	54.2	86.5	59.6	27.9	76.7	174.9
Mississippi	60.0	86.9	44.8	39.2	76.8	95.9
North Carolina	54.3	90.0	65.7	39.9	79.4	99.0
Oklahoma	94.6	97.2	2.7	61.0	90.7	48.7
South Carolina	55.0	85.1	54.7	35.9	73.1	103.6
Tennessee	73.4	92.8	26.4	45.8	85.1	85.8
Texas	80.3	93.2	16.1	47.5	86.6	82.3
Virginia	69.8	91.3	30.8	42.8	80.8	88.9
Total	68.8	90.8	32.0	41.8	81.0	93.8

Sources: Bureau of the Census, *Negro Population in the United States, 1790–1915* (Washington, D.C.: Government Printing Office, 1918), p. 428; and *Negroes in the United States, 1920–1932* (Washington, D.C.: Government Printing Office, 1934), p. 241.

Negroes in some states lagged behind, while those in others forged ahead. The percentage of change in the literacy rate experienced by the Negroes of Oklahoma, Florida, Arkansas, Texas, and Virginia fell significantly below the average maintained in the South between 1890 and 1930. Nevertheless, the rate experienced by Negroes living in Louisiana almost doubled, and it became almost one and one half times greater in Georgia and South Carolina. Apparently, most of this difference was due to the influence of the many private schools that Negroes were attending in these states. However, the Negro's literacy did rise, and long before midcentury the charge that Southern Negroes supplied the South with massive illiteracy had become statistically less justifiable.

Although the early period is spotty and the definitions of educational indices by which measurements must be made have been unstable, there is ample evidence for the conclusion that the Negro schools managed to facilitate the academic advancement of Negroes beyond the level of sheer literacy. By 1910 there were signs that Negro children were averaging 7 years of schooling as compared with 9.7 years for the white children at that time.[3] Some upward movement in grade level must have developed, for the median educational level of nonwhite adults in the South was 5.2 in 1940 and had reached 5.9 by 1950. Their progress during this decade was exactly the same as that of native whites whose median increased from 8.4 to 9.3.[4]

The Negro's reach for education at the higher level persisted strongly, pressing his average grade achievement level upward. The rush to colleges and universities that began immediately after the Civil War had not receded noticeably by 1900. W. E. B. Du Bois, reporting to the fifth conference of Atlanta University during that year, revealed that thirty Negro colleges were training 9,068 students. It is true that one third of these students were studying at the primary level, and almost one half were in the secondary departments. Nevertheless, the distribution of enrollment characteristic of these institutions indicated that young Negroes had begun to obtain a higher education.[5] The college departments of the higher institutions graduated 137 in 1876, but the number had increased to 1,883 by 1900. The growth continued into the twentieth century. In his study of a sample of 4,778 Negro college graduates who were alive in 1932 and whom he distributed according to the year of graduation, Charles S. Johnson observed a rapid and progressive tendency for the number to increase as the years passed.[6] Negro colleges conferred 69,453 baccalaureate degrees between 1939 and 1952, and 71,372 were graduated between 1953 and 1963. Chart 3 pictures the progress of this trend.

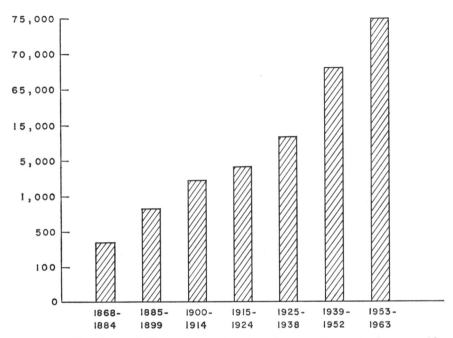

CHART 3. Number of Negroes graduating from college during specific intervals, 1868–1963

Sources: Charles S. Johnson, *The Negro College Graduate* (Chapel Hill, N.C.: University of North Carolina Press, 1938); Jessie Parkhurst Guzman, *Negro Year Book, 1952* (New York: Wm. H. Wise and Company, 1952); and Bureau of the Census, *Characteristics of the Population, 1960* (Washington, D.C.: Government Printing Office, 1963).

This persistent faith in formal education shown by Southern Negroes became a significant force and helped to enhance the quality of the Negro population in the South in accordance with community needs. The proportion of Southern Negroes having high school and college training gradually grew larger. There were 374,-015 Negroes (9.8 percent of the total) who had completed high

174

school in 1940. The number increased to 659,516 (14.4 percent) by midcentury. The proportion who had reached college level increased from 2.6 to 4.0 percent during this decade. Although the percentages were small, the progress was significant. Rates of increase at these academic levels were 47 and 54 percent, respectively. When compared with the rates of 124 and 18 experienced by whites who had moved to the high school and college levels, Southern Negroes appeared to be making more gains at the top of the academic ladder than at the middle.

Forced to meet many of its needs from within its population, the segregated Negro community of the South called for and received a more highly trained leadership. Of the 1,883 who had graduated from thirty Negro colleges of the South by 1900, over one third, or 37.2 percent, were serving as teachers in the region's colored schools at that time. Approximately one tenth, or 11.3 percent, were serving as clergymen, 4.0 percent as physicians, and 3.3 percent as lawyers. The others were employed as civil service workers, merchants, and store clerks. Only 1.4 percent were engaged in farming. Slowly but certainly the graduates were working their way into the community functional structure. Approximately one fourth had assumed some kind of responsible role of leadership on a voluntary as well as employment basis. Most of these were guiding religious societies, investing in Negro business enterprises, and contributing to newspapers or helping edit them. Many, spreading their leadership more thinly, had begun to work with charitable, agricultural, or health organizations.[7]

The college graduate's role in the Negro community had not changed very much three decades later. Indeed if any change had occurred at all, it was in the direction of anchoring the older pattern more deeply into the vitals of Negro community life. By 1930, schoolteaching, the ministry, medicine, Negro business, and the United States mail service had become the chief source of employment available to the Negroes who were being graduated from the various colleges and universities.[8] When evaluated in terms of role-needs, the winds of Negro education had blown the Negro community some good.

A FAITH OPENLY BETRAYED

Even as Negroes were enthusiastically accepting their special schools and were beginning to pass to higher grade levels through this newly found hope, there were already signs that they would get an education inferior in quality to that offered whites. There appeared first the brutal fact that their days of schooling each year were considerably shorter than for the white children. There was no way to detect this difference at the beginning of the public school movement. Each county did the best it could — ran its schools according to its own peculiar circumstances — and the Negro schools, wherever separated from the white, seemed to experience no more disadvantage than the white. By 1910, however, a policy of racial discrimination had quietly invaded public school administration in the South, and the average term for white children had grown 27 days longer than that for Negro children. Not all states were equally as guilty of this kind of discriminatory policy. Negro children fared best in Texas, Virginia, North Carolina, and Kentucky. Little difference existed in the length of school terms available to them and the whites in these states. They fared worst in Louisiana, Alabama, and South Carolina, where their school terms were 41 to 63 days shorter. As time passed, the length of terms for the Negro schools in Alabama grew closer to those for the whites. Table 2 shows that the differences against the Negro children in some states had increased severely by the 1928–29 school year and that the decreases in others were minor.

There were signs, too, that the system of farm tenancy would shorten even more the limited time for formal training which public policy had made available to Negro children. Most of these children lived in the rural areas of the South, where their parents were serving as sharecroppers. They constituted a large pool of unpaid family workers, and each day they spent out of school was a day of work on the farm. Since their absence from school was a decided economic advantage to landlords, they were frequently excused from school attendance through the influence of large landowners. Some were

TABLE 2. Average length of term (school days) for white and Negro public schools in the Southern states, 1909–10 and 1928–29

States	1909–10		1928–29	
	White	Negro	White	Negro
Alabama	131	90	159	129
Arkansas	94	70	152	132
Florida	123	106	163	128
Georgia	158	126	158	137
Kentucky	123	115	160	140
Louisiana	156	93	174	112
Mississippi	123	101	141	130
North Carolina	105	94	151	137
South Carolina	113	74	173	114
Tennessee	121	89	166	156
Texas	139	135	152	147
Virginia	133	123	174	151
Average	128	101	164	144

Sources: W. E. B. Du Bois, *Common Schools and the Negro American* (Atlanta, Ga.: Atlanta University Press, 1911); and E. B. Reuter, *The American Race Problem* (New York: Thomas Y. Crowell, 1938), p. 288.

kept out of school for sustained periods each year in order to accommodate the labor demands imposed by the growing and harvest seasons. Eventually, as evidenced by Table 3, the length of school terms available to Negro children of the various Southern states came to vary inversely with the rate of farm tenancy and the amount of cotton produced in the counties.[9] It was ironic that the Negro child's chance to learn became limited by an economy whose prosperity he helped to produce.

Whether intended or not, this disadvantage of the shortened school term helped introduce an adulterating factor into the South's educational standards. It was not reasonable to suppose that the Negro children were so smart that they could learn as much as white children while going to school for a much shorter period of time each year. Assuming a grammar school course of eight years and a high school course of four, under the 8–4 plan so prevalent in

TABLE 3. Percentage of tenancy and average number of school days attended by Negro children in the Southern states, 1930

States	Percent tenants	Average school days attended
Mississippi	87.6	74
Georgia	87.2	90
Louisiana	85.7	97
Arkansas	85.6	81
Alabama	83.0	101
South Carolina	79.3	86
Tennessee	77.6	121
Oklahoma	77.1	120
Texas	76.0	104
North Carolina	74.5	114
Florida	48.7	130
Virginia	38.2	128

Sources: Bureau of the Census, *Negroes in the United States* (Washington, D.C.: Government Printing Office, 1934); and Department of Commerce, *Statistical Abstract of the United States, 1935* (Washington, D.C.: Government Printing Office, 1935).

the South up through the thirties, the average Southern white child who finished the grammar grades spent 65.6 months in classroom study as compared with 57.6 months spent by the Negro child. Even if all other conditions were equal, a grammar school education achieved by the Negro child could not have meant the same amount of learning as one achieved by the white child. Indeed the adulteration factor failed to leave the white child's educational opportunities unaffected. Under the same assumption of equal conditions, white children graduating from the public schools of Mississippi, Texas, Georgia, and Alabama could not have achieved as much as those graduating in Virginia, Louisiana, and Arkansas. In fact, they could not have achieved as much as graduates of the Negro schools in some of the states. Therefore, special education for Negroes introduced more than a dual educational system. It imposed upon the South a dual pattern of educational standards.

Standards of the Negro schools were even more greatly imperiled by the smaller amount of money that accompanied the shorter school terms. The practice of providing less money for the Negro schools than for the white also crept unnoticeably into the public policy of school administration. When they were first established and before the special education program for Negroes was adopted by the South, all public schools in the region received substantially the same kind of economic support. Where differences did exist, they occurred as a result of variations in the tax base of the states and not as an effect of the racial factor. The opening of the twentieth century, however, saw a decided change, and by 1910, the Negro child's portion of the money spent for public education had fallen far below his proportional representation in the population. The Southern states aggregated a total expenditure of $72,051,460 for public education during the 1914–1915 school year, but only $8,792,137, or 12.2 percent of this amount, was spent on the Negro schools. The total expenditure had increased to $343,365,933 by the end of the 1929–1930 school year with only $40,073,312 or 11.7 percent going to schools for Negro children. Although the number of these children increased during this period, the percentage of the amount spent for their education was less than before and not even one half their proportional representation among the South's school-age population.

These racial differentials so inherent in the provisions for public education in the South become even more vivid when measured in terms of per capita expenditure. When the average Southern Negro child closed his school year in 1915, the people of his state had spent $4.01 in support of his educational opportunities. They spent $10.82, more than double the amount, on the white child in school that year. The passage of fifteen years saw an improvement in the actual amount which the Negro child was getting, but his position as related to the white child was not quite so well off. The state-by-state comparisons shown in Table 4 reveal a trend toward some improvement, but not much. Here, again, the Negro child's educational opportunities were considerably better in some states than in others. Particularly were they better in Kentucky, Oklahoma, and Texas. Also the Negro children of Tennessee received a greater per capita expenditure than did the white of Arkansas, Georgia,

TABLE 4. Per capita annual expenditure (dollars) for the education of white and Negro children in the Southern states, 1914–15 and 1929–30

States	1914–15		1929–30	
	White	Negro	White	Negro
Alabama	9.00	1.47	37.50	7.16
Arkansas	8.15	3.74	26.91	17.06
Florida	15.10	2.37	78.25	10.57
Georgia	10.09	2.08	31.52	6.98
Kentucky	10.30	8.91	25.27	25.77
Louisiana	16.44	1.81	40.64	7.84
Mississippi	8.20	1.53	31.33	5.94
North Carolina	7.38	2.66	44.48	14.30
Oklahoma	14.33	11.16	40.48	20.83
South Carolina	10.70	1.09	52.89	5.20
Tennessee	8.70	4.58	46.52	31.54
Texas	10.89	7.50	46.71	39.66
Virginia	11.47	3.20	47.46	13.30
Average	10.82	4.01	42.39	15.86

Sources: Monroe N. Work, *The Negro Year Book, 1916–17* (Tuskegee Institute, Ala.: The Negro Year Book Publishing Company, 1917), and *The Negro Year Book, 1931–32* (Tuskegee Institute, Ala.: The Negro Year Book Publishing Company, 1932).

Kentucky, and Mississippi. Nevertheless, before fifteen years had passed, many of these advantages had dwindled, and the Negro children in many Southern states dropped noticeably behind the white not only during that period but into the fifties.

Since the purse strings of the Negro school were short, relatively little was invested in its teaching force. The eleven Southern states that reported teachers' salaries according to race in 1909 paid $23,-856,914 to teachers of their schools during that year. This represented 74.4 percent of all the money spent by them for public education. Of this amount, not more than $3,818,705 or 12 percent was paid to Negro teachers for instructing approximately 40 percent of all the pupils. While the white teachers were receiving an average monthly salary of $60.60 over a longer school term, the Negro teachers were being paid $32.86 over a significantly shorter term. The

The Failure of an Experiment

Negro teachers' reward was better in Texas, where they received an average salary which approximated three fourths of that paid the white, and in North Carolina, Arkansas, and Virginia, where their salaries approached the two-thirds mark. Their reward was so much less in the deep South, however, that salaries paid the Negro teachers were hardly one half those paid the white.

The passage of time helped, but the average monthly salary of Negro teachers failed to equal that of the white teachers over a period of forty years. Beginning at slightly more than one half of the white teachers' average in 1910, the average salary of Negro teachers in the South was less than one third that of the white by 1929 and only about 85 percent in 1950. However, Table 5 shows noticeable exceptions to this general rule. The average salary of white and Negro teachers in North Carolina, Tennessee, Texas,

TABLE 5. Average monthly salary (dollars) of white and Negro public school teachers in some Southern states, 1909–10 and 1928–29

States	1909–10		1928–29	
	White	Negro	White	Negro
Alabama	53.76	24.47	117.18	54.46
Arkansas	40.52	30.36	96.40	69.08
Florida	61.97	31.98	130.12	66.25
Georgia	83.37	36.29	97.22	38.24
Louisiana	63.05	31.46	133.22	88.57
Mississippi	69.92	30.21	129.71	53.85
North Carolina	37.02	25.26	116.00	70.59
South Carolina	79.77	35.62	126.14	40.51
Tennessee	48.12	26.96	112.50	71.92
Texas	62.07	46.34	121.03	91.60
Virginia	47.18	29.37	111.36	69.72
Average	60.60	32.67	118.01	72.78

Sources: W. E. B. Du Bois, *The Common School and the Negro American* (Atlanta, Ga.: Atlanta University Press, 1911), pp. 107–115; Monroe N. Work, *The Negro Year Book, 1916–17* (Tuskegee Institute, Ala.: The Negro Year Book Publishing Company, 1917), and *The Negro Year Book, 1931–32* (Tuskegee Institute, Ala.: The Negro Year Book Publishing Company, 1932).

181

and Virginia had become substantially equal by this time. Nevertheless, the other Southern states, particularly Mississippi, had shown no signs of an equalization trend.

The equipment with which Negro teachers had to work was even more meager than the salaries they were paid. This, of course, was made mandatory by the mathematics of the situation. Since approximately three fourths of all expenditures for public education in the South was paid to maintain a teaching force, and since the Negro schools' total share was so small, there was little left for capital investment in plant and equipment. Of the $145,600,629 investment that the Southern states had made in public school property by 1915, only $13,996,342 or 9.6 percent had been made in the interest of the Negro schools.[10] In fact, the average white school child at this time was studying in an educational structure whose per capita investment value was $29.84. This was more than four times the $7.34 per capita value representative of the Negro schools. The investment values of white and Negro schools reached $812,873,522 and $77,326,009, respectively, in 1930, but the Negro school's proportional share remained constant.[11]

Given a shorter time to work with her pupils, paid a meager wage, and given inferior facilities with which to work, the Negro teacher was expected to produce results equivalent to the white teacher whose working conditions were far superior. School superintendents of the various counties reflected this expectation in their responses to Du Bois' questionnaire in 1910 concerning the efficiency of the Negro teachers under their supervision. The superintendent of Columbus, Georgia, complained of the teachers' lack of technical training. One of Baton Rouge, Louisiana, bemoaned their poor scholarship. From Asheville, North Carolina, came a complaint against their training in teaching methods. And the superintendent of Hillsboro, Texas, charged them with superficiality. But there were some superintendents who were more sympathetic. They seemed to know how much the Southern policy of racial discrimination was blocking the effectiveness of the Negro teacher. Out of Columbus, Mississippi, came a superintendent's confession, saying of his Negro teachers, "Their defects are not so great as their lack of opportunity to do good work." Similar confessions were made by superintendents of Gadsden, Alabama; Shawnee, Oklahoma; Chattanooga, Tennessee; and Abbeville, South Carolina.[12]

There is no doubt that the discriminatory policy under which the Negro schools eventually moved left scars which were to grow even uglier with the passing years. The schools had been asked to do too much with too little. Despite early planning, they had developed under very little supervision and care on the part of school officials. As W. K. Tate, state supervisor of elementary and rural schools in South Carolina, reported in 1910, the county superintendents frequently did not even know where the Negro schools were located.[13] T. J. Woofter, reporting on the Negro school situation in 1928, observed the lack of objectivity and care on the part of superintendents in the selection of Negro teachers. In too many instances it was possible for a teacher to get an appointment merely because some influential white person had recommended him. One woman who was appointed principal of a Negro school was recommended through a letter which read as follows: "I do not know Mary, but I believe she has the right spirit." A man who had been a waiter in a hotel was recommended for a teaching position by the hotel's manager who sent this letter to the superintendent: "I don't know how much James knows, but he has been a mighty good boy." [14] Cooks, maids, and yardmen whom white employers wanted to reward for faithful service often found the route to public school teaching made easier by their contacts with influential white people.

However, not all the blame for the inadequacy of Negro teachers during this period could be laid at the door of those who selected them. Most of it must be located in the total social order that allowed the institutions of higher education for Negroes to become second- and third-class imitations of white institutions. Basically poor machines turned out basically poor products. As Charles S. Johnson so aptly stated in 1930, the Negro teachers who had, even on paper, credentials equivalent to those of white teachers were themselves the product of an inferior educational system, one whose inferiority stretched from the primary department through the college itself.[15]

The causes of this inferiority were beyond the capacity of Negro educators to correct. They stemmed directly from financial neglect — from the bitter fact that the economic base on which the Negro colleges rested was not sufficient to support learning at the higher level. Of course a system of land-grant colleges had been established to train young Negroes in the industrial arts; many normal departments had been organized to train Negro teachers; and the private Negro colleges had been rejuvenated through the aid of philanthropy; nevertheless, the colleges for Negroes had fallen even further behind those for whites than the public elementary and high schools. All the Negro colleges in the nation spent only $4,028,356 during the school year 1914–1915, and only $281,000 of this amount came from the United States government. Despite their professed interest in industrial education and their commitment to train Negro teachers, the various Southern states provided only $422,356 of the total amount spent by these colleges. The colleges were constantly kept at a minimal operational level through the mercy of the philanthropic foundations that first nourished them. The contributions of these foundations and the income from student fees aggregated $3,325,000 or 82.5 percent of all the money spent by Negro colleges that year.[16] The aggregated income of all these colleges had reached $8,384,329 by 1930, representing an approximate increase of 50 percent over the fifteen-year period. When compared with the rate at which the financial structure of American colleges generally had been expanding, however, the increase the Negro colleges experienced meant little or no change in their relative position among institutions of higher learning in this country. There was considerable financial growth experienced by Negro colleges after the thirties. Their income increased to $38,318,254 in 1947–1948.[17] But here again, they were still behind. The income of American colleges in general had increased one-third faster.

Financial inadequacies grew as the programs of the Negro public schools and colleges expanded to incorporate practically all the curricula that the white institutions were offering the white students. For the most part, teachers, ministers, doctors, and other professionals who served the Negro communities absorbed the inadequacies that schools experienced. The institutions which trained them fell into the same categories as their white counterparts, but the adjective "Negro," heavily charged with lower standards, was used. The finished products of these colleges were "all right for the Negro community" but generally inadequate for service in the larger American society. Therefore the South's educational design became the same for both races, but the quality and content of that education created for Negroes was significantly below the American norm. When measured in these crucial terms, the South's promise to the Negro was broken.

AN ECONOMIC AND SOCIAL ADJUSTMENT DENIED

Contrary to what its designers had promised and what the Negro people had been led to expect, special education did not prove to be an effective tool of economic adjustment. The ideology and structure of industrial education failed to consider the trend of the American economy, despite the fact that our pattern of economic organization had already begun to make major shifts at the time the new educational idea was winning favor with Southern and Northern educators. Our primary economic functions had begun to recede; our secondary functions had begun to boom. From 1820 to 1900, the proportion of American workers in agriculture declined from 72.3 to 35.9 percent of the total working force, while the proportion in manufacturing increased from 12.4 to 29.6, and in commerce and service from 15.3 to 34.5 percent of all workers. Half the agricultural workers displaced during this period were absorbed by commerce, trade, and administration, while the other half went to manufacturing. The trend continued after 1900 until, by midcentury, less than one tenth of the United States workers were in agriculture, and only about one fifth of the South's workers were employed in agriculture. Although employment in manufacturing industries had remained more or less constant since the opening of the century, employment in trades, services and other industries had become a way of the American economy. These latter industries were employing over half the workers in the Southern states.[18]

Industrial education, as it was designed for Negroes, did not encompass the great shifts that the Industrial Revolution began to

push southward early in the nineteenth century. The county training schools, Hampton, Tuskegee, and the land-grant colleges emphasized training for an agricultural economy in which employment had
begun to shrink even before the curricular programs were well underway. These schools built courses in the manual arts around such
handicrafts as broom and mattress making, blacksmithing, and hand
laundering, while an entire system of manufacturing that would
require machinists and highly skilled laborers was already being
shaped. By the opening of the current century, these schools had
well solidified their programs for increased farm ownership until
relieved by the Federal aid that started in the thirties. But the aid
had come too late. The Southern plantation could not be made a
secure place either for the Negroes who had always lived there
or for those whom the industrial schools and colleges were training
for leadership there. In persistent search for an economic outlet,
Southern Negroes left the farms. Although their departure was
gradual, it picked up momentum as Southern agriculture adjusted
to mechanization and as Southern cities came more firmly into
the grips of industrialization. As Chart 4 clearly pictures, a Southern
Negro population that was almost completely rural in 1890 had become half urban by 1950.

Although the South's need for scientifically trained people in
agriculture was made more acute by the Industrial Revolution, its
traditions dictated a rejection of the Negroes whom the colleges
had given this type of training. In fact, what the industrial schools
were really doing was a job of training young Negroes out of the
agricultural tradition they had known and into a higher plane of
economic relations on which Southern landowners were not willing
to deal with them. The agricultural student who left these schools,
if he had been trained at all, was oriented toward farm ownership
and the essentials of scientific farming. He was able to count and
had learned some form of family gardening and home economy.
This type of orientation did not fit at all into the plans that the
South's landed aristocracy had for Negroes. These planters wanted
tenants, not landowners who would become their competitors both
for the market on which they sold their products and for the cheap
labor by which they produced them. The credit system had always

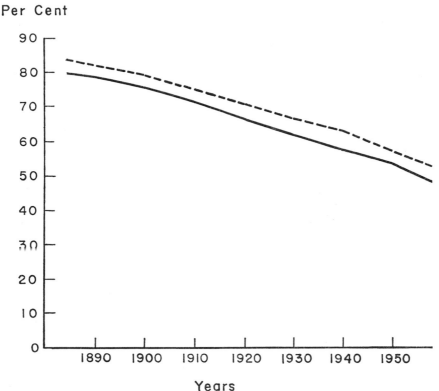

Per Cent

Years

Per Cent rural, South _____

Per Cent rural, Negro ‐ ‐ ‐ ‐

CHART 4. Total and Negro rural population (percent) in the Southern states, 1890–1950

Sources: Bureau of the Census, *Negro Population, 1790–1915* (Washington, D.C.: Government Printing Office, 1918), *Negro Population, 1920–1932* (Washington, D.C.: Government Printing Office, 1932), and *Characteristics of the Population* (Washington, D.C.: Government Printing Office, 1952).

been a rather lucrative source of income for them, largely due to the fact that their tenants either did not know how to count or were so intimidated that they would not dare question the white man's bookkeeping. College-trained Negroes, even if they were inclined to farm as tenants, contradicted the tenant system as the South had known it and threatened to place the landlord at a greater disadvantage than he was willing to chance. Finding the path to farm ownership closed to them, agricultural specialists produced by the Negro colleges turned to agricultural extension work and became farm agents, counselors to the dwindling Negro farm population left by the periodic tides of rural-to-urban migration. Even this occupational outlet was too limited for the large number of graduates that began to emerge from the industrial colleges. Most of them, therefore, went into public school teaching, where they trained more scientific farmers to become schoolteachers like themselves.

Industrial schools did not transform the Negroes into an industrial people. Those few who were graduated or certified in the manual arts each year, too, experienced consistent rejection by Southern industry not only because of policies of racial discrimination in employment but also because their training seldom fitted them for the new demands of the South's Industrial Revolution. These two conditions caused practically all the graduates of Negro land-grant colleges, industrial colleges, and even private universities to turn toward teaching as an occupational outlet. There were 4,367,278 Southern Negroes ten years of age and over who were gainfully employed in 1910, and 0.6 percent of these were teachers. The proportion of teachers had grown to 1.1 percent in 1930, and reached 2.3 in 1950. Apparently the expanding urban Negro communities of the South offered the only sure market on which the college-trained Negro could sell his services. While the aggregated proportion of teachers, preachers, physicians, and nurses increased from 1.1 percent in 1910 to 3.0 in 1950, the percentage of Negro workers who were machinists remained constant at 1.1. The position of the Negro workers in the building trades deteriorated steadily as the years passed. The proportion of Negroes in the major building trades decreased from 26.3 in 1910 to 15.2 in 1940. The greatest losses were suffered by Negro bricklayers, carpenters, and painters. Electricians and plumbers suffered losses too, but so small a proportion of the Negro labor market was involved that the Negro communities felt little effect of this.

The Failure of an Experiment

As time passed, the occupational pattern of the Southern Negro's labor force became neatly structured to accommodate the region's caste system rather than the product of its Negro colleges. There was the thin professional and managerial class whose economic support stemmed from the Negro institutions for which they worked in the segregated Southern communities. These involved only 2.5 percent of the Southern Negro labor force in 1940 and 3.4 percent in 1950. At the other extreme were the domestic servants and barbers, who represented 81.8 percent of the total Southern Negro labor force in 1940 and 69.2 percent in 1950. Craftsmen, who might have been trained by the Negro colleges, composed only 3.6 and 6.4 percent of the labor force during these respective years. In 1940, when census reports in terms of occupational class first appeared, the depressing future of the Negro college graduate became quite clear: the college-trained Negro had been condemned to the frustrating experience of having to limit the outlet of his talents principally to the Negro community from which he had sprung, or he could, if so complexioned, cross the color line by accepting employment on jobs for which he was qualified. Neither of these choices was geared to return to him an adequate dividend on his investment in a college education. The future of the white college student of the Southern region was considerably brighter. Having a chance to sell his talent over a broader labor market, even within the Negro community, this student could have aspirations for a college education about which the Negro student could never dare to dream.

Special education did not give the Negro any degree of favor in competition with the white workers who gradually invaded the labor fields in which blacks had held a monopoly. As Negroes ran to the cities in a desperate effort to escape the economic restrictions of sharecropping, they felt the pressure which white workers had already begun to place upon the labor market at certain industrial and occupational levels. Spero and Harris estimated that there were over 100,000 Negro artisans in the South at the close of the Civil War. By 1890, however, the skilled Negro had been virtually eliminated as a worker.[19]

Over the passage of time, the forces of economic and social discrimination exposed Negroes to forms of personal and communal instability that were beyond the capacity of Negro education to correct. The growing instability of their family life robbed the Negro child of his "father model" and exposed him to a growing matriarchy which, even now, threatens his manhood.[20] Crime rates soared among them, and the self-hate that segregation generated helped give them the highest incidence of homicide of any element of the American population.[21]

Making the Negro image even more unsightly was the insecurity of body and person that the segregated tradition encouraged and that the special education program was unable to correct. Out of persistent blockages to the economic mobility of Negroes came increased poverty and pauperism. The problem of dependency was particularly serious among those of the urban South, especially when the Great Depression first began to make its devastating impact upon family living. In 1935 one fourth of the Negro families as compared with about one tenth of the white were found to be receiving public assistance in nine large and middle-sized Southern cities. Negroes continued to receive a much larger share of the total relief benefits than corresponded to their population ratio.[22] The dependency rate would have been even larger had not the Negro families already developed a higher tolerance for economic need. The situation had not improved very much by 1950. At this time, Southern Negroes were living on half the income of Southern whites.[23] They composed 25.8 percent of the families of the region but received only 11.2 percent of the region's income.

Diseases spread among the Negroes, placing a severe pressure upon their small corps of physicians and the limited health facilities available to the race. During the period of slavery, when Negroes represented so much capital investment, their mortality rate was virtually the same as that of the whites. This was certainly true of those who lived in such Southern cities as Mobile, Alabama, Savannah, Georgia, and New Orleans, Louisiana. In fact, the Negro rate was significantly lower than the white in some instances. By 1910, however, the health picture had completely changed, and Negroes had begun to die at a rate almost double that of the whites. The most heavy loss was from the death of Negro babies, who died at the rate of 261 per 1,000 live births as compared with 129.7 for the whites.[24] Although most of the South was not included in the nation's birth and death registration areas until the middle of the thirties, city records were sufficiently reliable to indicate the Negro's continued disadvantage when compared with whites of this period. The Negro's death rate in 1900 was, on the average, one-third higher than that of the whites in the South. The rates of both races decreased over the years, but 1930 found the Negro rate 1½ times that of the white. Tuberculosis was probably the greatest single killer to which the Southern Negroes were exposed at that time. It killed Negroes in eight Southern states at an average rate of 210.3 per 100,000 in 1920, but decreased to 152.6 in 1930. The Negro rate generally remained three times as high as that of whites.

A QUALITY GAINED AND A BALLOT DENIED

The Negro's political future also failed to sparkle under the light of special education. Claiming his unreadiness for full participation in the general electorate, each Southern state had erected barriers against what they envisioned as a massive black ballot. In doing this they prescribed voting requirements which they knew the Negroes did not possess and instituted the "grandfather clause" as a means of exempting white men from the necessity of having to meet them. By the close of the nineteenth century, therefore, the Negro citizens of the South had been practically deprived of all voice in their own government.

Laws effecting this disfranchisement were obscurely drawn and not always easily understood.[25] Nevertheless, three kinds of tests aimed directly at restricting the Negro vote could be clearly gleaned. There was first the "tax test" in which payment of the poll tax was required of those who sought to vote in Alabama, Arkansas, Florida, Louisiana, Mississippi, North Carolina, South Carolina, Tennessee, Texas, and Virginia. There was the "property test," requiring the voter to own a certain amount of property and to have paid taxes thereon. Georgia required that all taxes legally imposed since 1877 be paid six months before the election in which the applicant sought to vote. It also required one to own 40 acres of land or $500 worth of property in the state. Alabama, Louisiana, and South Carolina required ownership of $300 worth of property on which taxes for the preceding year had been paid. Each state also imposed an "educational test" that the voter was required to pass. In Louisiana and Virginia, the applicant was required to be literate enough to make his application in his own handwriting and to prepare his ballot without aid. The other states required that applicants show their ability to read, write, or understand the state constitution at a performance level satisfactory to election officials.[26] Most of these requirements were instituted through laws passed between 1898 and 1910, but the effect of disfranchising Negroes occurred during the earlier years of this period. In South Carolina, for example, a simple educational qualification enforced with entire honesty would have disfranchised 60,000 to 70,000 more Negroes than whites in the early 1900s. Whereas universal suffrage would have allowed a Negro majority greater than 20,000, educational restrictions would have forced a white majority of approximately 45,000. Since the qualifications were not so impartially enforced, the extent of Negro disfranchisement was even greater than the letter of the law allowed.

Despite the many qualifications by which the South had limited their voting privilege, Southern Negroes maintained a kind of faith in the promise that their right of suffrage would be restored once these qualifications had been met. Confident that this achievement would be their gateway to an unrestricted ballot, many of them gained the qualifications required by Southern election laws. Almost half, or 1,202,107, of the 2,415,675 potential Negro voters living in the South in 1900 had achieved literacy at that time,[27] and, as has been previously indicated, progressed rapidly toward higher literacy rates as the years passed. Their property ownership rate had grown significantly, too, indicating a tendency for a larger proportion of the population to qualify as tax-paying citizens. Despite difficulties, the value of farms owned and operated by Southern Negroes increased from $123,754,391 in 1900 to $314,100,432 in 1930. At the same time a goodly number of Negro families in the region had begun to buy their homes. The number of home owners in this group increased from 264,688 in 1890 to 535,433 in 1930.[28]

Nevertheless, the ballot was still denied, and the major portion of qualified Negroes in the South remained disenfranchised through midcentury. In 1896, Louisiana had 130,344 Negroes who registered to vote, but the number declined in subsequent years until only 1,772 registered in 1916, and over one third of these were residents of New Orleans. In 1908, Alabama had 121,959 literate Negro males twenty-one years of age and over, but only 3,742 of them registered to vote at that time. Paul Lewinson observed that in nine Southern states from which he drew sample replies, only 22,980 Negroes voted during the 1920–1930 period, although these states had a potential Negro electorate of approximately 672,250.[29] In his study of Negro registered voters of 1936, Ralph Bunche reported the fewest number for Mississippi, where only a small number of "good" Negro aristocrats and schoolteachers were allowed to exercise their right of franchise. There were 2,007 registered voters in Louisiana at this time, but practically all of these lived in the vicinity of Baton Rouge and New Orleans. About 1,500 each were reported for Alabama, South Carolina, Tennessee, and Texas; and Kentucky had over 80,000.[30] Most voting occurred in and around cities where political machines had begun to absorb the Negro vote. Contrary to what he had hoped, the Southern Negro's growth to meet the educational and property qualifications specified by election laws did not gain him an unrestricted ballot. And so after operating for half a century, special education failed to do what both whites and Negroes thought it would do: keep educational opportunities equal, secure the Negroes economically and socially, and gain an unrestricted ballot.

VIII · IN QUEST
OF EQUALITY

The Southern experiment failed to make permanent the interracial accommodation for which it was planned. Carrying the seeds of its own defeat, it merely served to develop a further stage of inter-group conflict — a stage in which the Negro American's persisting need for racial equality would be revived and a new accommodation in American race relations made necessary.

The dynamic force behind this historical process was two-dimensional: It grew out of changes that the experiment created within the Negro population and out of the discontent that resulted from the South's refusal to grant Negroes the chances for upward mobility that they believed they had earned. Although the experiment had succeeded in segregating the Negroes spatially and socially, in keeping them out of the mainstream of American culture and civilization, it had necessitated and supported the development of a leadership class whose talents could be directed against the great detour. It created a mass of Negroes who were professionally and technically trained beyond the demands of the segregated Negro community and unable to win acceptance in the larger national economy.

When the faith the Negroes had placed in the special educational system was broken — when the equality that they had been led to expect was not forthcoming — their collective aspirations for first-class citizenship were revived. Moved to discontent by sheer disillusionment, they set their trained leadership to the task of securing through other means the goals the great detour had failed to achieve. They set upon a quest for equality of opportunity within a legal structure that formally asserted that this equality was their right.

Negro responses to disillusionment were basically aggressive and mixed as to effectiveness. Some, obviously instances of misdirected verbal complaints, were drowned out by the sound of mere talking. Others became shaped into literature, the collective expression of a people; they pierced the public mind and tapped the public conscience. One, more powerful than all the rest, eventually found its way into the established social structure and became the foundation for more effective social action. None can be given an order of temporal priority over another. They started largely at the same time, aimed at the same target.

The attack began mildly, not as a rebellious move against the walls of segregation itself, but as a neat and tidy program to stimulate equality of treatment within what the institution itself would guarantee. First, there was the drive for a new self-image, an attempt on the part of Negroes to prove to themselves that they were *somebody*. Beginning mildly and subtly, the drive developed into a kind of catharsis — a series of pep talks — in which a goodly number of Negro voices were heard. Some of the talking was done cleverly through the many anecdotes about white people that Southern Negroes composed so prolifically. Projective in nature, these folk tales reflected the black man's protest against the white man's enforced position of superiority and served as a kind of shield against the eroding force of Negro inferiority.

As early as the days of slavery, Negroes had invented a system of humor by which they could permissibly laugh and make fun of their white masters. Newbell Niles Puckett illustrated this well in the many such anecdotes he recorded. One example is his story of the new field hand who did not understand the meaning of the plantation dinner bell — finding him still working after the bell had rung, the master angrily commanded him to "drop whatever he had in his hand and run for the table" whenever he heard the bell ring. The next day at noon he was carrying his master, who had taken sick in the field, across a footlog over the creek when the bell rang. He dropped the white man in the water and nothing was done to him, for he had only obeyed what his master had commanded.[1] Stories of this kind, well known to all the plantation Negroes in the eighties and nineties, were revived after the dawn of the century. They were told and retold by Southern Negroes who sought mental relief and a reenforcement of their dignity. Probably the most institutionalized instance of this subtle method of verbal aggression may be found in the Br'er Rabbit and Uncle Remus stories preserved by the Southern white journalist, Joel Chandler Harris, and analyzed by the folklorist, Bernard Wolfe. According to Harris, Negroes of the eighties gleefully related stories in which the weak Rabbit persistently outwitted the strong fox. Far into the twentieth century, Southern Negroes were relating these stories in which they identified themselves with the rabbit and associated the white man with the fox. In their minds, the rabbit not only saves himself from the fox by his cleverness on many occasions, but he also strikes back at the fox and inevitably causes his death.[2] These stories seem to have conveniently accommodated the Negro's conflict of loyalty to the white man and to his own race. As Harris interpreted their projective intention, it was apparently not virtue that was allowed to triumph but helplessness, it was not malice but mischief.[3]

With the turn of the century, Negro Americans began a protest against the white order which was more direct, far less subtle, but still verbal in nature. Individual Negroes who were trained in the Negro schools and occupied strategic positions of leadership in the various communities frequently raised their voices against certain indignities imposed upon the race. Speaking from whatever "platform" available, they carried the protest as far as their voices could be heard. No complete record can be given. There were too many voices. Nevertheless, individual protests did follow a pattern: They were cries against any threat to black dignity which Negroes were experiencing at the moment.

Even Booker T. Washington, in response to the rising tide of "Jim Crow Car Laws" that had begun to sweep the South by 1914, sent out a circular letter asking that June 7 and 8 of that year be observed as Railroad Day. Feeling that this was a fertile ground in which to place the plow of mild protest, Washington advised, "The interest of the railroad people has been aroused in many ways. They are beginning now to see that it is worthwhile to treat 10,000,-000 people with consideration. One of these days, go directly to the railroad authorities and put before them the difficulties under which we labor in cases where there is in existence unjust treatments." Railroad Day was widely observed, and many communities urged the railroads to provide better facilities for Negro patrons.[4] The play, "Birth of a Nation," caused heated discussions throughout the press, pulpit, and other mass media in 1915. The Negroes objected to the play on the grounds that the scenes depicted them in a bad light; that the play tended to stir up race prejudice generally, and particularly prejudiced young people of the North with whom young Negroes had to live and work out their destiny. The Bridgeport, Connecticut, *Herald* called the complaint unjust. It was joined by the *Houston Chronicle* whose editor, M. E. Foster, said that the play would prove beneficial to the Negro race rather than harmful. However a number of editorials of Northern papers agreed with the Negroes,[5] thus encouraging more verbal protest.

A new issue did appear. It appeared soon after April 6, 1917, when the United States declared war upon Germany. On June 22 of that year, the *Houston Chronicle* proudly displayed the list of young white men who had "played their part as heroes in answering their country's call on registration day." Knowing that he had also registered along with other Negroes, F. T. Wright made a protest in behalf of his people and raised this question with the editor: "Why was it that our names were omitted? We did not look for our names to be mingled together with the whites, but they could have been somewhere near some corner in the paper stating how many of the colored had played their part." [6] This kind of discontent with the Negro's position in the war effort became widespread. In 1918, a group of Negro leaders, including 31 newspapermen, called upon the War Department and the Committee on Public Information to discuss the matter.[7] They drew up a "bill of particulars" as a kind of price for keeping quiet. They did gain something, for a result of their protest was the assignment of regularly commissioned Negro war correspondents to the Western front. The calm did not last very long, and at war's end came the Negro's sharpest protest. In their thinking, the democracy for which they had fought seemed far away. The ever-aggressive *Houston Informer* expressed this feeling forcefully in its issue of October 11, 1919:

When called upon to defend this country's honor and integrity and to save civilization from the clutches of the cruel and heartless Huns of Europe, the black American went forth to battle the mighty Goliath of autocracy, militarism, and kultur. Having performed a "brown skin" job "over there," he now expects Uncle Sam to clean up his own premises and since the BLACK MAN FOUGHT TO MAKE THE WORLD SAFE FOR DEMOCRACY, he now demands that AMERICA BE MADE AND MAINTAINED SAFE FOR BLACK AMERICANS.[8]

In May of that same year, *Crisis* magazine turned the complaint into a national chant when it said, "We stand again to look America squarely in the face and call a spade a spade. . . . This country of ours, despite all its better souls have done and dreamed, is yet a shameful land. It lynches. . . . It disfranchises its own citizens. . . . It encourages ignorance. It steals from us. . . . It insults us." [9] The Negroes felt justified in such bitterness and open expressions of disappointment, for they had already received a promise of improved conditions from President Wilson. Speaking to a group of prominent Negro ministers who held a conference with him at the White House on the evening of March 14, 1918, the President had given this encouragement:

> I have always known that the Negro has been unjustly and unfairly dealt with; your people have exhibited a degree of loyalty and patriotism that should commend the admiration of the whole nation. In the present conflict your Race has rallied to the nation's call, and if there has been any evidence of slakerism manifested by Negroes the same has not reached Washington.
>
> Great principles of righteousness are won by hard fighting and they are attained by slow degrees. With thousands of your sons in the camps of France, out of this conflict you must expect nothing less than the enjoyment of full citizenship rights — the same as are enjoyed by every other citizen.[10]

There was another vexing problem that plagued the Negroes and kept them reminded of their inferior social position. This was the persistent use of objectionable terms by the white press in referring to the race and all things related to it. Leading stores of Washington, D.C., advertised in a daily paper that they had "nigger" goods for sale. Houghton and Dutton Company stores used the term "nigger curl" as an advertisement for some black astrachan cloth. The terms "wench" and "negress" were constantly used by the white press in referring to Negro women just before World War I.

Various types of protest actions were taken by Negroes in an effort to stop these practices. Booker T. Washington, speaking at the August 1915 meeting of the National Negro Business League, urged delegates to use all their influence to do away entirely with the word "nigger" and to have the word "Negro" spelled with a capital "N." So strongly were leaders opposed to racial epithets that some wanted to drop the use of the word "Negro" altogether. Monroe Trotter's *Boston Guardian* did just this. In defense of his position, Trotter said, "Daily papers, speaking of the respectable element, refer to the 'colored citizens.' Daily papers unfriendly to the race speak of 'the burly negroes.' " [11] This phase of the Negro's campaign continued into the twenties and had some effect in winning normal salutations for Negro women.[12] It had little effect, however, in breaking the barrier of interracial etiquette which had been erected across the Negro's path to respectability in the South.

While this spontaneous type of verbal protest was going on, the Negro's quest for self-respect was taking a more lasting form. What was later to be called the "New Negro" was being shaped, and through the literary efforts of this new breed, America's black people were to find a new conception of themselves and a deeper spiritual orientation. The new group aspired to reestablish the Negro's racial heritage, for they felt as Arthur A. Schomburg interpreted so well: "The Negro must remake his past in order to make his future." And so they wrote of African kings, black warriors, black leaders of slave rebellions, Negro jockeys, and the problems of being Negro.[13] The historical significance of this movement rests not solely upon the literary talent that it revealed but also upon the change in the Negro's intellectual convictions which it symbolized. The change was from an attitude of compromise to one of challenge. It meant that the Booker T. Washington philosophy that had prevailed for more than a generation had been condemned and was to be rejected by the Negro masses.[14]

The explosion was touched off by W. E. B. Du Bois who had studied at Fisk University, Harvard, and the University of Berlin.

199

Du Bois was well equipped for the task. There were so many great scholars at Harvard who had shared in the shaping of his mind. There were William James in psychology, Palmer in ethics, Royce and Santayana in philosophy, Shaler in geology, and Hart in history. Naming these and several others, he wrote in his autobiography: "By good fortune, I was thrown in contact with many of these men. I was repeatedly a guest in the house of William James; he was my friend and guide to clear thinking; I was a member of the Philosophical Club and talked with Royce and Palmer; I sat in an upper room and read Kant's Critique with Santayana." [15]

As if catching a glimpse of the future years, the founder of the new movement wrote these words in a theme which he submitted to Barrett Wendell, the great Harvard English scholar, on October 3, 1890: "I believe foolishly perhaps, but sincerely, that I have something to say to the world, and I have taken English 12 in order to say it well." [16] His aim was not in vain. He published *The Souls of Black Folk* in 1903, and through it presented the Negro problem more clearly than it had ever been presented before. He explained what emancipation really meant to the Negroes and the South; he traced the development of the "personal leadership" that followed, and he hurled what proved to be a paralytic blow against the philosophy and leadership of Booker T. Washington. He explored the black and white worlds and accurately predicted that segregation, if not challenged, would be its own perpetuator. Three years later he wrote "A Litany at Atlanta," on the occasion of a bloody riot in that city, and captured the prayers of every Negro American who had begun to feel hate for the white world. Included in his stirring poem were these words of vitriol: [17]

> Sit no longer blind, Lord God, deaf to our prayer and
>   dumb to our sufferings.
> Thou too art white, O Lord, a pale bloodless, heartless thing?

Inspired by the imaginative and creative mind of Du Bois, other Negro intellectuals combined their literary talents in the task of building race pride, defining race heroism, "and burying Uncle Tom." James Weldon Johnson, born at Jacksonville, Florida, graduated from the public schools of that city and from Atlanta University to become a poet, essayist, lawyer, librettist, diplomat, and reformer. He contributed as much as any man to the development of race pride among Negroes of his day. He gave them their national anthem, "Lift Every Voice and Sing," which he composed in 1900 on the occasion of a celebration of Lincoln's birthday and which, thereafter, was always sung by Negroes on the opening of their public programs. He gave them status through his librettos in *Goyescas,* a production at the Metropolitan Opera House. He helped to restore the Negro's pride in his past by extolling the virtues of being black. As an expression of his literary inclination along this line, he wrote this inspiring verse of reverence for his ancestry:

> O Black and Unknown Bards
> How come your lips to touch the sacred fire?
> How, in your darkness, did you come to know
> The power and beauty of the Minstrel's lyre? [18]

Claude McKay, Countee Cullen, Langston Hughes, and a host of other Negro poets and novelists gained national recognition through their writings in the twenties, and "made race a new and interesting note in American literature." [19] They expressed, with intriguing styles, the mixture of their emotions which derived from being black and American too. Claude McKay, Jamaican by birth, had tasted Negro life as a student at Tuskegee for a few months and as a "citizen" of Harlem for many years. His first American publication, *Harlem Shadows,* appeared in 1922 and with it came the most defiant protest theme to appear in the literature of Negro intellectuals of his day. The following lines of one of his poems are most often used to illustrate this protest spirit:

> If we must die, let it not be like hogs,
> Hunted and penned in an inglorious spot,
> While 'round us bark the mad and hungry dogs,
> Making their mock at our accursed lot.[20]

Showing the split loyalty that was to haunt the pen of every Negro intellectual, McKay expressed this kind of ambivalence:

> Although she feeds me bread of bitterness,
> And sinks into my throat her tiger's tooth,
> Stealing my breath of life, I will confess
> I love this cultured hell that tests my youth.[21]

Countee Cullen, though Northern-reared and Harvard-trained, was no less involved in this crusade for self-respect. He, too, had a racial axe to grind. *Color,* one of the best known of his works, appeared in 1925. It gave renewed zest to the protest theme and more vivid evidence of its ambivalent nature. Signs of this characterization appeared crisply in his work as illustrated in this short verse:

> Yet do I marvel at this curious thing,
> To make a poet black and bid him sing.[22]

And still this poet yearned for the sense of belongingness that he felt was rightly his under the flag which he and his ancestors had come to love. In expression of this yearning, Cullen wrote:

> We shall not always plant while others reap
> The golden increment of bursting fruit.[23]

Langston Hughes graduated from Lincoln University at Pennsylvania in 1929 but had published his first significant book of poems, *The Weary Blues,* three years earlier. He became one of the most influential writers of this new group, though he put as much bitterness into his pen as any of the rest. In vigorous expression of pride of nationality and protest against being "left out," he cried, "I, too, sing America"; and as if reinforcing his claim with equal vigor in his poem "Mulatto" he warned, "I am your son, white man!" In a passionate expression of a great pride of ancestry, he bragged, "I've known rivers as ancient as the world and older than the flow of human blood in human veins." But still bound to his native land, he begged, "Let America be America again." [24]

These are but a few examples of the Negro's collective expression of a will to win self-respect and to create a new self-image. No attempt has been made here to develop fully this literary movement, which made significant impressions upon the minds of the Negro masses. No mention has been made of the many short stories, novels, and dramas that were also expressions of this creative urge. This type of development has been described more adequately elsewhere.[25] Nevertheless it must be noted that the Negro's experiences under racial segregation gave him a split self-image — made him love and hate himself and his native America at the same time. His literature of this period, therefore, was more than an artistic expression. It was therapeutic in nature — an attempt to work out this mental conflict. It went some distance toward building his self-respect and making it possible for him to live as a black man and as an American too. As the drama of the "Negro Renaissance" approached its dénouement, both whites and Negroes had come to see the Negro people in a new and more appreciative light.

Another verbal pattern that Negroes employed to gain self-respect appeared in the form of a massive accumulation of research reports pertaining to their history and their contemporary life. What they had tried to do in all their various movements was to gain a feeling of worth and a sense of freedom from guilt. These reports served as a means of realizing such motivations by glorifying their history and locating the basic causes of their problems within the realm of segregation. By objective research, it seems, the Negroes tried to say "I am somebody" with one voice and "my problems are not my fault" with another. These voices were largely those of a corps of Negro scholars who, serving as teachers in the various Negro colleges, acted as spokesmen for the race.

This movement was started by Carter G. Woodson, who in 1912 had received a Ph.D. in history and government from Harvard, after having taken his earlier degrees from the University of Chicago. In 1915 he founded the Association for the Study of Negro Life and History in a dedicated attempt to focus the Negro American's cultural tradition before the world and in a manner that would extol the image of the race. White historians were thought to be biased in their preconceptions about Negroes and had been charged with negligence in omitting significant portions of the Negro's history from their writings. Hoping to rectify these wrongs, Negro scholars vigorously joined Woodson in collecting and publishing historical and sociological facts about the race.[26] The *Journal of Negro History* was established as an official organ of the association, with Woodson as editor, and became the main medium through which the Negro's history was communicated to all who would take the time to read it.

Though somewhat propagandistic in nature, the historical reports which appeared in the *Journal* — and often stood alone in published volumes — followed conventional historical methods rather closely. The methodological rigor by which they were developed increased as time passed, and their propagandistic tones became softened as the scholarship of the authors matured. But like the Negro press, which was growing along with it, the association's mission was a special one, not susceptible to conventional evaluations. The Negro scholars who became involved in the movement inevitably guided their historical inquiries according to this "mission of grandeur." They tried to show that the Negro race did not originate entirely out of savagery; they bolted the Negro's origin tightly to African history, Egyptian nobility, and the descendants of the Pharaohs. They uncovered ancient cities in the heart of Africa, having well-planned streets, improved wharfs, and conveniences for trade.[27] They endeavored to show that Negroes, even before their enslavement, were mechanics and artisans; that some, in slavery as well as freedom, were creative inventors whose ideas were often stolen by whites.

Those most responsible for presenting the history of the Negro to himself and the rest of the world were largely products of the Negro college. Although a few had never studied in these institutions, most of them had taken their first degrees there, had moved to the large Northern universities for their graduate work, and had returned to the Negro colleges as teachers. Heading this list was Charles H. Wesley, historian, who took the baccalaureate degree at Fisk University, the M.A. at Yale, and the Ph.D. at Harvard. He was a Guggenheim Fellow and distinguished himself by the publication in 1927 of the first organized treatise to trace the development of Negro labor in the United States. William S. Savage and Luther P. Jackson, two other historians prominent in the Negro history movement, received doctorates at Ohio State University and the University of Chicago, respectively. Jackson, too, was a graduate of Fisk and concentrated his scholarly interests around the Negro in Virginia. Wesley served as dean of the graduate school of Howard University and later as president of Wilberforce University in Ohio. Savage was professor of history at Lincoln University in Missouri, and Jackson was a professor of history at Virginia State College. Benjamin Quarles came out of Shaw University to secure an M.A. and a Ph.D. at the University of Wisconsin. In 1948 he published the first systematic account of the life of Frederick Douglass, using more highly sophisticated methods than had ever before been employed in Negro biography. He published a complete historical account of the Negro's role in the Civil War, using a style that has proved significantly attractive to students. He was professor of history and dean of the college of Dillard University at that time and later took a professorship in the department of history at Morgan State College. Lorenzo Green, Rayford Logan, and Merle Eppse are but a few of the other fine scholars who have employed their talents in developing the story of the Negro's cultural heritage.[28] The findings of these historians invaded the Negro public schools, the Negro colleges, and even some of the white institutions. White women who became involved in interracial work in the South drew heavily upon this literature. They used it as a basis for making speeches, and some studied Negro history in their clubs.

As Negroes attempted to develop their feeling of worth through the works of their historians, so did they try to explain their problems through the studies of their sociologists. These social scientists, also mainly a product of the Negro college, directed their scholarship almost entirely to the race question. Although guided by scientific procedure, their works embraced environmentalism often to the point of strain and located the causes of social disorganization among Negroes almost wholly within the realm of segregation. As one examines the social science reports that Negro scholars produced between 1920 and 1940, one sees, in many instances, a Negro life totally at the mercy of the world that surrounded it. The Negro mind was compared to Locke's *tabula rasa*. This "guilt-freeing" theme, so characteristic of the works of these scholars, was very clearly identified by William T. Fontaine in 1944. After reviewing an excellent sample of these researches, Fontaine drew this conclusion about the Negro scholar and his work: "Born and confined to a milieu within which struggle against out-group and counter-race status has been waged for generations, his action and thought have become interwoven with 'defense mechanisms.' " [29] Despite the inevitable bias of personal involvement, these scholars were successful in showing the influence of certain environmental forces upon the existing disorganization of Negro community life. Later, psychologists like Kenneth Clark, Mamie Clark and Eli S. Marks showed how segregation tended to distort the value judgments and self-conception of Negroes.[30]

Practically all this literature originated within the Negro colleges, but not all of it appeared in journals published by Negroes. Some of it found its way into social science journals of national and international circulation and won positions of distinction for Negro scholars. Such was the case with the works of sociologists like Charles S. Johnson of Fisk, E. Franklin Frazier of Howard, Ira DeA. Reid of Atlanta University, Bertram Doyle also of Fisk, Oliver Cox of Tuskegee and Lincoln University in Missouri. Some of the scholars pushed beyond the limits of the Negro college and joined their forerunner, Du Bois, in gaining a highly distinguished rank among social scientists throughout the world. Particularly representing these were Abram Harris and Allison Davis of the University of Chicago; Ralph Bunche of Harvard and the United Nations; Robert Weaver, now Secretary of the Department of Housing and Urban Development; Ira DeA. Reid, later of Haverford; E. Franklin Frazier of Howard; and Kenneth B. Clark of the City College of New York. Scholars like these, in what was probably their most significant influence, gave young Negroes a sense of academic worth and inspired them to emulate their high scholarship.

There were Negro scholars in the field of education who also made a distinct contribution to the Negro's drive for equality. In the early phases of the movement, their works served to increase the feeling of discontent and urgency. The *Journal of Negro Education* was established at Howard University in 1932 under the editorship of Charles H. Thompson. Through the *Journal* and Thompson's leadership, the most influential researches concerning racial inequalities in American education found their way into print. The facts which these researches presented later supplied the basis on which many court cases were filed and prosecuted.

THE SPREAD OF GROUP DISCONTENT

Whatever protest and discontent the Negro scholars softened through the subtlety of their literature and the attempted objectivity of their investigations was brought vividly into the open and spread widely to the masses by the Negro press. Making this diffusion possible were the Negro's increasing literacy, his concentration in Southern as well as Northern cities, and the growth of the professional and proprietary classes. As these changes occurred, newspapers owned and operated by Negroes sprang up in various cities and grew to constitute the only organized channel of uninhibited mass communication available to the race at that time.

At first progress was slow, growing out of the feeble efforts at journalism which were made long before the South's special education program for Negroes was instituted. John B. Russwurm published and edited the *Freedom's Journal* in New York in 1827, and the *Colored American* was established at Augusta, Georgia, just after the Civil War. But these made little impact upon the Negro masses and were little noted by the few Negro intellectuals who were active during this time. Once political disfranchisement got under way, however, and segregation had begun to set in, Negroes increased the tempo of their journalistic efforts and by 1880 had established 30 newspapers in 18 Southern and 12 Northern cities.[31] Eighteen years later, as Du Bois reported, the Negro press had expanded to include 3 magazines, 3 dailies, 11 school papers, and 136 weeklies. The dailies were published at Norfolk, Virginia, Washington, D.C., and Kansas City, Kansas. Of the weeklies for which information was furnished, 13 were published by religious and secret societies.[32] It had become clear that the Negro's serious move for equality would spring from within the race and the institutional structure of the segregated community.

The organized militancy that the Negro press was to foster actually began with the *Boston Guardian,* established by Monroe Trotter in 1901. This paper dedicated itself to voicing the opposition of educated Negroes to the conciliatory attitude Booker T. Washington had taken toward the denial of the Negro's citizenship rights in the South. Trotter himself joined Du Bois in a vicious fight against Washington's ideology and kept the industrial education idea alive as a highly controversial issue. His *Guardian* also crusaded against the segregation of the races in government departments at Washington. Trotter headed a delegation of Negroes who, representing the National Equal Rights League, went to the White House to consult with President Wilson. He and others had supported the President in the political campaign of 1912. They called this to his attention, but the President insisted that segregation was not a political question and that he would not take it up on political grounds. He objected to the manner and tone adopted by Trotter and told the committee that if it called again, it would have to get a new chairman. The "Trotter Incident," as this affair came to be called, was widely discussed in the press. White papers of the North and South were divided on the issue, but the Negro papers were in common agreement: They looked with hostility upon President Wilson and his attitude toward segregation.[33]

However, it was the *Chicago Defender,* established in 1905 by Robert S. Abbot, which was to set the tone of militancy for all other Negro papers. It forced the use of headlines and sensationalism upon Negro journalism, popularized many issues that grew out of World War I, and stimulated the northward migration of thousands of Negroes by picturing the advantages of the North as opposed to Southern oppression. Other Negro papers followed the *Defender's* example. They praised the valor that Negro soldiers showed in the war and underscored the discrimination with which they were met on their return home from the battlefields. They said good-bye to the "Black Mammy" and Uncle Tom and demanded firmness, courage, manliness, and aggressiveness of those who presumed to lead in the new era they felt opening before the race.[34]

From the point of view of its power to generate a state of discontent and a will to act, the Negro press eventually emerged as one of the most important institutions in the Negro urban community. It became the main channel through which racial protest was expressed and the most militant agitator that the community possessed. Wherever an incident unfavorable to Negroes occurred in the nation or in the world, the fact would be known to the majority of the Negro population by the week's end. The facts were admittedly slanted, though not willfully abused, for the mission of the Negro press was to foster militancy and fight complacency. There was little difference between editorials and news, for both were organized to serve the same ends.

Freed of direct reprisals from the white world, the Negro press could take stands on racial issues which Negro teachers and others who were more dependent upon whites for employment could not take. It therefore supplied Negro leaders of these groups with a stone wall behind which they could retreat after throwing a rock. It has been difficult to keep track of all the different newspapers and magazines that made up this vital institution of Negro life. Nevertheless it is known that 155 Negro newspapers had an aggregate circulation of 1,270,000 in 1940. It was reported that 84 of these newspapers in the South had combined circulation of 474,500 at that time.[35] Through this magnitude of circulation, the papers were able to sow irritation over a wide area of the nation and to reap a harvest of solidarity concerning issues about which the Negroes would have been otherwise seriously divided.

THE RISE OF PROTEST ORGANIZATIONS

A group of protest organizations grew up with the Negro press, and each of these institutions complemented the other's power because Negro intellectuals and the organizations that they formed found a common ground at the close of the nineteenth century and began to coordinate their pursuit of equality and full citizenship. The organizations ranged in degrees of aggressiveness from compromise methods to court litigations.

Once again, Du Bois' appropriate leadership set the movement on its course. His controversy with Booker T. Washington, sustained over a period of years, had begun even at this time to win Negro leaders over to his side. He had resigned from the Committee of Twelve which Washington had assembled at New York in January 1904, and his faith in the essential education of what he called the

"talented tenth" had been maintained as the heart of his basic difference with Washington. The preservation of the Negro college as
a source of educated Negroes who could guide their own destiny
was to him an intellectual and emotional commitment. He believed that the Negro, acting as a member of the human race and
backed by historical experience, "is capable of improvement and the
acquisition of culture to any degree; and that he is entitled to have
his interests considered and respected according to his numbers in
all conclusions as to the common weal." [36] When President Bumstead
of Atlanta University asked him to join his staff to direct work in
sociology and take charge of the new conferences the university was
inaugurating on the Negro problem, he eagerly accepted the invitation. Beginning therefore in 1896 the Atlanta conferences systematically accumulated information on Negro life. They dealt with
such topics as mortality, urbanization, efforts of Negroes to improve
themselves, Negroes in business, college-bred Negroes, Negro artisans, the Negro church, and Negro crime. In all, they published
2,172 pages, which together formed a current encyclopedia on the
American Negro problem.[37] The Atlanta University studies were
widely distributed in all the libraries of the world and were freely
used to document the works of many scholars who wrote about the
Negro between 1896 and 1920. Most important for the protest
movement is that they projected Du Bois as the Negro's champion
against racial discrimination.

Stimulated by Du Bois' influence, numerous organizations came
into existence with strong resolutions directed against the "unbeara-
ble conditions" the conferences had revealed. In the year the Atlanta conferences were organized, the National League of Colored
Women and the National Federation of Colored Women combined
to form the National Association of Colored Women. The association became affiliated with the National Council of Women in
the United States in 1900 and developed into a very strong public
influence.[38] These women directed their efforts against lynchings by
appealing to the sentiments of the Christian world. They also appealed to legislative bodies and courts in an attempt to secure the
protection of the rights of all citizens. They condemned segregation
on public carriers, and their affiliated clubs united to induce Ne-

groes to refrain from patronizing facilities under conditions so discriminatory, as had been pointed out by the various reports available to them.

What was to become the most effective of all the Negro's attempts to secure equality for himself was launched by Du Bois in 1905. On June 13 of that year he directed a letter to a selected group of Negro leaders throughout the nation, proposing the formation of a new organization and outlining what he felt the purpose should be. Twenty-nine men from fourteen states answered his call in a meeting held near Buffalo, New York, on July 11–14, 1905. To symbolize the power it was hoped the movement would generate and because of its proximity to the Falls, it was christened "Niagara." The Niagara Movement, aiming to pull all Negro organizations more closely toward one large national push, directed its program against all the barriers to first-class citizenship erected against Negroes: disfranchisement, curtailment of civil rights, limited job opportunities, inadequate and unequal educational opportunities, and the squalid conditions under which Negro children were being reared in the various cities of the nation. It was not unmindful of the corresponding obligations which these efforts would impose upon the Negro people themselves. Therefore, included in its declaration of principles were reminders that Negroes be urged to vote, respect the rights of others, work, obey the law, be clean and orderly, send their children to school, and respect themselves even as they respect others. These were the principles, complaints, and prayers that the leaders of the Niagara Movement submitted "to the American people and Almighty God." [39]

The Springfield riot of 1908 fed additional life into the protest program, which had begun to slow down under the Niagara effort because of lack of funds. The riot also prompted a group of white people to seek justice for the Negro.[40] Accounts of the riot were spread throughout the country, picking up influential white sympathizers as they moved. One sympathizer, the most influential of all, was William English Walling whose vivid article entitled "Race War in the North" appeared in the *Independent* on September 3, 1908. Moved by Walling's appeal, Miss Mary White Ovington assembled a few interested persons in a small room of a New York apartment and there founded an organization which was to become, in May 1910, the National Association for the Advancement of Colored People. The next year, this organization, later known as the NAACP, adopted the following objectives from which little variation would occur in the subsequent years:

> To begin immediately a scientific study of Negro schools.
>
> To organize a Legal Redress Committee of national scope, whose work shall be dealing with injustices in the courts as it affects Negroes.
>
> To publish *The Crisis,* a monthly magazine devoted to race topics. Also to publish pamphlets dealing with the work of the committee.
>
> To hold mass meetings, memorial exercises, etc., and to place on the platform members of other bodies of thinking people who are recognized authorities on matters pertaining to the race question.
>
> To establish a bureau of information by which the press, magazines, and individuals may be given unbiased information on all questions pertaining to the Negro.
>
> To form local groups, to which may be referred questions of race discrimination or injustice arising from race prejudice, and thus prepare the ground work for the vigilance committees.
>
> To take an active part in the matter of reapportionment of congressional districts by Congress.
>
> To form a national committee for the purpose of studying the question of national aid to education.
>
> To make foreign propaganda, to which end W. E. B. Du Bois, director of publicity and research for the Association, will make a European trip in April, May, and June, culminating in the Race Congress in June, of which Mr. Du Bois is one of the Secretaries.

Other organizations joined the protest movement, but compared with the NAACP, their voices were soft winds before a hurricane. The National Urban League, founded in New York in 1911, appeared at a crucial period in the Negro's history. It came when Negroes were moving to the cities in great numbers and were experiencing many of the economic and social handicaps that tend to haunt urban newcomers. Headed by philanthropists, social workers, and professionals of both races who believed that Negroes needed not alms but opportunity, the league established local units in practically every large Northern industrial center where Negroes aggregated. It received substantial financial support from such philanthropists as John D. Rockefeller, Julius Rosenwald, William H. Baldwin, and Alfred Stone. It received an excellent set of programs from the leadership of George E. Haynes. Using the methods of a social service agency, the league worked to create employment opportunities for urban Negroes, to give them industrial counsel, to secure for them more adequate housing, and to encourage the training of Negro social workers through its fellowship program. It published *Opportunity* magazine, which became the platform of many Negro intellectuals and a great influence in the cities. It pushed the Negro's cause, both industrial and social, as far as the range of tolerance of local interracial norms would permit. Many new jobs were opened to Negroes as a result of its influence, and one can well conclude that Negroes never would have adjusted so smoothly to the complexities of Northern industrial cities without its aid.

The great strain in Negro-white relations after World War I stimulated the rise of a second organization involving the combined efforts of the two races. This organization was the Commission on Interracial Cooperation, which was organized in 1919 under the leadership of W. W. Alexander, Jessie Daniel Ames, Emily H. Clay, Howard Odum, and Arthur F. Raper. Its support came largely from foundation grants but was indeed bolstered by membership dues. Operating through the process of conciliation, moral persuasion, and education, the commission brought a gradualistic approach to the field of race relations in the South. It blocked the development of anti-Negro movements in the region, helped reduce lynching, and stimulated the study of race relations in Southern colleges. It was never very bitterly attacked in the South, but this was probably due to its softer touch.

THE DRIVE TO EQUALIZE
EDUCATIONAL OPPORTUNITIES

Although Negroes had acquiesced to segregation, they had not surrendered their rights to equality as citizens of the United States.

Consequently, as their self-respect, discontent, and inclination to organize increased, they became more bold in directing pressure against the various inequalities from which they suffered. Some gains were made this way, and the culmination of each attack left them in a better position than before. Not all the inequalities they were able to eliminate fell at the same time, for the attacks were not made upon them simultaneously. Moving first against the unequal educational opportunities that had become so obvious, and backed by the constitutional provisions which forbade such inequalities, Negroes widened their pressure to include more areas of their community life.

Like the move for self-respect which it paralleled, the drive for equality in education began almost spontaneously and without much organization. As early as 1885, small groups of Negroes turned against their limited educational opportunities and sought greater equality through the courts. During that year, some citizens of Arkansas petitioned the state supreme court for a writ of mandamus to compel the directors of their common school district to provide schools for the education of their children. Appearing as residents of the district and as parents of forty children of school age, they charged that a school had been maintained for the white children for three months and that none existed for Negro children during an equal period of time. They were successful in changing the situation. The court, ruling in their favor, held that it was the duty of the school directors to provide equal facilities for both races and that school funds could not be apportioned nor could the school terms be limited to each class according to its proportion of the scholastic population.[41] J. W. Cummings, James S. Harper, and John C. Ladeveze sought, through the state courts, to enjoin the school board of Richmond County, Georgia, from appropriating money for a high school for white children when there was no such school for Negro children. Their aim was to force greater support for the Negro elementary schools of their county. Although the court ruled that withholding assistance from a high school for white children was not a proper remedy for the board's error in failing to provide one for Negro children, the moral issue was defined, and such a school for Negroes was established.[42]

This type of small-group action in favor of improved educational opportunities for Negroes continued well into the century. W. A. Lowerly and other parents of Kernersville, North Carolina, took action against their board of graded school trustees to prevent a graded school "for whites only" from being established in that town. The state's supreme court did not support the plaintiffs, but it did, in its ruling, force the establishment of a similar facility for Negro children. Basing its decision upon an implied interpretation of the state statute authorizing the school, the court ruled: ". . . inasmuch as it is provided in Section 4 of the Act that all children resident in the district within school age shall be admitted, the statute must be construed as directing the establishment of one school in which the children of each race are taught in separate buildings and by separate teachers, and in so construing, this is not a violation of the Constitution."[43] The aims of the plaintiffs were, in fact, achieved. Similar educational facilities were provided for the Negro children of that district. William J. McFarland turned to the Mississippi courts in 1909, seeking to enjoin the tax collector and treasurer of Jasper County from collecting a special tax levied for the support and maintenance of white youths. His bill of complaint alleged that he was a resident citizen and freeholder of the county, a Negro with children of educable age, and that the law under which the school was established was unconstitutional in that it abridged his privileges and immunities and those of other citizens of his race. The Supreme Court of Mississippi supported his allegation and ruled that the statute under question did violate the privileges and immunities clause of the Fourteenth Amendment. In making this decision, the court stated: ". . . the very law itself creates the school for white children only and imposes on all taxable property for the purpose of raising revenue for the support of the school, and by its very terms excludes the idea that, whatever conditions may exist, any such colored school can be created." [44] The Supreme Court of North Carolina gave similar support to the maintenance of schools for Negroes when, responding to a case instituted by a purchaser of school bonds, it ruled that bonds issued by the school district of Camden County for the purpose of erecting a school building for the whites were invalid. The court held that the act which provided for the issue for the stated purpose violated the mandate of the Constitution which required that "there shall be no discrimination in favor of or to the prejudice of either race." [45]

A Kentucky statute that tended to base the support of Negro schools on the taxable resources of the Negro population was attacked and overthrown by a group of citizens who sought relief through the state's courts. Negro trustees for the Negro grade schools of Mayfield instituted action against the white trustees in order to secure for the Negro children their prorata share of taxes collected from corporations. The white trustees contended that since corporations were white, Negro children could not share in the taxes collected from them. But the court ruled the statute on which their claim was based to be invalid and a violation of the equal protection clause of the state's constitution. It held further that a corporation was neither white nor black. This being true, the court reasoned, the Negro school was entitled to a prorata share of all taxes collected from corporations.[46] This kind of persistent effort on the part of Negro citizens pushed the movement for equal educational opportunities at least to the degree of the availability of schools.

Nevertheless, these attempts at equalization could not reach the full potential of their power until the motivations became common and the efforts were unified. The movement had to become centered around an instance of discrimination felt by all Negroes, and it had to be backed by an organization with which all of them tended to identify. These two conditions seemed to have met in the early thirties, and the equalization movement seems to have begun in earnest near that time. The common ground of discrimination was supplied by the sizable differentials that existed between the salaries paid white and Negro teachers. It is estimated that these differentials amounted to a loss of approximately 10 million dollars annually to Negro teachers. The organized support came through the NAACP, whose program was originally designed to handle such problems and whose local branches had begun to take special interest in the Negro's unequal educational opportunities.

In 1936 the NAACP began a legal campaign to equalize the salaries of Negro and white public school teachers in 15 of the 17 Southern states maintaining separate schools for the races at that time. The litigations were not instituted by the NAACP but by individual teachers or their organizations who brought suits through the counsel of the Association's Legal Department and the support of its rapidly growing financial resources.

One of the earliest cases of this campaign was that of William B. Gibbs, a school principal, who sued the school board of Montgomery County, Maryland, in December 1936 at the instance of the Maryland State Colored Teachers' Association. Disposition of the case came by consent decree, in which the board effected a compromise with the teachers to equalize salaries in 1939. In November 1937, Elizabeth Brown, an elementary teacher of Calvert County, Maryland, sought a writ of mandamus to compel the board to equalize her salary. Her petition alleged that she received $600 annually, whereas white teachers in the same category were paid $1,100. Her case was also settled out of court, but with some relief coming earlier. By consent decree coming in that same year, the board agreed to equalize salaries by 1939 but ordered salaries of the Negro teachers increased immediately to one third of the differential against which the complaint was made. Negro teachers of Prince George County and Anne Arundel County, both in Maryland, filed similar writs the following year. Their cases, also, forced the equalization of teacher salaries by consent decree. By the end of 1941, the NAACP was able to announce that almost one half of its campaign had been won. Eight Southern states had been forced to defend their practice of paying lower salaries to Negro teachers for equal work and requirements, and the policy of salary equalization had been definitely established in five.[47] But the campaign continued to grow in subsequent years, taking in some 38 cases. Of this number, 27 had been brought to successful conclusion by 1948 and had resulted in the addition of millions of dollars to the salaries of Negro teachers.[48]

School boards of the Southern states did not yield to this pressure without making severe counterattacks in support of their discriminatory policies. Some of the attacks came in the form of "legal smoke screens," which attorneys for the respective boards laid across the courts. Before the case of Charles Stubbins against the Palm Beach, Florida, County Board of Public Instruction was settled in 1943, the defendants filed additional defenses, claiming that it was impossible to equalize the salaries of Negro teachers because the money paid all teachers was raised by taxation in the special tax school district in which the particular teacher was employed, and that the distribution of these taxes was fixed by the trustees of that district. What the board was actually attempting was to hide behind the screen that Negro teachers in Palm Beach County were, in some instances, governed by Negro trustees. However, the court struck this defense, opening the way for the consent decree that followed two years after the Stubbins suit was filed. Soon after the salary equalization cases hit the Louisiana courts, the school board of Baton Rouge announced, effective June 20, 1943, that it would operate on a salary schedule that took into consideration "merit" and "responsibility." Nevertheless, the action did not stop Eula M. Lee and Wiley B. McMillan, respectively of Jefferson and Iberville Parishes, from winning their salary equalization rights during the same year.[49] After Viola Duvall of Charleston had won her case for salary equalization, the South Carolina Legislature, under the leadership of Cotton Ed Smith, began laying plans to sabotage the NAACP's program. The legislative plan was to destroy all existing teacher's certificates and to institute a new system of certification which would permit the local boards to give Negro teachers inferior certificates and less salary on that basis. But white teachers and interested white citizens fought this proposal on the grounds that it would have destroyed the effectiveness of white as well as Negro teachers. The *Columbia Record,* condemning the bill in its editorial on March 16, stated crisply: "The legislators of South Carolina are playing with dynamite. They are playing with the whole educational system. They are playing with the future of South Carolina's sons and daughters. And these things are not play things." [50] The bill was defeated by the legislature, and Albert N. Thompson of Richland, South Carolina, won a court decree favoring the equalization of his salary one year later.

Finding their discriminatory policies blocked by the courts, school districts turned to the strategy of attempting to intimidate those teachers who had filed suits against them and those members of the NAACP who had supported the equalization movement. Charles

Stubbins, plaintiff in the teacher's salary case at Palm Beach, Florida, was fired by his board subsequent to his victory over them. The Negro trustees of his district demanded the removal of a Negro principal whom they could not remove because he had the backing of the county school board. However, the county board agreed not to reappoint the principal in question providing the Negro trustees would not recommend the reappointment of Stubbins. In this manner the offended board was able to dispense with the services of Stubbins without giving the appearance that they had fired him because of his activities in the salary equalization case.[51] A similar reprisal was taken against teachers who were plaintiffs in the Newport News, Virginia, cases of 1943. Three school principals who were among the leaders of the equalization movement in that city were not reelected to their positions. They had been serving the city's school system from eleven to twenty-three years. Reprisals in Louisiana were directed against members of the NAACP. Some white citizens, protesting the court actions in the salary cases, instituted a reign of terror against officers of the association. Officials of the branch in New Iberia were beaten and driven out of town. The branch responded by reorganizing its forces and acquiring 150 new members in the city. Negro teachers known to be members of the NAACP found little security in their employment with some school districts of the South, and many of these teachers found it necessary to keep their membership in secret. Nevertheless, by midcentury, the NAACP's campaign was complete. There was hardly a state in the entire nation that was not paying its Negro teachers salaries that equaled those paid to whites of similar positions and experience. At least this phase of the Negro's drive for equal educational opportunities had been achieved.

EQUALIZATION IN SUFFRAGE

Recognizing that education is largely a public institution and under the administration of elected officials, Negroes moved against barriers to their citizenship in the field of suffrage rights. But, here too, the attack was first launched by individuals or small groups who did not have the advantage of the support from the strong Negro organizations that were then being formed. The attacks started in Texas, where the "white primary" had emerged as the South's strongest tool of Negro disfranchisement. In 1918 the Negroes of Waco sought relief from their disfranchisement through the courts, demanding that they be permitted to vote in the primaries which were about to be held in that city. On February 28 of that year, Judge E. F. Clark of the Nineteenth District Court ruled that keeping Negroes from voting in the white primaries was a violation of Federal law, the Texas constitution, and the Terrell Election Law of the state. Freed by this ruling, Negroes voted in the primaries of Waco and Houston.[52]

Relief was only temporary, however, since the Texas Supreme Court, in a decision in 1922, ruled that any political party has the right to prescribe the qualifications for persons voting in its primaries. Negroes voted in the 1922 Democratic primary election at San Antonio, but the party's committee on salaries and platforms influenced the state Democratic convention to take action against their voting in the future. Responding to the action taken by the convention, the Texas Legislature passed a law prohibiting Negroes from participating in Democratic primaries. Negroes challenged this act in the *Chandler v. Neff* case, argued before the Texas district court in 1924, when they entered suit to restrain the enforcement of the 1922 law on the grounds that it violated the Fourteenth and Fifteenth Amendments. Although the suit was dismissed through the ruling that a primary election was "not an election," the case received wide public attention, especially from the legal profession, and built up a strong sentiment against the Negro's disfranchisement. The discriminatory nature of the decision caused some lawyers to brand it as "probably the most efficient and boldly daring deprivation of the political rights of Negroes." [53]

But the antidiscrimination program that the NAACP had designed a decade before had become fairly well established by the close of the twenties, and the association's legal department had entered the suffrage field. It carried the case of Dr. L. A. Nixon (*Nixon v. Herndon*) on appeal from El Paso to the United States

Supreme Court. The Nixon case had also arisen out of the new Texas "white primary law." On March 7, 1927, the court declared the Texas law unconstitutional by unanimous decision. In handing down the decision, Justice Oliver Wendell Holmes declared, "It seems to us hard to imagine a more direct and obvious infringement of the Fourteenth Amendment." [54] Similar victories were won by Negroes in Virginia, Arkansas, and Florida.

Nevertheless, the Negro's suffrage rights remained in almost universal jeopardy until some legal frame of reference prohibiting the persistent retaliation of state legislatures could be found. The frame of reference came in 1941 through the Supreme Court's decision in the case of *U.S. v. Classic*. In this case, the Court ruled that where the primary is an integral part of the election machinery, or when the primary determines the final election, the exclusion of an elector from such a primary is prohibited by the United States Constitution.[55] This was a significant decision in that it reflected the tendency of the Court to prevent state legislators from giving state functions to private organizations in order to escape condemnation as state action within the scope of the Fourteenth Amendment.[56]

Using the *Classic* case as a foundation, NAACP lawyers filed the case of *Smith v. Allwright* in 1941. Two years later, the United States Supreme Court rendered its decision in this case, ruling unconstitutional the Resolution that the Texas Democratic party had passed in another vain attempt to keep its primaries white. This decision broke the barrier of Negro disfranchisement in Texas and paved the way for the political freedom of Negroes in other states of the South. Georgia responded by repealing the poll tax as a prerequisite for voting.[57] A Florida judge ordered that Negro voters be registered "forthwith" in the political party of their choice, citing the opinion in the *Smith v. Allwright* case.[58] And Federal Judge T. Hoyt Davis of Macon, Georgia, ruled that Negroes must be permitted to vote in the Democratic primaries of that state.[59] Despite strong opposition from Southern legislators, the number of Negroes permitted to vote in Southern states grew rapidly, and Negroes gained more power to influence public policy as related to their schools and other aspects of their institutional life.

ATTEMPTS TO EQUALIZE
RESIDENTIAL AND JOB OPPORTUNITIES

Without apparent awareness of its tremendous effects upon the entire school question, American Negroes carried their fight for equality into the areas of residential segregation and limited job opportunities. In a large measure, the fight in the former instance was forced upon them either by the passage of racially biased city ordinances or by court litigations instituted by white people.

Ordinances designed to draw the rope of residential segregation more tightly around the Negro's neck were passed between 1912 and 1914 by such Southern cities as Winston-Salem and Mooreville in North Carolina; by Atlanta in Georgia; and Richmond, Norfolk, and Roanoke in Virginia. But it was not until 1914 when Louisville, Kentucky, passed its ordinance providing for residential segregation in that city that the NAACP became involved and took the cases of complaining Negroes to the courts. The association won its first victory in this field when, on April 27, 1917, the United States Supreme Court, ruling in the Kentucky case of *Buchanan v. Waverley,* invalidated the Louisville ordinance on the ground that it violated the Fourteenth Amendment. The association's legal department also helped to fight residential segregation in Richmond, Atlanta, and Huntington, West Virginia.

Not all the battle against residential segregation was confined to the South. Pressure to confine the Negroes to certain areas of the cities prevailed in the North as well, where the Negro's attempt to escape the urban ghettos was met with prohibitive litigations under the sponsorship of those whites who wanted to maintain all-white residential areas. When several Negroes purchased property in the predominantly white Entwistle Tract of Los Angeles, George H. Leaten and other whites entered a suit against them, using Pauline Ellis, a Negro woman, as their target. The plaintiffs asked that the Negroes be enjoined from living in the tract because a clause in the deeds provided that lots should never be sold, rented, or leased to people of Negro descent. However, Judge Carl I. Stutsman, ruling for the defendants on August 3, 1928, held that Negroes had been living in the area since 1909, and the clause, therefore, had never been enforced and was naturally void.

Under a ruling handed down in January 1930 by Superior Judge Vicini, Sally Trainor, a Negro preacher, was forbidden to occupy her property on East 4th Street of Los Angeles or to permit any other "non-Caucasian" to live there for 99 years. The decision came in an action brought by Neil D. Ross and thirty others who sought an injunction in the area.

However, some progress against residential segregation had been made by 1926. The NAACP won the Sweet case of Detroit that year. The city of Indianapolis passed a residential segregation law in March, and Judge Chamberlain of the Marion County Circuit Court of Indiana ruled, in November, that the ordinance was unconstitutional. But the big blow came on May 3, 1948. On that day the NAACP tasted a victory that virtually put the finishing touches on its campaign to outlaw the restrictive covenants which had kept residential segregation alive. The United States Supreme Court, in a unanimous decision in four restrictive covenant cases, held that Federal and state courts may not enforce restrictive covenants which bar persons from owning and occupying property because of race or color.[60] Although the decision left open the door to discriminate by private agreement, the passage to mass discrimination in this field had been closed.

The Negro's attack upon equal job opportunities had been hesitant and slow because the constitutional grounds upon which the attack could be made had not been clear and are still clouded. Consequently the NAACP, in taking the leadership in this attack, had resorted to pressure tactics rather than court litigations.

Economic expansion during World War II afforded the association with a much needed occasion to apply its pressure tactics. As government agencies began to let contracts for defense production, the NAACP began placing pressure on the government in order to force the reduction of racial discrimination which was inherent in the employment policies of many firms holding these contracts. Justification for the pressure became even stronger when, on July 19, 1941, President Franklin D. Roosevelt appointed a six-man committee, making Mark F. Ethridge of the *Louisville Courier Journal* head, for the purpose of investigating discrimination against Negroes seeking defense and government employment.

The NAACP, using its far-flung scheme of branch-locals, became a virtual "watchdog" for the committee. Its Tulsa, Oklahoma, branch supplied the Fair Employment Practices Committee with affidavits that evidenced racial discrimination in the employment policy of the Manhattan Construction Company. Affidavits were submitted from Detroit against the Briggs Manufacturing, Bud Wheel, Timken Axel, and Kelsey Hayes Companies.[61] The following year, the tri-cities, Alabama, branch, representing the committees of Tuscumbia, Florence, and Sheffield, investigated discrimination against Negro workers in the knitting mills that held defense contracts. The branch also attempted to break down discrimination in national defense vocational training courses but experienced little success in each instance.[62] Strongly urging the investigation of a layoff of 800 laborers in Savannah, 500 of which workers were Negroes, the city's NAACP branch sent the following wire to the War Manpower Commission on November 30, 1942: "Strongly protest lay-off of 800 laborers at Southeastern Shipyards for failure to sign agreement which smacks of collusion between Company and union which would deprive workers of rights." [63] The Fort Worth branch of the NAACP protested to the Commission because of the refusal of the United States Employment Office to permit the registration of qualified Negro applicants for skilled employment. One of the applicants was a World War I veteran, holding the Master of Arts degree. Another had been a mathematics teacher.[64]

Fighting for more than one third of a century in a battle for human rights had produced spotty results but had made Negroes battle-wise. They did not gain full respect from the American people, but they gained a sense of power. They did not get the schools equalized, but they forged a tool that could do it. They won the battle for the ballot, but they still faced the job of getting Negroes to use it. Some of the occupational barriers had been knocked down, but Negroes still hesitated to take advantage of their opportunities.

IX · THE BID FOR DESEGREGATION

Finally, the power of organization which the Negro Americans had generated was made ready to attack the total system of segregation — an institution that had restricted them since the *Civil Rights Cases* of 1883. The system of special education to which Negro children had been consistently exposed for more than four decades had created personality types that had not been planned for by those who had sponsored the great detour. It had produced leaders who were filled with discontent, possessed of a will to act in relief of their grievances, and capable of plotting a way, however tortured, to a desegregated life that was in fact their goal. The Negro community had matured into a discontented and strong force. The NAACP had won its place as the most respected of all the Negro organizations, and its influence had permeated the entire complex of Negro urban communities in the North and South. Its local branches, scattered as they were, had so handled the probing elements of the protest program that every Negro, sooner or later, would feel some blessing as a result of its effectiveness. Its success in the courts, where sheer equality was at first sought, was to inspire a new kind of confidence in American law and order, and many Negroes would come to believe that the overthrow of segregation itself was a possibility. Most significant of all was the high level of intraracial morale that the association was to induce: the growing tendency for individual Negroes to serve readily as plaintiffs in cases guided by the NAACP's attorneys and supported by its funds; the unmistakable martyrdom that was to await those who felt the retaliation of the white community because of their NAACP activities; and the halo of racial patriotism that was to crown all who were to be identified with the NAACP's litigations.

First, there was the strategic move to test the strength of the "separate but equal" doctrine. Early in the 1930s, the American Fund for Public Service, established by Charles Garland, joined forces with the NAACP in a program designed to foster a doctrine favorable to civil rights. The fund gave the Association $10,000 to be used exclusively for a campaign of legal action against the unequal apportionment of public funds for education and the many discriminations in public transportation from which Negroes had suffered. Charles H. Houston, vice dean of Howard University's School of Law, was retained to direct the campaign.

The actual casework, launched with suits against graduate and professional schools, was specifically built around the legal strategy Houston created. The strategy called for attacking segregation in public education at its point of greatest vulnerability — the point where no claim of "separate but equal" could be reasonably made, and where no promise of equalization could be realistically given. Houston reasoned that inequality in higher education could be proved with ease. There were virtually no public graduate and professional schools open to Negroes in the South, and it was thought that judges, by virtue of sheer academic affinity, would understand the shortcomings of separate legal education with which some of the cases were concerned. Since it would be financially impossible to furnish true equality, it was expected that desegregation would be the only practicable way to fulfill the constitutional obligation of equal protection. Also, small numbers of mature students would be involved. This fact was expected to forestall any argument based upon the possibility of violence or the threat of social revolution. It was the "soft sell" element of the strategy, designed to cope with a judicial climate that had been an apparent barrier to favorable court decisions in the field of civil rights. The strategy would let Negroes eat their cake and have it too: Negro leadership would be augmented, whether the cases resulted in the desegregation of the old professional and graduate schools that were all-white or the creation of new ones that would be all-Negro.[1]

Beginning in 1935 and with the border states where resistance was believed to be softer, the NAACP instituted in June of that year the case of *Donald G. Murray v. The University of Maryland*. In doing so it opened a legal campaign to break down the color bar of all public colleges of the segregated South. Having been refused admission to the University of Maryland's law school by its registrar, Donald Murray filed a mandamus suit against the school in a Baltimore city court. His demand was based solely on the grounds of his constitutional rights as a citizen of the state and his educational qualifications as a law school applicant. He was a resident of Baltimore and a graduate of Amherst.

Several loopholes had been shaped by various Southern states to cope with such cases, but Maryland had not been thorough in developing this kind of strategy. Some of the states wishing to maintain segregation in their institutions of higher learning had passed standby statutes which authorized "separate but equal" facilities when and if Negroes applied for them. Some, too, had enacted legislation that provided scholarships for Negro applicants, enabling them to study outside the state and in other states where the courses they sought were available to them. At the time Murray entered his suit, however, Maryland had not authorized the establishment of a law school for Negroes, and its out-of-state scholarship grant was only $200. These facts prejudiced the state's position and forced a decision for the plaintiff in the Maryland Circuit Court of Appeals. This court ruled that since there was no authorization to establish a separate law school for Negroes, it could not undertake to remedy the inequality of treatment by ordering the establishment of such a school. Therefore, a writ of mandamus requiring Murray's admission to the law school was properly directed to the officers and regents of the University of Maryland.[2]

When the Murray case was finally settled, the NAACP had broken an important link in the chain of segregation. Lloyd Gaines filed a similar suit against the University of Missouri in an attempt to gain admission to its law school. A Missouri statute of 1921 had authorized the establishment of a law school for Negroes at the segregated Lincoln University, and had also instituted out-of-state scholarship grants for Negroes seeking professional training not offered at Lincoln. Although the NAACP's lawyers based their plea on the Murray case, the lower court of Missouri accepted the state statute of 1921 as a point of difference and ruled against the plaintiff on the grounds that he did not exhaust all remedies available to him before filing his suit.[3] Nevertheless, Gaines' attorneys appealed to the United States Supreme Court, and on December 12, 1938, this body ruled that he could not be excluded from the University of Missouri law school on the grounds of color or race. The Court through this decision outlawed out-of-state scholarships as a device for meeting the "separate but equal" doctrine. It held that scholarship provisions in effect did not furnish equal facilities.[4] Although the Missouri Supreme Court ordered a rehearing of the case in the lower court in order to comply with the United States Supreme Court mandate, the case was dropped because Gaines could not be found to appear in court. Nevertheless, the cause of segregation suffered irreparable damage as a result of the decision.

Spurred by these cases, some states continued their efforts to meet the Negro demand for professional and graduate education by establishing out-of-state scholarships and makeshift departments. Missouri's plan paid off when, in the case of *State ex rel. Bluford v. Canada, Registrar of University,* the state's supreme court ruled against Lucile Bluford of Kansas City in her attempt to secure admission to the university's school of journalism.[5] Tennessee shared a similar success in the case of *State ex rel. Michael et al. v. Witham et al.*[6]

Despite these reversals, the trend toward desegregation on the level of higher and professional education pushed forward. Less than one decade after its significant pronouncement in the Gaines case, the United States Supreme Court handed down an equally meaningful decision. This came in the case of *Sipuel v. Board of Education.* In this instance Ada Lois Sipuel sought admission to the University of Oklahoma's law school. On January 13, 1947, the Court ruled that the state was compelled to provide for the plaintiff, and all others similarly situated, not only equal opportunity to commence the study of law at a state institution but an opportunity to commence such a study at this institution at the same time as citizens of other groups. Although the decision was clouded by an announcement that the state would establish a law school for Negroes, the persistence of the plaintiff and the NAACP attorneys who handled the case resulted in Miss Sipuel's admission to the law school of the University of Oklahoma in 1949.[7]

The legal precedent that had been so firmly planted in the Murray and Gaines cases was reinforced in the case of *Sweatt v. Painter* and virtually ended the segregation of graduate and professional education as a legal issue. On May 16, 1946, NAACP attorneys filed a suit on behalf of Heman Marion Sweatt in the District Court of Travis County at Austin, Texas, against the board of regents of the University of Texas. They were seeking a writ of mandamus compelling the board to admit Sweatt to the University's law school since it was the only such school maintained by the state. Less than one month later the Court ruled that Sweatt was entitled to relief because he had been denied equal protection of the laws as guaranteed by the Fourteenth Amendment. The ruling had a catch, however, for it stipulated that the order was to become operative after six months so that the state of Texas might have time to establish a separate but equal law school for him. As evidence of good faith, the state's attorney filed copies of minutes of the board of regents of the Texas A. and M. College system showing that a law school for Negroes was to be established at Houston in February 1947 under the supervision of its Negro branch at Prairie View. The case was appealed, but the appellate court remanded it to the lower court for a new trial. In the new trial of May 1947, NAACP attorneys presented evidence which showed that the three-room law school that had been set up at Houston was unequal to that for whites at the University of Texas. After the lower court had denied admission to Sweatt on the grounds that the make-shift law school was equal to that of the University of Texas and that the Texas Supreme Court had refused to review the case, NAACP attorneys appealed to the United States Supreme Court. In June 1950 the Supreme Court found in favor of the petitioner. Through Chief Justice Vinson who read the decision, the Court ordered the University to admit Sweatt to its law school.[8]

The attorneys for the NAACP had hoped, through this case, to test the legality of segregation per se, but the Court, in dodging a head-on collision with the "separate but equal" doctrine, cleared the way for a later collision. It identified the requirements of separate equality piece by piece and did the job in such a manner that it was made impossible for a state to afford to establish a law school for Negroes with equal facilities. In the end, the Court buttressed the Negro contention that separate schools and equality of educational opportunities cannot coexist. And on the same day the Court upheld George McLaurin's complaint against the differential treatment that he was receiving as a graduate student in education at the University of Oklahoma. It decreed that once a school admits a student it must not discriminate against him but must accord him the same rights and privileges accorded other students. Thus, by midcentury, the NAACP had successfully abolished segregation in public education at the graduate and professional levels.[9] There was still some bickering on the part of the states that were to resist the desegregation process, but in the end, racial segregation in this area of American life was to disappear.

The Negro's legal campaign to invalidate the "separate but equal" doctrine was not confined to the service area of public education. It spread to incorporate other services where the public interest was directly touched. The policy of racial segregation in the law library at the District Court Building of Washington, D.C., was ended as a result of a suit filed in 1938 by Huver I. Brown, a Negro lawyer of that city. George Wilson, a Negro lawyer of Alexandria, Virginia, secured the use of the public library of that city as a result of a suit filed in its corporation court. Although a Negro branch library was subsequently organized, the case established the precedent for the use of a public library by Negroes. Two years later, the Chancery Court of Knoxville, Tennessee, upheld Negro physicians in their contention for equal privileges with white doctors in their city's tax-supported general hospital. And in 1941, Congressman Arthur Mitchell secured a ruling from the United States Supreme Court to the effect that discrimination against a Negro passenger with a first-class ticket by the refusal of accommodations equal in comfort and convenience to those offered first-class white passengers violated both the Interstate Commerce Act and the guarantees of the Fourteenth Amendment.[10] This case was merely the forerunner of a more far-reaching decision about segregation on public carriers. On June 3, 1946, the United States Supreme Court in the case of *Morgan v. Virginia* held that the separation of passengers by race in interstate bus travel could not be accomplished by state statute.[11] Although the ruling involved travel by bus, its influence was to spread to the transportation by railroad.

THE DEATH OF JIM CROW SCHOOLING

Having established the virtual impossibility of equal but separate schools, the NAACP entered the decisive phase of its legal campaign to gain equal educational opportunities for Negroes. This phase, radically different from all the rest, aimed to destroy the legality of segregation as a public school policy. Early in 1951, and under the guidance of the legal department of the NAACP, Negroes entered suits in an attempt to get the court to do what it had refused to do in the case of *Sweatt v. Painter:* to rule on the legality of segregation itself and to consider as a basis for its judgment nonlegal materials that would possibly assess the inequalities inherent in segregation more realistically than would conventional legal evidence.

At that time, Oliver Brown and twelve other parents, in the famous *Brown et al. v. Board of Education of Topeka et al.* case, brought suit in the district court for the district of Kansas on behalf of the educational opportunities of their children. They sought to enjoin enforcement of a Kansas statute which permitted, but did not require, cities of more than 15,000 population to maintain separate school facilities for Negro and white students. The Brown case was consolidated with four other cases in which Negro school children were seeking similar relief. Harry Briggs, Jr., and sixty other Negro children brought suit against the school board of Clarendon County, South Carolina. Dorothy E. Davis *et al.* had likewise entered suit against the school board of Prince Edward County, Virginia. And Ethel Louise Belton, joined by Barbara Bulah, had instituted suit against Francis B. Gebhart and other school officials of the state of Delaware. In each of the four cases the plaintiffs were denied admission to public schools attended by white children under state laws requiring or permitting segregation according to race.

There was no looking backward on the part of these plaintiffs. They refused to settle for the promise of equality under the traditional system of racial separation. The Federal district court ruled against Oliver Brown and his daughter, Linda Carol, on August 3, 1951. Considering itself bound by the "separate but equal" doctrine, the special three-judge court ruled that the Negro and white schools were substantially equal and that in the maintenance and operation of the schools there was no willful, intentional, or substantial discrimination. The NAACP's attorneys immediately began preparing for an appeal to the Supreme Court. The Federal court also denied relief in the case of *Harry Briggs, Jr., et al.* Although the segregated schools of Clarendon County, South Carolina, were found to be inferior to those afforded the whites, this court, too, invoked the separate but equal idea and ordered the defendants to take steps to equalize the public schools promptly and to report back in six months. The three-judge district court of Virginia admitted the inadequacy of the Negro school in Prince Edward County but merely ordered the board to pursue "with diligence and dispatch" the building program which it had already begun. On April 1, 1952, the Delaware Court of Chancery ordered immediate admission of Negro students to schools previously attended by white children only. This judgment was affirmed, in unanimous decision, by the state supreme court on August 28, 1952. Lacking the vigor of the lower court, however, the affirmance implied that segregation laws might again be enforced if and when school facilities were equalized.[12] The nature and development of these cases clearly showed that it was the inequality inherent in segregation and not the inequality inherent in schools which was under attack. When these cases reached the Supreme Court, therefore, the basic issue was clearly the legality of segregation. This was vividly brought out by Chief Justice Warren who, in delivering the opinion of the Court in the Brown *et al.* cases, said, "The plaintiffs contend that segregated public schools are not equal and cannot be made equal, but that hence they are deprived of the equal protection of the laws." [13]

Strange as it may seem, the strength of the Negro's attack in this crucial legal battle rested in large measure upon conditions that had been created by the forces of segregation. Forced to turn to the study of their own life and history as an outlet for their talents, Negro intellectuals, particularly social scientists and psychologists, had revealed many facts about the damage done by segregation. Ever since 1915, Negro leaders had been very much concerned about the crowded conditions of their communities and the social problems that resulted. Through the local branches of the NAACP they had been waging legal campaigns against residential segregation and restrictive covenants.[14] They had been fighting unequal educational opportunities for more than fifteen years. Consequently, when they entered the courts in the Brown *et al.* cases, they pursued a thoroughly tested legal strategy and a large number of objective facts to underscore their contention that segregation in and of itself was damaging to Negro children.

The most influential element in the legal strategy of the attorneys for the plaintiffs was the use of social science materials in their briefs. The employment was not easy to achieve — as some observers have clearly stated, the use of direct evidence is a more firmly established tradition in judicial procedure.[15] Nevertheless some issues cannot be resolved on the basis of firsthand evidence. Involving matters beyond the competence of the court's "fact-finders," they call for experts who, by training and experience in the areas from which the issues stem, are freed by the courts to testify beyond the limits of direct fact.

Social scientists and psychologists, some of whom were Negroes, took the witness stand in the four cases before the court and freely testified that "segregation is detrimental to Negro children." [16] Kenneth B. Clark, a Negro psychologist at City College of New York contributed a forceful statement to the brief. His report, previously made before the Mid-Century White House Conference on Children and Youth, brought together the available social science and psychological studies that were related to the problem of how

233

racial and religious prejudices influence the development of men-
tality and personality. Clark highlighted the fact that segregation,
prejudices, and their social concomitants potentially damage the
personality of all children — all children of the majority group in
a way somewhat different from that experienced by the more obviously damaged children of the minority group. Probably most
significant of all, the report indicated that as minority-group
children learn the inferior status to which they are assigned — as
they observe the fact that they are almost always segregated and
kept apart from others who are treated with more respect by the
society as a whole — they often react with feelings of inferiority and
a sense of personal humiliation. A report by Ira DeA. Reid, a
Negro sociologist at Haverford College, challenged the "colored
world" in which segregation forces Negroes to live. His view, shared
by other social scientists whose testimony was entered into the record,
scored the point that segregation imposes upon individuals a dis-
torted sense of social reality. All thirty-two of these American
scholars, some the products of the Negro college, testified directly
or by implication against the policy of racial segregation and on
behalf of the values to be derived from its elimination.

Although the evidence from social science was merely entered
for the purpose of supplying information for the judges, it apparently
carried the day on May 17, 1954. "Whatever may have been the
extent of psychological knowledge at the time of *Plessy v. Ferguson*,"
said Chief Justice Warren in reading the opinion, "this finding is
amply supported by modern authority. . . . We conclude that in
the field of public education the doctrine of 'separate but equal'
has no place. Separate educational facilities are inherently unequal.
Therefore, we hold that the plaintiffs and others similarly situated
for whom the actions have been brought are, by reason of the
segregation complained of, deprived of the equal protection of the
laws guaranteed by the Fourteenth Amendment." Thus came to an
end the legal basis for Negro education as it had been known for
more than three quarters of a century.

Once the Supreme Court had spoken, several school districts, in
sincere expression of the will to comply with the judicial order,
began almost immediately to desegregate their schools. Within one

year after the order was handed down, two districts in Arkansas, nine in Delaware, one in Maryland, two in Missouri, two in Texas, and the District of Columbia had abandoned their separate school policy either voluntarily or in direct response to a specific court decree. School desegregation in West Virginia started in 1955 at Magnolia County and progressed rapidly thereafter to involve all forty-three of the state's districts with white and Negro pupils.

There were apparent reasons for the early compliance of these states. One of these was the fact that many of them were border states, neither completely Northern nor completely Southern. Therefore, the changeover was less revolutionary in nature and was less of a disturbance to their traditional social order than to that of the more Southern states. Also, they fell at the extremes of the continuum formed by the proportional representation of Negroes in the total school enrollment of the respective segregated states. The racial composition of those districts earliest to comply was almost all Negro or almost all white. The apparent economy resulting from the changeover seemed far to outweigh any breach of tradition that could possibly result. For example, when Charleston, Arkansas, voluntarily desegregated its school in 1954, there was hardly one Negro pupil for each 100 pupils enrolled. Conditions were the same for the school districts of Delaware, except at Wilmington where Negro students constituted almost half the total enrollment. The other extremes operated in the District of Columbia and the city of Baltimore. Negro students of these integrating districts composed over half the total school enrollment. Only in Kentucky and West Virginia was there a trend toward a general integration of the Negro pupils during these early years of desegregation.[17]

Despite the more flexible customs and the relatively small proportions of Negro pupils characteristic of the states within which compliance with court decisions was earliest, the success experienced during these pioneering efforts must be attributed mainly to the careful planning that preceded the desegregation programs. Immediately following the Court's decree, the Board of Education of St. Louis began to make definite plans for the desegregation of the schools under its jurisdiction. At its meeting of June 22, 1954, it unanimously adopted and publicly announced a step-by-step program of desegregation to be started in September of that year and to be completed by September of the following year.

The scheme did not catch the city's population unprepared. Although a segregated pattern had been a way of life for St. Louis, a number of its key civic, religious, and social agencies had during the preceding years become increasingly active in working to change that pattern. As a result of this kind of action, the city's two universities, its Catholic schools, leading hotels, municipal recreational facilities, a major league baseball park had all been desegregated. Desegregation in employment opportunities had also progressed significantly. The line of communication between whites and Negroes had been kept open, preventing the sharp delineation of in-group and out-group attitudes that had been allowed to develop in some other cities with segregated facilities. Ever since 1877, when Negro teachers were first employed in St. Louis, it had been general practice for meetings of teachers and principals called by the administrative office to be held on a nonracial basis. For more than twenty years prior to the Court's decision, courses of study had been written and textbooks had been selected for the St. Louis public schools by committees on which white and Negro teachers and principals had worked side-by-side. The integration of teachers' professional organizations had been going on since 1918 and had reached virtual completion by 1950. Possibly of greatest importance is the fact that by the school year 1944–1945, one decade before the Supreme Court's decision, teachers of the St. Louis public school system had organized and instituted an effective program of intergroup relations. Their work in this area had become so well known that their school district in May 1945 had been invited to become a participating unit in the eighteen-city experimental study of intergroup education being conducted by the American Council on Education. The students, teachers, and the civic-minded residents, whom the press had kept so well informed, were ready to desegregate when the St. Louis school board made its move on June 22.

In keeping with the Court's 1954 decree, the St. Louis school board designed its "prompt and reasonable start toward compliance" according to three basic steps: Junior and teacher colleges and special schools providing services on a city-wide basis were to be desegregated in September following the decision; all high schools except technical, and all adult education programs were to be desegregated at the beginning of the second semester, January 31, 1955; and desegregation of all technical high schools and elementary schools was to start in September 1955. This tended to give more time for solving problems that, apparently, were expected to vary with the academic level of the school facility that was being desegregated. In an attempt to respect the rights of students and school personnel, two basic guidelines were employed. All tenure rights were preserved, and all future employing was to be done on the basis of merit — examination scores for teachers and job competency for other personnel. New school boundary lines were to be drawn on a nonsegregated basis and published November 15, 1954. Students would be required to attend school according to their boundaries, except that school authorities might have transfers to relieve overcrowded conditions or to accommodate students already enrolled in a school but not residents in the light of district changes. Such students were to be allowed to remain in their school until graduated.

In September 1954 initial steps in the implementation of the program were taken. The teachers and junior colleges of the system were reorganized on a nonsegregated basis. Stowe Teachers College for Negroes was consolidated with Harris Teachers College for whites, and the integrated institution was housed in the building formerly occupied by the white students. Schools for orthopedically handicapped children were similarly consolidated, thus integrating students, teachers, and all other workers. Schools for the deaf were desegregated according to the same pattern — the consolidation of duplicated facilities and personnel. Residents of any part of the city were free to enroll in adult education courses for which they were qualified wherever those courses were offered. The consolidation of such courses effected an economy which made it possible for the institution to concentrate more upon course improvement.

The second step of the program was introduced by the creation of new district boundary lines for the high schools. The central office, on the basis of information secured from each high school student, prepared an IBM card for each of the approximately 6,000 city blocks in St. Louis. On each card were punched data showing, by grade, the total number of public high school students residing in that block. All indications of racial identity were purposely omitted from the card. Using the statistics thus assembled, together with consideration for building capacity, distance, and transportation facilities, planners of the program divided the city into nine high school districts. This redistricting method resulted in the enrollment of 862 Negro students in six of the seven high schools of the city that were formerly designated as white. These students constituted 9.4 percent of the 9,181 pupils enrolled in these high schools at the beginning of the desegregation period. Slightly more than 40 percent of the students already enrolled in the former all-Negro high schools were eligible for transfer under the redistricting system, and slightly less than 60 percent of these elected to transfer.

A similar method of redistricting was employed in desegregating the elementary schools of the city. Preliminary estimates showed that this method produced thirty-seven schools, formerly for whites, in which the percentage of Negro children eligible to attend them ranged from 56 to less than 1 percent; thirteen schools, formerly all-Negro, in which the percent of white children eligible to attend ranged from 18 to less than 1. Thus, the check revealed, white and Negro pupils in varying proportions would be attending classes together in 50 St. Louis public elementary schools. According to the plan, approximately two thirds of the city's 40,000 elementary school pupils would be enrolled in schools at which some children of both races would be in attendance. As the plan actually operated, however, a somewhat larger number of white and Negro pupils enrolled in the same school than was initially estimated.

Just before the St. Louis program went into operation, community resources were again called upon to facilitate the spread of information about the plan throughout the city. Parent-Teacher associations and mothers' clubs at neighboring white and Negro schools sponsored discussions of the project; area associations of white and Negro community leaders worked to facilitate the transition; and other community agencies, including the press, carried an explanation of the new plan far beyond the limits of the more specialized associations. When the elementary school staff was properly located and all necessary facilities were adequately assigned, the St. Louis board had completed the implementation of all the steps outlined in its plan. By September 1956 it felt that it had fulfilled the purposes that were enunciated at its meeting of June 22, 1954: "to expeditiously and wisely assure for every public school child full, equal, and impartial use of our school facilities, and to secure for our employees fair and impartial treatment." [18]

Despite this careful planning, however, the dynamics of urban growth were to upset the racial balance at St. Louis, and more serious problems in the area of school desegregation were to plague subsequent school boards in that city. Soon after school desegregation was under way, certain factors began disturbing the city's population in such a way that *de facto* segregation threatened to override all the progress that had been made. [19]

First, there was a tendency for the white population of St. Louis to move out of the central city and to shift toward the periphery, while the number of Negroes in the central city was increasing. Between 1950 and 1960 the percentage of whites in the central city decreased from 81.5 to 78.4, and that of nonwhites increased, although only slightly, from 95.2 to 96.2. The total population of the city decreased 14.2 percent in this period while the nonwhite population increased 39.8 percent. It was not the metropolitan community area that was beginning to lose the white people; it was the central city. The population shift so characteristic of metropolitan America was at work; the whites were moving to suburbia; the Negroes were moving to town. Second, also characteristically common to American cities was the fact that the Negroes remained spatially concentrated in their racial islands. As they expanded outward to the new areas contiguous to those they occupied, whites ran to avoid them, taking up residence in suburban districts that had a greater chance of remaining lily-white.

Even though the school desegregation plan which was first introduced succeeded in effecting some integration of the Negro pupils, the dynamics of black and white population shifts quickly made the schools virtually all-Negro again. When St. Louis schools were integrated in 1955, Soldan High was 74 percent white in school population. By 1963 it had become 99 percent Negro. With the shift of Negro residents to the West End, elementary schools of that area experienced a similar change.

Population changes gave the city persistent problems of overcrowding, even prior to desegregation. Some of the pupils in congested schools were assigned, pending new construction, to schools where space was available. Movement to and from the "receiving schools" was either on foot or by bus at public expense. During the school year 1962–1963, all but one of the sending schools were all-Negro or predominantly Negro; twenty of the receiving schools were all-white or essentially so. Almost all, or 95 percent, of the transported children were Negro, carried as "room groups," each traveling under teacher supervision. Each transported group was taught at the receiving school in what "may fairly be called a contained unit." In both classroom and extracurricular activities, commingling with resident pupils was inconsequential. Urban dynamics had created *de facto* segregation, and the St. Louis school board had not been able to overcome it.

Such instances of the extension of segregation did not escape the notice of Negro parents and some of the leaders of the Negro community. Nevertheless, criticism was restrained, for the image that Negroes held of the St. Louis school board was one of good faith, and there was not apparent evidence that this faith was being broken. During the winter and spring of 1961–1962, Superintendent Hickey had appointed a committee to study such matters. Its report, released to the press on June 13, 1962, very strongly recommended intensification and expansion of efforts toward the full integration of the transported pupils.

Less than one year later, however, the calm that had gathered around the receiving school problem broke. The board made known its plans to shift Harris Teachers College from the heavily populated Negro West End to the Vashon High School in central St. Louis; to build a football stadium at Soldan High School in the West End; and to build six new elementary schools in this area. Responding to these moves, groups of Negroes attacked the change and charged that school officials had introduced policies which had brought about a "resegregation" of the schools. Criticism of varying degrees of intensity came from the West End Community Conference, the

NAACP, the two Negro members of the school board (James Hurt and the Reverend John J. Hicks), and from the city's Negro alderman, William L. Clay. Direct action taken in legal suits, public demonstrations, and boycotts kept the St. Louis school situation in turmoil for over a year.

By the spring of 1964, however, a new calm had begun to form. Progress against *de facto* segregation had become more apparent. The school board's committee had reported that for the first time, in September 1963, no high school in St. Louis was either all-white or all-Negro. This report also noted, in its reference to transporting 4,653 Negro children from overcrowded West End, that complete desegregation had been achieved in eighteen classrooms at five receiving schools; where full classroom integration had not become "possible," all other aspects of school life had been integrated.[20] It was apparent, however, that the city's policy of residential segregation had placed its board of education on a segregation-desegregation treadmill from which the board could not escape by its own efforts.

School desegregation at Louisville, Kentucky, developed in a manner very similar to that of St. Louis: It started early on the basis of a well-laid plan. Immediately after the 1954 decision the city openly accepted the decree. Superintendent Omer Carmichael released a statement to the local newspapers stating that the decision was the law of the land; that he as superintendent would carry it out without resort to subterfuge or undue delay; that in carrying it out, children would have first consideration; and the teachers would come second, with the parents of the pupils following in that order. On the same day Governor Lawrence Wetherby issued a statement announcing that Kentucky would comply with the law.

In the light of the pattern of race relations which the city had already developed, this official attitude was a logical trend. There was never a separation of the races on street cars and buses in Louisville. Negroes had been on the police force since 1923, and the Y-organizations of the city had sponsored many programs and activities to promote good race relations. The Louisville Free Public Library had opened its main building to Negroes in 1948, and ten branches had opened to them in 1952. Almost within the same period, the University of Kentucky, the nursing school of the city hospital, and the city's public golf courses had desegregated. The Greyhound Bus terminal desegregated in 1954, and so did the publicly owned amphitheaters.

A significant trend toward desegregation had already been established within the operational policies of the school system's administrative family. A permissive policy whereby white and Negro teachers did professional planning together was already in operation. A Negro woman was made assistant supervisor of music in 1948 and had been given office space in the main administration building along with other supervisory and administrative personnel. A young Negro woman had been employed and placed in charge of mimeographing. Another had been employed to serve as clerk for two supervisors. The Regional Conference of Jews, established in the city at the close of World War II, had been sponsoring human relations institutes, involving the cooperation of the superintendent and the participation of the teachers.

It was against this type of background that the Louisville school system launched its desegregation program. With the opening of schools in September 1954, intensive work was begun to "create the proper climate in Louisville so that desegregation could take place orderly." A faculty study plan was instituted and possible problems of desegregation were anticipated and noted. This program was later "fanned out" into the entire community. PTAs were asked to conduct public programs, and local papers cooperated by giving wide publicity to their activities. Churches, church-related groups, women's clubs, civic clubs, and other community organizations began arranging meetings on desegregation. School administrators, supervisors, and teachers served as speakers for these occasions. Members of the board of education, ministers, and other interested citizens served likewise. Such discussion groups gave the public a feeling of participation; they involved the citizenry and inculcated some sense of public responsibility.

The students were also directly involved in the program. From the beginning of the 1954–1955 school year, all teachers were working with their children on the desegregation problem, "preparing them, whether Negro or white, to go more than halfway to make desegregation work." Negro pupils appeared on white assembly programs and white pupils appeared on the programs of the Negro schools. Students of the two races, working together, were allowed to develop these programs and activities. This apparently helped to break down the strangeness that segregation had fostered between the children of the two races over the years.

Once this groundwork had been laid, steps toward official action were taken. Superintendent Carmichael, author and director of the program, reported his activities to the board, recommending that it request him to submit a desegregation plan in mid-November of 1955, calling for desegregation to begin in September 1956. The board unanimously adopted his recommendation. When the plan was completed, copies were sent to all organizations, the press, parents, and leading citizens, inviting written suggestions for improvements.

As prescribed in the plan, the entire city was redistricted for elementary and junior high schools without regard for race. Cards were sent to parents, informing them of the schools to which their children had been assigned and allowing them, if such was desired, to indicate their first, second, and third choices. When the cards were received from the parents they showed that 37,247 of the 41,762 elementary and junior high school children involved had accepted the school to which they belonged according to the redistricting. Only 11 percent had requested transfers. Of the Negro children included in this dissatisfied group, 45 percent had requested transfers back to what had been Negro schools. Of the white children who had fallen into formerly all-Negro schools, 85 percent had requested transfers. No redistricting was done for senior high schools. A card was sent to the parents of high school pupils announcing that each senior high school was open to pupils of both races who lived in the district that it served.

The end of the third day of school found 10 elementary schools and 1 junior high school with white pupils only; 5 elementary schools, 3 junior high schools and 1 senior high school with Negro pupils only. Of the 73 schools, only 20 were serving one race exclusively as of the fall of 1956. Approximately 74 percent of Louisville's public school children were attending mixed schools at that time.[21] In apparent satisfaction for having planned well, Superintendent Carmichael wrote:[22] "As I evaluate the first year of work under the program which we developed, I feel that we planned more wisely than we knew. Some of the problems that were anticipated did not arise. The thorough preparation which had been made and the fine poise of our teachers and parents enabled us to handle the specific problems which arose with at least reasonable satisfaction."

By the school year 1961–1962, however, the Louisville School Board found itself in a position similar to that of St. Louis and for similar reasons. About half of Kentucky's Negro students were attending all-Negro schools, and the state's pattern of desegregation had taken on an indecisive quality. Some districts had desegregated high schools but were still maintaining segregation at the elementary level. Others had desegregated their elementary schools but were sending their Negro high school pupils to a public all-Negro school. Still other districts forbade any Negro child to attend school with a white child. The situation at Louisville was more decisive, but the process of population shift involving the mobility of whites and Negroes inhibited the decisive trend toward school integration that the Carmichael plan first initiated. Almost half the city's 73 schools were either virtually all-white or all-Negro. A liberal rule permitted any child, upon written request of his parents, to transfer out of the school zone of his residence to any other school of the same grade level in the city which could accommodate him. Nevertheless population mobility continued to keep school desegregation off balance and tending toward resegregation. Parents of white children at the elementary level increased their request for transfers as the school enrollment ratio tipped to a Negro majority. As in the case of St. Louis, the Louisville School Board was unwittingly blocked in its desegregation plan by the force of residential segregation along racial lines.[23]

The District of Columbia public schools also launched a desegregation program soon after the Court's decision, but the action was taken against a background of preplanning somewhat less thorough than that designed by school administrators and citizens at St. Louis and Louisville. The first steps in the District's program were taken in September 1954.

Although with less care than in the case of Louisville and St. Louis, the District had experienced some degree of preparation for the changeover that was instituted. For several years prior to desegregation various activities were initiated by Negro educational leaders for the purpose of giving pupils an opportunity to participate in interracial groups.[24] Through the leadership of school principals, discussion groups were held on how children of other races should be received: Courtesy and good manners were stressed; what children of the host schools were expected to do in making newcomers welcome was defined; and ways and means of acceptable behavior were taught. Roscoe Evans, then principal of Shaw Junior High School for Negroes, sponsored a Better Conduct Program, using jingles to emphasize swimming-pool behavior.[25] A similar program, possibly on a broader scale, was put into operation at the Burville School. Each year, even before the Court's decision, a Parents' Institute brought together citizens who were interested in child guidance, and led these parents in the exploration of problems of intergroup behavior.[26] Despite these and other such efforts, preparation for desegregation at Washington, D.C., seems to have operated merely through the Negro community and without too much involvement of the total community.

School desegregation in the District of Columbia, therefore, was instituted without "too much deliberation." One week after the Supreme Court's initial decision in the school desegregation cases, the District's Board of Education made this declaration of policy:

> We affirm our intention to secure the right of every child, within his own capacity, to the full, equal and impartial use of all school facilities, and the right of all qualified teachers to teach where needed within the school system.
>
> And finally, we ask the aid, cooperation and good will of all citizens and the help of the Almighty in holding to our stated purposes.[27]

Accompanying this declaration of purposes was a five-point antidiscrimination policy. The policy included declarations that pupils and teachers were to be assigned to schools without regard for race; boundaries of former white and Negro schools were to be redrawn without racial distinction, but for convenience of location as related to pupil residence. When school opened September 13, 1954, the plan went into operation only for students who were registering in Washington schools for the first time or who had moved from one part of the city to another. In addition, 3,000 Negro students were transferred from overcrowded schools into formerly white schools that were far less crowded. One week later, as provided by the desegregation schedule, other students were given a choice of remaining in the schools they were attending or transferring to the schools re-zoned to serve their community.[28] In this way, the District of Columbia schools were desegregated. But all was not to go well.

Of the school districts first to comply with the Court's order, those of Baltimore, San Antonio, Texas, and Nashville, Tennessee, made the least preparation. Baltimore was the first to announce desegregation plans. Its announcement came on June 10, 1954, less than one month after the Court's decision. At this time the city had over 55,000 Negro school children, constituting 39 percent of the school population.

Although little preparation for the changeover had been made, Baltimore's school officials had experienced some contact with the problem prior to their desegregation announcement. The city's board of school commissioners had apparently long favored desegregation to some degree. It had desegregated high schools two years before the Supreme Court ruled, when Negro students asked and secured admission to an accelerated college preparatory course in Polytechnic Institute, a formerly all-white school. When the request came, the board's first inclination was to set up a similar course in a Negro school. On second thought, however, its feeling was that a segregated course could never be equal to "Poly's excellent reputation." Consequently, Negroes were admitted without drawing too much public attention. The superintendent merely told a special assembly of the students that there were not going to be "two kinds of boys; just Poly boys."

The city's wider program of desegregation was instituted with no more preparation than this. The plan was simple. Having established no previous policy of school districting, the board merely continued its policy of allowing children to attend schools of their choice and dropped all racial distinction. However, this free-choice policy actually produced little race mixing. As late as the third year of the city's desegregation program, 80 percent of the schools reported mixed classes but only 30 of these had a 10 percent or higher Negro enrollment in what had been all-white student bodies. In fact, 34 schools remained all-white and 53 all-Negro.[29]

School desegregation in San Antonio, Texas, had the advantages of good race relations and a clear-cut statement of policy. With its small Negro population, relatively a large number of Spanish Americans, and an economy considerably based upon large military establishments, this city had a reputation for being the bright spot of interracial relations in Texas. Superintendent Thomas B. Portwood in July 1955 announced that the San Antonio school district hoped to "make a beginning at integration the following fall," and a plan for such was set up to begin operation in September of the school year 1955–1956. His announcement was backed by three important proclamations: The first was his own, proclaiming that the recent court ruling required a prompt and reasonable start toward school desegregation. The second was made jointly by the state board of education and the Texas Education Agency. Both announced that local districts might begin a desegregation policy without the loss of state funds. And the San Antonio school board passed a resolution instructing the superintendent to draw up a plan for beginning desegregation that fall. The plan was to take into consideration the distribution of the pupil population, the ability of the schools to handle the load, any educational loss that might result from a change of school, the most efficient use of existing school facilities, and the educational welfare of all pupils and teachers.

The plan was set into operation by way of specific steps. Negro children who were eligible to attend first or second grade in September 1955, and who resided within any all-elementary school district, were allowed to enter the school of their desired district. If they did not wish to enter any of those schools, they were permitted to return to one of the schools that were formerly provided for Negroes.

The number of students transferred to the formerly white elementary schools was limited. Designated areas were set up within the regular districts of these schools, and Negro children of the first and second grades who resided in these areas were permitted to enroll there. Those who did not wish to make this change were allowed to continue in the all-Negro schools. Negro pupils of grade 7B were transferred to the junior high schools according to the policy followed in the instance of the elementary schools. Negro children entering senior high school for the first time were allowed to attend any San Antonio high school of their choice, but those who had been enrolled in high school prior to September 1955 were required to enroll at the Negro senior high. All special schools were desegregated on a free-choice basis.[30]

School desegregation in Nashville, Tennessee, was court ordered,[31] and Superintendent W. A. Bass began the institution of the city's grade-a-year plan in the fall of 1957. There were about 3,200 first-grade pupils in the system, and 41 percent of these were Negroes. Some attempt to involve the responsible elements of the community was made, but this was on a relatively small scale. The superintendent presented an eight-point program of action to both Negro and white PTAs, calling for the establishment of study groups in the various communities for the purpose of informing as many citizens as possible of the Supreme Court's ruling and making a careful positive explanation of the board's policy. The desegregation program was discussed with interested parents. Lectures were given to teachers; preliminary talks with the mayor were held; and endorsements from leading white organizations were secured. On August 27, 1957, thirteen Negro children were registered in five formerly all-white elementary schools to inaugurate the first step of the grade-a-year plan to complete school desegregation at Nashville.

Many segregated school districts cleverly avoided early compliance with the Court's decision by erecting a variety of subterfuges, which they included under the label of "all deliberate speed." Early after the judicial order several of the large urban school districts adopted the "study-group method" as a delaying tactic. With about 100,000 school pupils under its jurisdiction, the School Board of

Atlanta, Georgia, set itself up as a committee of the whole in July 1955 to study desegregation problems. A professional research staff was appointed to bring in a report. The School Board of Greensboro, North Carolina, had said a year earlier that it was going to make a study, and boards of Asheville, Charlotte, and Winston-Salem had expressed similar intentions. Winston-Salem appointed a biracial citizen's desegregation study group. During this same period, the School Board of Mobile, Alabama, reported that it would study desegregation and added an assurance that it would work toward compliance with the Court's order. The spread of desegregation in some of the larger cities of Tennessee was also "deliberate." Knoxville, after turning down Negro requests for admission to white schools, announced that it was "studying methods of complying." Chattanooga's board was first to announce a readiness to comply but postponed its action in the face of community opposition.[32]

The delaying tactics of Houston, Texas, were based upon the claim that time was needed to build the proper buildings and to prepare the Negro schools for the changeover. Mrs. Frank Dyer, president of Houston's school board, accounting for the city's delay in school desegregation, begged for time to "upgrade Negro teachers." This was a new note coming from a board that had contended that the Negro schools were equal to the white in every respect.[33] Through the Dyer leadership, a summer program was developed whereby Negro teachers were to become "upgraded" by watching, through the use of a one-way screen, white teachers teach Negro children. Dubbed "the peeping plan," this program was quickly aborted as a result of strong objections by Mrs. Charles E. White, the sole Negro member of the Houston School Board, and protests from the city's Negro community. Speaking for the Houston Church Women's League, a Negro organization, Anna Dupree called the plan "an insult which can breed only more enmity and strengthen the existing misunderstandings between minority and majority races." [34]

A study group that the Houston board had appointed brought in a report justifying the delaying tactics which the school district had adopted. In its report to the board on May 1, 1957, the study group advised that school desegregation begin in the district after its "present" building program — not later than 1960 — and that the program should proceed one grade at a time for twelve years. H. E. Lee, a Negro physician and lone dissenter in a study group that included only two Negroes, presented a minority report calling for desegregation the following fall.[35]

Eventually, however, deliberation ran its course and several reluctant school districts found themselves under compulsory court orders. The United States District Court, in the case of *Calhoun v. Latiner,* ordered desegregation of the Atlanta schools. Final approval of Atlanta's proposed desegregation plan was given by the court on January 20, 1960, with an order that the plan be made effective on May 1, 1961. And so, on August 30, 1961, the first common school district of Georgia became desegregated when nine Negro students transferred to four Atlanta public schools that had previously been all white. The change occurred with great calm and exemplary order. The United States District Court of Chattanooga in 1960 also granted summary judgment in the case of *Mapp et al. v. Chattanooga Board of Education,* and ordered the board to present a desegregation plan by December of that year. The persistence of Negro parents pushed Houston nearer desegregation in 1960. Responding to the case of *Houston ISD v. Ross,* filed in 1956 in the United States District Court, the trial judge ordered "desegregation with deliberate speed," and in August 1960, ordered desegregation on a grade-a-year plan to begin with the first grade in September 1960. This order was upheld by the United States Fifth Circuit Court of Appeals, and eleven Negro children entered the first grade with white children that fall.

A WILL TO RESIST

Resistance and compliance were twin born. While the people and officials of some states vigorously searched for a way to mix the races in their schools, others searched, with greater diligence, for a way to keep the races apart. The scale was never balanced for popular sentiment kept the force pointed in the direction of the old tradition. Whereas those who deliberated accepted desegregation as an inevitable policy but tried to postpone the changeover as long as they could, those who resisted bluntly rejected the policy and tried vainly to erect barriers that would protect them forever against it. Although patterns of resistance were varied and can be classified in many ways, one can say with certainty that they assumed two forms: those that operated outside the legal machinery and those that operated within it. One can say, too, that the degree of success experienced through the use of either method depended squarely upon the extent to which actions of resistance were able to break through such lines of legal and moral defense as were thrown up by the constituted authority and the general citizenry of the desegregating communities.

There were dramatic instances in which popular discontent exploded into violence and fostered open rebellion against constituted authority. One of these occurred at Baltimore, where the nation's first step toward compliance with the Supreme Court's decision had to be fought for vigorously partly because no adequate preparation had been made for it. Here, desegregation proceeded smoothly for a month but in nearby Milford, Delaware, a spark destined to become a conflagration was lighted. Bryant Bowles, head of the "expedient" National Association for the Advancement of White People, closed a desegregated school, forced the school board to resign, and drove Negro students from the school which was formerly all white.

Moved by this action of defiance, some discontented citizens of Baltimore began a duplication of the Milford rebellion on the same day. In a neighborhood near the B & O Shops, inhabited largely by home-owning semiskilled workers, women picketed an elementary school containing about 12 Negroes and 700 whites. Parents who were apprehensive about what was happening took their children out of school. On the following day resistance spread to Southern High School, where 50 Negro children had been placed as a result of desegregation. Conditions reached riotous proportions, and the operation of the desegregated schools was disrupted.

Nevertheless, such determination as school officials had shown in developing the desegregation program withstood a most violent test.

Civic leaders rallied courageously to its defense. Ministers preached brotherhood in their churches; the Mayor pleaded for calm; and the school board stood firm. Both the school officials and the police adopted tougher policies when things were at their worst. School officials telephoned parents and warned them that it was illegal for them to keep their children out of school. The police commissioner went on television to declare that anybody who disturbed the school or induced a student to be a truant would be arrested.

At Baltimore constituted authority kept faith with its responsibilities. This worked. One day after school officials and police authorities had spoken, school reopened, and the pickets were chased home. Three days later attendance was back to normal. By 1957, three years after the city's school board had announced its desegregation plan, 28.7 percent of the Negro pupils were attending mixed schools. Faculties had been desegregated also, and more than one hundred Negro teachers were working in formerly all-white schools. Indicating a collapse of the will to resist at Baltimore, one man said, "there aren't many people really cheering but there aren't many trying to halt or delay it either." [36] As Superintendent Fischer concluded, the plan had succeeded because the school board was unanimous and unwavering in its stand, and the move was backed by the local government and the community's leaders.

In Sturgis, Kentucky, less than 200 miles away from Louisville — where later developed one of the best desegregation programs in the nation — constituted authority did not show official courage so great as that shown at Baltimore, and violent rebellion did not suffer so decisive a defeat. There, discontented citizens sought to block with mob action what school officials had done with too little deliberation. The rebellion started when, on September 4, 1956, Negro children who had been admitted to all-white schools at Sturgis and nearby Clay appeared for assignment to class. They were turned back in each instance by jeering crowds of five hundred at Sturgis and one hundred at Clay.

In taking this step as Kentucky's first desegregated students, the Negro children were not facing a community that had been prepared for them in any way. The superintendent had merely given his approval for their enrollment. School officials had hinted that

Dunbar High School for Negroes would be closed in 1957 because of its small enrollment, and all Negro students would be integrated at Sturgis or Morganfield High Schools. However no announcement of this was ever made. Back of the plan was no history of planning for desegregation and no involvement of the communities.

On hearing that the Negro children had been admitted to these two formerly all-white schools, members of the White Citizens Council began writing antidesegregation letters to local newspapers and spreading "hate literature" throughout the communities. Their actions fostered a boycott that kept Negroes out of Clay High School, and they began action to secure the same results at Sturgis, where a boycott had begun but was fading. Mass meetings held by the council in Mansfield on September 15 and in Sturgis two days later rekindled a boycott of Sturgis High School by white students. Attendance dropped to about fifty whites and eight Negroes. Believing local law enforcement agencies incapable of handling the situation, Governor A. B. Chandler called in the Kentucky National Guard. Order was restored but not before the county board, responding to the pressure of lawlessness, had ousted the Negro students.[37]

Violence also won a temporary victory over weak authority in Mansfield, Texas. There bitterness followed desegregation despite the fact that San Antonio schools made the transition with relative ease. Desegregation was ordered at Mansfield in November 1955, when the Fifth District Circuit Court mandated the school board to admit students without regard to race. No organized preparation was made for the changeover, however, although the city's climate of race relations warranted it.

Relations between the races had been quite strained. The Ku Klux Klan had been active in Mansfield fifteen or twenty years before, and at least one lynching had occurred in the history of the city. A long-standing enmity had existed between a white cafe owner and a Negro operator of a barbecue stand. The white owner had been waging a vicious campaign in an effort to get school officials to prohibit white students from patronizing the Negro's stand. In addition the conditions of the Negro school had been considered deplorable by the Negro citizens. The school had no indoor toilet; no running water, no teaching materials, no flagpole on the grounds, and no school bus. Since all the city's Negro students who wanted a high school education had to go to Fort Worth to secure accommodations, the local chapter of the NAACP had brought suit in an effort to gain relief for these children. Their effort had resulted in the district court's decision. *When Negro students tried to enter a whit sch*

It was against this background that the Negro students marched when they presented themselves for proper registration at the all-white high school. There on the school grounds a crowd of about 250 disgruntled citizens had gathered to stop them if they tried to register. They carried threatening signs that read: "Nigger stay out, we don't want niggers, this is a white school"; "A dead nigger is the best nigger"; "Coons ears $1.00 a dozen." A dummy figure of a Negro was displayed hanging from the school building.

Quantities of hate material had been so well distributed that the organizers of the antidesegregation demonstration developed a "little dictatorship" where once law and order had ruled. Despite the large number of law enforcement agents on hand, the Negro children who sought to register got no protection. In fact, the superintendent who had stayed away from school during the first day of the protest, came the second day and told the crowd: "Now you guys know I'm with you, but I've got this mandate hanging over my head." The Fort Worth attorney who represented the Negro children vainly issued a plea for additional law enforcement officials. He sent a telegram to the governor, requesting his aid. He tried to get the governor by telephone without success. He telephoned the director of public safety at Austin, but the director merely said that it was his policy to respond only to requests from local law enforcement agents and that such a request had not been forthcoming. The Mansfield press did not prove to be a responsible community force. Instead of pouring water on the conflagration, it added oil. It said that the Supreme Court could not make laws, cited biblical quotations in defense of segregation, and claimed that the "separate but equal" policy works no injustice against the Negroes. The *Mansfield News,* sole newspaper of the town, wrote a scorching editorial claiming that "Our Precious American Heritage is at stake." Only ministers raised a dissenting voice against lawlessness, but they were criticized by the editor of the local paper and called "pin-headed preachers." Frightened by their exposure to lawlessness, the Negro children failed to appear at the school for a chance at registration which was due them by law. They retreated to fight another day.[38]

On January 4, 1956, District Judge Taylor ordered the desegregation of all three high schools of Anderson County, Tennessee, by the fall of that year. Consequently, twelve Negro children registered for admission to the all-white high school in compliance with this order. They did this against a background that was steadily becoming more favorable to them and with the cooperation of a constituted authority that was not to yield to the pressure of extralegalized violence.

The situation in Clinton, Tennessee, where the trouble centered, was already in transition. "Creeping integration" had already begun as a result of the economic expansion of nearby Oak Ridge, where Negro professionals were being employed. A Negro had been elected to the city council there; the public swimming pools had been desegregated; and, in the light of the Court's decision, the junior and senior high schools had been open to all races. There had been no high school for Negroes in the county prior to this time, and Negro high school pupils had been compelled to travel to La Follette, 24 miles away, or to Knoxville, which was 15 miles distant.

Nevertheless, the Anderson County Federation for Constitutional Government responded to the desegregation move by circulating petitions in protest against the change. Its members filed an injunction suit, demanding that the state cut off funds to Clinton High and restrain the county officials from desegregating the school. They invited others of the county to join them in working toward "an orderly solution to the problem." But on August 25, several days before the opening of school, Frederick John Kasper, twenty-six-year-old executive secretary of the Seaboard White Citizens Council, arrived in Clinton and began gathering support for a picket line against desegregating the school. He made house-to-house visits, talked with members of the Anderson County Federation, and made speeches before mass gatherings. Agencies of law enforcement, accepting desegregation as their duty, met with Kasper and tried to persuade him to leave town. This failing, the agitator was arrested for inciting to riot. Although he succeeded in stimulating even greater demonstrations after his release from jail, lawlessness was controlled by the Tennessee National Guard. School enrollment returned to normal, and the Negro children enrolled in school as the Court had intended.[39]

It was at Little Rock, Arkansas, however, that the national government exercised its greatest force against violent reactions to desegregation, by taking decisive steps in support of a local school board that had begun to weaken.

After more than two years of careful planning and the development of a Court-accepted scheme for desegregation, Little Rock's school board experienced serious trouble. On September 3, 1956, its school desegregation program was blocked temporarily by troops of the Arkansas National Guard whom Governor Orval Faubus had prematurely ordered into action for the purpose of restoring a peace that had not been broken. On the evening before the schools were to open, these troops appeared at Little Rock Central High School and surrounded it. Governor Faubus, speaking on radio and television an hour later, said the guardsmen were there to maintain or restore peace and good order; that they were not to act as segregationists or integrationists; that peace and good order would not be possible "if forcible integration" were carried out; that the schools "must be operated on the same basis as they have operated in the past."

The school board, completely surprised by this action, responded by an attempt to gain time. It issued a statement which in effect recognized the Court's order, announced the presence of troops, and asked the Negro students not to try to enter the school the following morning. The ten Negro students who had registered in the all-white Central High School complied with this request. None of them went to school on the opening day. In the afternoon, the school board sought directions from the Federal court as to what it should do. Federal Judge Ronald N. Davis, who was serving the Little Rock District temporarily, ordered the board to go ahead with the desegregation schedule. He said he was taking the governor at his word — that the troops were there "to preserve peace and not to act as segregationists or integrationists." Nine Negro students appeared on the second day of school, but the troops turned them away. After refusing the school board's second plea, which asked, this time, that the desegregation plan be delayed indefinitely, Judge Davis ordered injunction proceedings against Governor Faubus, Major General Sherman T. Clinger, and Lt. Col. Morrison E. Johnson — all connected with the presence of the National Guard at Central High School. While a Faubus conference with President Eisenhower was breaking down, Judge Davis was hearing and ruling on the injunction proceedings which he had ordered. A temporary injunction against interference with the court desegregation order by Governor Faubus or the National Guard was promptly granted, and the governor ordered removal of the guardsmen three hours later.

In this collision between a state's chief executive and Federal authority, the American people had won. Despite the presence of a crowd of approximately 1,000 people, who had assembled before the school on the following Monday morning, the Negro children did enter the school. Once again, however, the school board registered fear and removed the Negro students. But President Eisenhower, after an appeal to the interfering crowd, ordered the Arkansas National Guard into Federal service along with a part of the 101st Airborne Division. Their orders were simple. They were to surround the school and see that the Court's will was enforced. On Wednesday morning, nine Negro boys and one girl entered the school.[40] President Eisenhower had done what his successor was to do later and in the deeper South: He had preserved the constitutional authority of the United States.

Resistance to school desegregation was most persistent in the field of legislative action, where several states, particularly those of the Deep South, attempted to avoid compliance with court orders by means of complicated administrative procedures. As James M. Nabrit, Sr., occasional attorney for the NAACP, described these procedures, they were "worded so as to make it difficult to separate pseudo-administrative difficulties from valid ones." [41]

One of the major techniques of resistance along these lines was the pupil placement law. Two years after the 1954 decree, laws of this type were passed by Alabama, Georgia, Florida, Louisiana, Mississippi, North Carolina, South Carolina, Tennessee, and Virginia. Alabama created a pupil assignment act providing that boards of education may assign pupils to schools on the basis of such factors as psychological aptitude for types of teaching and association involved, effects of the pupil's admission upon the prevailing standards of the school, and the possibility of threat or friction or disorder among pupils and others. A Florida law permitted the assignment of students to the school "for which he is best fitted." Louisiana legislation authorized local school superintendents to designate each school a student may attend. North Carolina, pioneering in this type of legislation, transferred complete authority over enrollment and assignment of pupils from the state board of education to local boards. And a South Carolina legislation not only gave local boards exclusive authority to operate any public school and to transfer pupils "so as to promote the best interest of education," but it also gave them permission to transfer pupils from one county to another without the necessity for the parent to own property in the county to which the transfer was made.

These various kinds of "resistance laws" were designed to serve three purposes: to make it necessary for Negroes to sue each school board or superintendent and thereby diffuse the impact of litigation aimed at desegregating the schools; to make it possible for desegregated schools to disappear for want of white students; and to make it possible for superintendents caught under the force of a court mandate to exclude Negro pupils from all-white schools on spurious grounds that were not susceptible to clear validation.

Another device of legal resistance was that of putting discretionary control over the purse string of public education. Georgia made it a felony for any school official — whether state, county or municipal — to spend tax money for public schools in which the races are mixed. It fixed the penalty for such a violation at two years in prison in addition to an imposed personal liability for the money expended. Provisions for cutting off state financial aid for any school which mixed the races were planted in the state's constitution before 1952. However, a constitutional amendment was ratified in 1954 to allow the general assembly to provide for grants of state, county, or municipal funds to citizens of the state for educational purposes. Louisiana gave its state board of education authority to withhold approval from any school violating the state's segregation provisions, and prohibited the granting of free textbooks and other supplies or state funds for the operation of a school lunch program to any school violating the segregation provision. The South Carolina legislature of 1955 wrote into Clarendon and Calhoun County supply bills and the general appropriation act provisions for cutting off funds to any school from which or to which a child may be transferred in compliance with a court order contrary to the assignment of the school authorities. This state also joined North Carolina in placing disciplinary pressure upon teachers. In both instances continuing contracts were eliminated. As additional means of intimidation, laws were created to allow school boards to cancel the contracts of any teachers advocating desegregation or to require teachers to sign an oath to uphold and defend the constitution and law of the state. Such laws were enacted by Georgia and North Carolina. The Texas legislature also passed a series of resistance laws, the most threatening of which was the requirement that desegregation occur where public approval by referendum was secured.

Some states, rather than comply with the desegregation order, prepared to abolish their public schools if it should become necessary. They created "readiness legislation" along these lines soon after the court decree was rendered. Mississippi amended its constitution to provide for the abolition of public schools by a two-thirds vote of both the houses of the legislature. The amendment provided that a county or school district may be empowered to abolish its schools by a majority vote of both houses. South Carolina made similar enactments. It repealed its compulsory school attendance laws and its code authorizing school boards to regulate the opening and closing of school terms. Alabama legislation permitted the state to discontinue the public schools whenever necessary to avoid friction or disorder, and allowed the state and its subdivisions to appropriate public money for the aid of private education when adequate public facilities were lacking or public operation involved the adoption of coercive policies.

While enacting laws of resistance, Mississippi was building another defense line — one, it was hoped, which would make school desegregation less desirable to Negroes. The state tabled its move toward interposition, slowed down its laws of "massive resistance," and started a program of public school equalization. It appropriated large sums of money in an attempt to bring Negro schools up to the standards enjoyed by the white. Salaries of teachers in the Negro schools were increased, new buildings were constructed, and more varied courses were offered.

Despite all the law making, these resistance patterns gradually lost their power under the force of litigation that proved them unconstitutional. During the period from 1954 to 1958, eleven states passed 145 laws in defense of the maintenance of their segregated schools. Pupil placement acts were held invalid, teacher firing laws were overthrown, voluntary segregation was ruled insufficient, and control of public education through police power was outlawed in Virginia, Tennessee, and Louisiana. Further collapse of the massive resistance movement appeared with the opening of the 1960s. The attorney general of Texas ruled unconstitutional the state's 1957 law requiring referendum approval by public school districts before desegregation could begin. And the United States Fifth Circuit Court of Appeals declared that Houston's "brother and sister rule" on pupil placement assignment was discriminatory.

Although the validity of many of these laws is still untested, the degree of their effectiveness in halting the desegregation program is currently assessable.[42] By 1961 small but definite progress had been made toward school desegregation. Of the 2,804 school districts which had Negro and white children in separate schools in 1954, approximately one third had been desegregated by this time, and 233,509 of the 927,146, or 7.3 percent of the Negro children as of early 1960, were in school with white children. Only Alabama, Mississippi, and South Carolina had managed to escape desegregation at this time.

When viewed over-all, the pace of public school desegregation in the South has been embarrassingly slow, and the Supreme Court's order that desegregation be carried out "with all deliberate speed" has come to be the most disregarded edict the high tribunal has ever handed down. Ten years after the historic decision, only 1.18 percent of the 2.9 million Negro children enrolled in schools of the Deep South were attending with white children. No child was attending a desegregated class in Mississippi prior to September 1964, and less than 600 Negro pupils in all had been admitted to formerly white schools in Alabama, Arkansas, Georgia, and South Carolina. Mississippi had Negro students registering in some of its schools for the first time in September 1964. When the six border states and the District of Columbia are added to the Southern totals, the record still shows that Negro children had not been able to derive significant benefit from the May 17 decision. Less than one in ten had been desegregated.[43]

In the border states — Delaware, Kentucky, Maryland, Missouri, Oklahoma, and West Virginia — the Court's order had meant complete desegregation in some instances, slow and token compliance in others. Approximately 55 percent of the Negro children in these states and the District of Columbia were attending schools with white pupils ten years after desegregation was ordered. Almost all or 97 percent of the total Negro enrollment in the border region were in desegregated districts. Nevertheless shifting neighborhood patterns and deteriorating downtown districts have contributed heavily to resegregation in the cities of the border states.

In complete defiance, Prince Edward County, Virginia, closed her schools in 1959 and spent $2 million to support a white students' private academy and to fight legal efforts to compel desegregation. The approximate 1,600 Negro pupils who were left without schooling finally won access to education through the "free schools" which Attorney General Robert F. Kennedy initiated three years later. Financed by $1 million in private contributions and staffed by a crack faculty of 93 teachers recruited from all parts of the United States, the "free schools" claimed, through standardized test evidence, significant success in building the national achievement rates of the Negro pupils. Nevertheless, this movement was merely a stop-gap, not at all causing the traditional public schools which Negroes had lost to be no longer necessary. In fact the Court took this position while showing its impatience with the delay so obvious in the entire school desegregation program. On May 25, 1964, Justice Hugo Black wrote this statement in his opinion directing the Prince Edward County to reopen its public schools: "The time for more 'deliberate speed' has run out, and the phrase can no longer justify denying these school children their constitutional rights to an education equal to that afforded by public schools in other parts of Virginia." [44]

It is fair to say that although there has been some small progress in desegregation in the South, the national desegregation record had hardly improved by the end of 1966. "The great majority of American children attend schools that are largely segregated," stated James S. Coleman in the summary of a comprehensive report that he and his associates submitted to the United States Office of Education.[45] More than 65 percent of all Negro pupils in the first grade in the United States were attending schools that were between 90 and 100 percent Negro. In the South most public school children were attending schools that were 100 percent white or Negro. Court orders for school desegregation now blanket the South. Only the strength of human patience remains to be broken.

A CONTINUATION OF THE COLLEGE PUSH

Although the NAACP had made substantial progress in the desegregation of public education at the higher and professional levels, there remained the job of opening public colleges to Negro undergraduate students. Progress along this line was considerably enhanced by the Supreme Court's decision of 1954.

Of course some Southern states had assumed the role of pioneer in this field even before the Court's ruling appeared. As early as 1948, the University of Arkansas admitted Edith Mae Irby to its medical school. With greater timidity, the University of Delaware moved toward desegregation when, also in 1948, it announced that Negroes would be accepted for all courses not offered at the Delaware State College for Negroes. And in 1950 the university admitted Negroes without restriction under the force of a court order. Kentucky voluntarily launched a college desegregation program during this period. The University of Kentucky began admitting Negroes to its graduate school in 1949; Paducah Junior College began accepting them under a court order in 1953; and the university's undergraduate division voluntarily opened its doors to them in 1954.

Once the ground had been broken in the higher education field, several other states picked up the desegregation trend. Louisiana State University began admitting Negroes under a court order in 1950, but three other colleges in Louisiana, acting under similar compulsion, opened their doors to Negroes in 1954. Until 1950 only the law school of the University of Maryland admitted Negro students. During the fall of that year, however, its graduate school was opened to them, but they were not admitted to the undergraduate school until four years later. A state court ordered the admission of Negroes to the University of Missouri in 1950, but all universities and colleges of the state had desegregated by 1954. Negro students enrolled in the law school of the University of North Carolina as a result of a court order, and North Carolina State College desegregated voluntarily in 1953. After the desegregation of the University of Oklahoma by court order in 1948, other public colleges of the state followed the trend. One white junior college of the state desegregated voluntarily, and nine white senior colleges followed the example in 1955. In Texas all the white junior colleges began desegregating in 1950, and by 1955, twelve of the thirty Texas colleges of this class had desegregated. Desegregation at the higher level in Virginia first occurred at the University of Virginia, where a Negro was admitted to the law school under court order in 1950. By 1953, however, desegregation had occurred voluntarily at four other public colleges of the state. West Virginia University voluntarily admitted Negroes to its graduate school as early as 1938, but all the state's eleven colleges were desegregated voluntarily in 1954.

When the 1956–1957 school year opened, desegregation on the level of higher and professional education had been almost assured. Three states had opened all their public colleges to Negroes: Kentucky, Maryland, and Oklahoma. Negroes were attending all but one of the seven colleges in Tennessee; ten of the fifteen in Missouri; and, in short, twenty-seven of the seventy-three colleges operated by other Southern states, excluding only such Deep South states as Alabama, Florida, Georgia, Mississippi, and South Carolina.[46]

By the fall of 1961, desegregation in the South's public colleges seemed only a matter of course. Of the 285 tax-supported institutions of higher learning operating in the Southern region at that time,

152 were known to be desegregated in practice or principle. There were probably other colleges willing to accept Negro students, but the racial status was unknown due to the fact that their enrollments were not kept by race or that no policy of desegregation had been announced. With the exception of the Authurine Lucy case at the University of Alabama and the James Meredith incident at the University of Mississippi, the admission of Negro students to public colleges in the South has been far less stormy than the desegregation of the public elementary and secondary schools. Also, little notice had been given to the several instances in which previously all-white private colleges were admitting Negroes. Except where court orders are required to free trustees of charter commitments against desegregation, as in the case of Tulane University of New Orleans, desegregation in private colleges progressed quietly and without praise.

The 1954 Court decision, to some degree, set desegregation to operating in reverse. Of the fifty-one original Negro colleges now operating in the United States, fifteen will accept white students. Morgan State College at Baltimore has been opened to white students since its inception in 1867, but its trustees reiterated a desegregation policy in 1954 after the Supreme Court had spoken in the instance of the public school cases. Probably the most dramatic instance of this "two-way passage" may be found in the cases of West Virginia State College, Lincoln University at Missouri, and Texas Southern University at Houston. Ever since May 18, 1954, when a white student called the registrar of West Virginia State College saying that he would like to enroll there, and inquiring if this was permissible in the light of the Court's ruling of the previous day, this college at Institute has been desegregated. More than one thousand white students registered there in the fall of 1957.[47] Approximately one-half of the students enrolled at Lincoln University are white and, like West Virginia State College, the institution runs a high probability of shifting to a predominantly white college in the near future. The instance of Texas Southern University is made dramatically significant not because of its number of white students — indeed the number is relatively small — but because it is the only formerly all-Negro college in Texas that is

264

desegregated; the only one of all the state's colleges with a desegregated faculty;* and probably the only institution of higher learning in the nation before which white students demonstrated for admission on the ground that their constitutional rights were being violated. The demonstration was moot, however, for the board of directors of Texas Southern University had desegregated the institution the year before. Wherever student desegregation has occurred in previously all-Negro colleges, faculty desegregation has accompanied it.

When the 1963–1964 school year ended, Negro Americans had spent approximately thirty years in a campaign of sustained court litigations, seeking to secure school desegregation and equal protection of their constitutional rights. Accepting the United States Constitution seriously, they had utilized established institutional channels in pursuit of relief. The relief had come much more in words than in deeds, and the Negroes had begun to turn their faith more toward direct action and noninstitutionalized ways of attaining in fact what the courts had decreed.

* The University of Texas has since employed its first Negro as a full-time faculty member.

X · THE MOVE
TO CHANGE
A SOCIAL ORDER

The legal action movement, though successful in part, did not effect the kind of changes for which the Negroes had hoped when they launched it. Like the great experiment, the national policies that were instituted as a result of its force conflicted with popular sentiment, generated even deeper needs within the Negro population, and made additional national reforms in the area of race relations necessary.

Of course the court decisions established school desegregation as a legal function of our political democracy, and even carried hope for the elimination of racial discrimination in other areas. At least on paper, the Negroes had made three basic gains. The desegregation of their schools had been decreed, promising opportunities for their children to move out of the great detour and into the roadway that is the main artery of American education. A free and unrestricted ballot for them had been accepted as a working American commitment, promising them some participation in the determination of the nation's destiny through political processes. The national government had accepted as a normative fact the right of every citizen to buy property from any owner who was willing to sell and had thereby freed the Negroes from the residential limitations formerly ensured by the restrictive covenants.

But once again, changes in the intended objectives of the national society carried their own set of serious conflicts. They instituted major conversions in our political democracy that were radically inconsistent with the system of moral democracy by which the public tended to guide its behavior. The American dilemma, as Gunnar Myrdal had described it,* was still with us. Old constitutional provisions that guaranteed civil liberties for all Americans had been more strongly confirmed, particularly as they applied to Negro Americans, but apparently, the democratic values as related to this element of our population had not been internalized by the majority of the American people.

Consequently, failure of this internalization resulted in forms of public resistance that rendered the changes in political democracy virtually inoperative. What this really meant was that the Negroes had won the battle but not the spoils. Segregated schools had been declared illegal, but nine out of every ten Negro school children were still studying in racially separated classes. States of the Deep South, continuing their massive resistance to the Court's decree, had relatively no Negro children attending formerly white schools, and even the border states, where compliance had been so pronounced, were gradually being pushed back into their old ways by the force of shifting populations. *De facto* segregation was taking up where *de jure* segregation had left off.

In the meantime, other areas in which racial segregation was traditional were apparently as securely segregated as before the legal victories were won. The ring of disfranchisement which the South had thrown around its Negro citizens was just as tight as before, especially in those states where resistance to school desegregation was strongest; and there was no hope of changing the situation through established political processes. Employment opportunities for Negroes had been improved somewhat by various Presidential orders related to the expenditure of government funds, but the progress along these lines was not spectacular.[1] The relative position of the race in the national occupational structure had changed little since 1940,[2] and it had become apparent that, given no radical improvement, relative economic stagnation would become the Negro's fate. Even though restrictive covenants had been broken through the legal action program, and Presidential orders against discrimi-

* This is the continuing conflict between the values prescribed in the "American creed," and those operative in individual and group living; see Gunnar Myrdal, *An American Dilemma* (New York: Harper and Brothers, 1944).

267

nation in federally aided housing had been issued,[3] the Negro was still not able to escape from the ghetto.[4] Shifting populations had been causing the South's Black Belt to grow lighter, but the survival of urban ghettos had been inherent in this trend. The Negro's settlement in other places had merely meant the exchange of smaller black ghettos for even larger ones.

As with the failure of the great experiment, many Negroes were disappointed, especially those composing the higher social classes or who were attending the Negro colleges. The disappointment was a bitter one, having derived from a very crucial area of the Negro's relations with instituted governmental authority. His confidence in the power of court decisions had been so strong that he had given little or no thought to the possibility that these decisions would encounter such public resistance to their enforcement as to render them meaningless. Prolonged resistance undermined this confidence and installed a weak image of the power of American law enforcement. For the first time in our history the Negro American saw the national government as an agency too weak to enforce the decrees of its own courts. The disappointing experience so shaped the minds of Negroes that the slightest threat to their aspirations, when properly dramatized, could trigger them into collective action.

The conditions that fostered their discontent also helped make possible the success of the campaign they eventually launched. Court decrees and the administrative actions had removed almost completely any legal question about the civil rights of Negroes. Although enforcement had lagged seriously behind court action, it had been made clear to the public that Negroes had rights that the public was bound to respect. The uninhibited leadership that had served the race so well in both its drive for equality and in its bid for desegregation was still available. Ministers, doctors, lawyers, proprietors, and other professionals produced by the Negro college and the segregated community had continued to enjoy protective insulation against white reprisals. They were still free to give directions and undisguised support to those who chose to involve themselves in open rebellion against the hard core of America's traditional caste system.

The Move to Change a Social Order

Some success at massive demonstrations was already behind them and served to prepare them for a bigger fight. Late in 1955 they had launched and won an organized boycott in hostile rebellion against racial discrimination on city buses in Montgomery, Alabama. The movement had projected Martin Luther King into a leadership role never before played by a Negro American and had introduced a strategy of nonviolent coercion never before employed on so large a scale in the Deep South.

The leadership had supplied a brilliant example. It had been produced by the Negro college and was protected against white reprisals by the economy of the Negro community. Du Bois, who started the earlier thrust, had studied at Fisk University; King, who started the latter, had been trained at Morehouse College. Du Bois had secured the doctorate from Harvard; King had received his professional training at Crozer Theological Seminary and his doctorate at Boston University. Du Bois had been a professor in a privately endowed Negro college; King was the pastor of a Negro church. Despite these parallels, however, their leadership had served different purposes. One had started a movement that led to litigation in the courts; the other had inspired a set of rebellious tactics that led to demonstrations in the streets. Each had come to see his mission from the vantage point of his own day: for Du Bois, it was "The Dusk of Dawn"; for King, it was "The Stride toward Freedom." If any comparison of their respective commitments is ever made, one must conclude that King's mission was by far the more dangerous. It called for taking a nonviolent course in the face of great hostility.

And so about one decade after they had won their favorable decision in the famous school cases, and school desegregation had been instituted as a national though inoperative policy, the Negroes responded to their disillusionment by launching a type of direct action movement that went beyond the Montgomery boycott in its rebellious intent. They took up action aimed at changing the entire American social order; they aimed to erase completely all institutionalized forms of racial discrimination from our national society. There was a desperation about this action. They were to risk all for which they had fought; they were to leave little ground

269

for compromise. They started what was to be known as the "Negro Revolt"; they were to achieve what some would call the "Second American Revolution."

THE SIT-INS FROM COLLEGE

Against this background of rising discontent and exemplary leadership, the first great protest to open the new movement got underway. It sprang spontaneously from the ingenuity of Negro college students who, in addition to having been influenced by the success of King's nonviolent boycott, had directly experienced the inconveniences of persistent delays in the implementation of the desegregation orders. Slowly and clearly the threatening possibility that complete desegregation would not come during their lifetime became apparent. Through learning they had felt, and justly so in many cases, that they had been filled to overflowing. As one demonstrator later explained, they were "all dressed up with an AB degree and nowhere to go." *

And so in the winter of 1960 the movement that was to be known over all the civilized world as the "sit-in" was started. Four Negro students, freshmen at North Carolina's Agricultural and Technical College of Greensboro, walked into Woolworth's five and ten cent store and sat down at its all-white lunch counter for service. When requested to leave, they, like Mrs. Rosa Parks in the Montgomery case, chose to stay. The manager closed his counter but the students remained and studied as they sat. Their actions were merely exploratory if not completely impulsive. In trying to explain what later became a national movement, David Richmond, one of the original four, gave this report: "For about a week we fellows sat around the A. and T. campus, where we were in school, talking about the integration movement. And we decided we ought to go down to Woolworth's and see what would happen." Their discussions apparently caught on with the other students who told reporters they had been ready to do something like that for a long time.

* As reported to Lane Kerr, staff reporter of the *Greensboro Daily News,* 1960.

The explorations begun at Greensboro spread to cities within commuting distance of a dozen North Carolina colleges and then to cities across the nation. It soon became the voice of protest of the nation's Negro college students.

Within one week after the movement first began, the attack had spread over all of North Carolina; it included students at High Point, Winston-Salem, Durham, Charlotte, Raleigh, Fayetteville, and Elizabeth City. It had reached every Southern state except Mississippi by the end of the year. The traffic was extremely heavy. A group of 100 students marched upon nine lunch counters in Tampa, Florida, and demanded service. Atlanta, home of some of the best of the Negro colleges, witnessed the daily trudge of hundreds of students who had long viewed the city with the ambivalent emotions of love and hate. Hardly did a single Negro college fail to supply students for this campaign. Even colleges in Mississippi joined in the march in 1961, and white students, North and South, participated or sent funds to assist in the payment of bail bonds for those who were arrested. When the sit-in campaign subsided, some 70,000 students in twenty states across the nation had participated in the rebellion.

As members of the power structure of almost every Southern city were soon to learn, the students were not playing. They efficiently involved the adult element of the Negro communities as sources of support, gathered their moral courage, and coordinated their strategy as if they were in combat against a hostile military force.

Members of the Negro professional and proprietary classes backed every move the students made. Presidents of the colleges they attended, with only a few exceptions, tolerated the inconveniences in school operation which the movement caused; they failed to yield to pressure from white people and took a new look at the degree of maturity shown by the youngsters they watched. Negro consumers, whose purchasing power had long stood as dependable sources of income for the many white businesses they patronized, religiously practiced "economic withdrawal," and dealt the white community a telling blow in payment for the discrimination it had allowed to exist. This kind of economic boycott, launched at Nashville under the leadership of Professor Vivian Henderson, played an important part in forcing concessions for the students who held protests in that city. Negro leaders and organizations gave even greater support in the form of financial assistance. Attorneys had to be retained, bails had to be posted, and fines had to be paid. The NAACP, Congress of Racial Equality (CORE), civic clubs, and just plain people shouldered these obligations and thereby gave the students a feeling of security that could not have come any other way.

Individually, however, the students had accepted the possible consequences of personal harm. They had reinforced their nerves with self-discipline. They had been well schooled by the instructions in nonviolent tactics that King personally gave them and by the realistic practice sessions in learning to take personal abuse to which Len Holt of CORE had exposed them.[5] These instructions served the students well, for before one month of the campaign had passed, 1,300 of them had been arrested.[6] Indeed they were jailed, over 4,000 of them in all. They were jailed so much that to be arrested was an honor. They were afraid, but not for long. Signs of their collective strength gave them greater courage. When asked about fear, one young participant replied, "I was afraid at first, but after a while, I knew I would never be afraid any more." The Negroes had apparently broken through a barrier of fear that had blocked their rebellion since the slave insurrection of Nat Turner.

The degree to which these college students were dedicated to the objectives of the sit-in protests is also indicated by the care with which they organized their activities. Students representing eight Southern states convened at Raleigh in the spring of 1960 to coordinate their campaign and give it greater direction.[7] The Student Nonviolent Coordinating Committee, later to be called SNCC, was born at that time. But C. Eric Lincoln's case study of the operation of the movement at Atlanta gives us the clearest picture of the students' ways of protest.[8]

The Atlanta attack was opened with fair warning. It was initiated through a full-page advertisement in the city's morning and afternoon papers. The students appealed for human rights, made clear the rights they wanted for themselves, expressed their impatience, and announced their intentions of using "every legal and nonviolent means" at their disposal to secure their full citizenship rights "as members of this great Democracy." They skirmished in the spring, but when the colleges opened in mid-September, introduced what came to be known as their "Fall Campaign." They negotiated. This failing, they created a regimental organization modeled after that of a military unit in combat. The general staff, having concluded its deliberations, selected a corps of pickets on the basis of class schedules and the nature of the day's objectives. Pickets, later called "picketeers" by the students, were assigned by the Deputy Commander to a downtown district identified on a large map which was their guide. An area commander was placed in charge of each district and was held responsible for directing the picketeers under his command. Assignments called for three kinds of roles: picketeers, sit-ins, and a flying squad called "sit-and-runs." The role of the latter corps was that of closing lunch counters by merely putting in an appearance and requesting service. When the merchant chose to close his counter rather than serve Negroes, the sit-and-runs were expected to move to another target and start the process all over again. All attacks were synchronized through field commanders who kept in constant contact with each other by way of short-wave radio sets handled by students who were licensed operators. Stand-bys, a selected squad, served as replacements. They spotted trouble and communicated the information to the mobile radio units that relayed the data to headquarters, which the students called "The Ramparts."

This is the kind of organization that broke the South's resistance to desegregation in many areas of public accommodation long before the 1964 Civil Rights Bill was passed. These demonstrations effected more changes in the balance of race relations in the South than all the litigation that Negroes had carried through the courts since the opening of the century. Their effect would not have been nearly so pronounced, however, had not the NAACP, through its litigations, secured some important judgments and inspired some genuine support from law-abiding American citizens. On March 7, less than one month after the demonstrations had moved out of Greensboro, six Negro college students were served without incident at drugstore lunch counters in Salisbury and at a store in Winston-Salem. San Antonio, Texas, desegregated its lunch counters on

March 16. A large department store in Charleston, West Virginia, desegregated its counters after two years of boycott and demonstrations conducted by the students of West Virginia State College. Quickly and slowly the barriers fell before the onslaught of this mass of Negro college students. According to a report released late in 1961 by the Southern Regional Council, sit-in demonstrations had produced desegregation in 93 cities of 10 Southern states by that time. The Deep South was not cracked, but the students had succeeded in effecting some changes in Georgia by the middle of that year. And there were fringe benefits that resulted from the movement. Communities were forced to look more realistically at their race problem, interracial committees were put to work, and, in some instances, institutions like hotels and playgrounds were desegregated under voluntary plans. When the sit-ins subsided, the way for desegregating public facilities in the United States had been considerably eased.

However, there were other kinds of results that loomed with equal importance. There was the psychological impact of the sit-ins on the minds of white people, and the corresponding change in Negro-imagery that resulted. White people were compelled to see the Negro (whom many thought they had always known) in a new light. They were shocked at what they found. A white Houston heckler, on the occasion of the Texas Southern University student sit-in campaign, told a television news reporter, "After all we've done to try to educate them, this is what they do to us." Members of the white power structure suddenly found themselves sitting at the bargaining table, negotiating with Negro students whose parents they were wont to call "boys" and "girls." These were the whites who were first to know that a revolution had come to the South.

ARMY OF THE DISCONTENTED

Ordinarily collective behavior is short-run. It tends to die after the limited goals it seeks to reach are either reached or aborted, but this did not prove to be true in the Southern case. The rebellious practices established through the Montgomery bus boycott

and the sit-ins pushed the protest movement nearer institutionalization by inspiring a complex of organizations which came to be
a kind of army of the discontented. The Southern Christian Leadership Conference (SCLC) was created to perpetuate the momentum
gained at Montgomery; CORE was revitalized as an advisory and
supporting agency of the sit-ins; and SNCC was formed to give more
pointed direction to the sit-in campaign. Showing a surprising degree of mutability, these organizations managed to survive the crisis
period of rebellious incidents, to gain national recognition, and to
present themselves as the most vigorous element of the Negro's
drive for racial integration.

CORE was the first organization to give leadership in the establishment of this institutional trend. It was probably the first to
sponsor protests after the sit-ins subsided. When the student protest
movement was begun at Greensboro, CORE was a little-known
organization. It had achieved some degree of success in desegregating
housing projects and restaurants in New York and Chicago, but it
was virtually unknown in the South. It had developed some skill
and sophistication in the use of nonviolent tactics and had become
a vital part of the sit-in movement incidental to a frantic call for
help sent to James Farmer, its national director, by Dr. George
Simpkins, President of the Greensboro branch of the NAACP, when
the students started protesting there.

But CORE remained vital. It intensified the use of nonviolent
tactics through its aggressive project which came to be known as
"The Freedom Rides." On March 13, 1961, CORE announced its
intention of conducting freedom rides through the South, and later
wrote President Kennedy to this effect, requesting Federal protection for those who were to participate in the project. The Supreme Court, in the case of *Boyton v. Commonwealth of Virginia,*
had just ruled that discrimination against interstate travelers in
bus terminal restaurants to be illegal. The purpose of the rides was
to test this ruling. The freedom rides started from Washington,
D.C., on May 4, after three days of training under the leadership of
CORE's national director who had been three months preparing for
the risky undertaking.

The story of the rides has been fully told,[9] though there may be need to recall that the riders were not of local origin and that they made a significant impact upon the American conscience. They were made up of groups of whites and Negroes who entered Southern cities by bus and sought service at terminal restaurants in racially mixed parties. Their travel route carried them through practically every Southern state, and their reception was almost as varied. According to the schedule that Louis E. Lomax cites, the riders met their first dispute at the Trailways terminal in Danville, Virginia, but this was settled quickly. One rider was arrested at the Union Bus terminal in Rock Hill, North Carolina, and one at the Trailways terminal in Atlanta. Riders on a Greyhound bus, traveling to Birmingham, were met by a mob in Anniston; the passengers were blocked from getting off; an incendiary device set the bus on fire, and 12 passengers had to be hospitalized before the group moved to Birmingham, where it encountered its most threatening resistance. Conditions became so disturbing in Montgomery that Governor John Patterson proclaimed martial law in that city on May 21, 1961. But three days later, Martin Luther King and his associate, James Lawson, joined the movement, giving riders further instruction in the philosophy and techniques of nonviolent action.

Including ministers, college students, and leaders of organizations, the freedom riders fanned out to touch many other Southern cities. They were outsiders invading the South in defiance of its long-standing tradition of keeping the races separated. Their activities were widely publicized through the various mass media, and, particularly as a result of television, the entire world could see the South's system of segregation at its worst — at the point of unprovoked brutality. The marches that were begun at Birmingham under King's leadership helped considerably to focus world attention upon the most brutal aspects of the American race problem.

What purpose did these demonstrations serve? King gave the spiritual answer in his letter from a Birmingham jail in response to eight of Alabama's top white religious leaders who had issued a formal statement calling the Birmingham demonstrations unwise and untimely. In his answer, King pressed one basic and inescapable historical truth: "Oppressed people cannot remain oppressed forever. The urge for freedom will eventually come." [10]

There is another answer, more brutal in its sociological impli-
cations. The various protest movements tended to strike differently
the minds of scholars who attempted to assess their effectiveness.
Some felt, and with some evidence behind them, that the effectiveness had been overemphasized; they thought that the social order
was tending to settle back to normal. Others, obviously influenced
by the dramatic methods employed, hailed the movements as creators
of the social revolution it really was. However, the viewpoints of
both schools seem to have merit. The South had changed but had
not become what it was to be. The Negroes had been able to find
a weapon from which the South tended systematically to retreat.
They could dramatize the evils of the race problems for the nation
and the world; they could expose bigotry and impose public ridi-
cule upon a bigoted class. They still have the army capable of holding and consolidating this ground. Though individuals come and
go, the organizations of protest seem to remain with us. King's
SCLC, Farmer's CORE, or the students' SNCC are all quite capable
of persisting through time and transcending locality. They are now
special interest rather than locality groups. CORE has been known
to be operating in several different places on the same day in response to different occasions of protest. It has acted in the capacity
of a trouble shooter. On Tuesday, August 11, 1964, Dallas, Texas,
Negroes filed a suit in the Federal court, asking for complete desegregation in the city's schools. The Reverend Earl Allen, local
minister and regional director of CORE, made this significant statement of alternative in case the court failed to rule favorably in acting upon their suit: "We will have no alternative but to send for
outside resources of civil rights groups and leaders." [11] The Southern voter registration project in which SNCC participated so heavily
included only a few students who had sit-in experiences and even
less who actually lived in the South. Drawing upon the American
right to protest, Negroes had made nonviolent rebellion a noble
cause. The old order seemed bound to yield under this pressure.

XI · EPILOGUE: NEW CONFLICTS AND THE NEW CHALLENGE

This book has been designed to give an historical explanation for the great changes we are now experiencing in American race relations. In particular, we have tried to trace the development of educational opportunities for Negro Americans in the South and to show how these opportunities became the means by which the race gained greater personal emancipation.

We have shown how members of the Negro race were able to move, through a hidden passage in the South, from the status of slave to that of freedman during the period from 1619 to 1863; from freedman to segregated citizen from 1863 to 1954; and, finally, to desegregated citizen ten years after the Supreme Court's historic decision.

In closing this phase of the evolutionary process, the Civil Rights Act of 1964 was meant to be the last legislation necessary in this area. It appears that this legislation will hold, leaving the Negro American's desegregated life to go unchallenged. Millions of Americans now in their teens are expected to grow up accepting desegregation as an established institutional practice. They have really known little other than this. They have never known an America in which segregation exists as a legal prescription or a permissive custom. Millions who are older, though having experienced this racial limitation upon our citizenship, have also begun to accept the change. Both groups seem to have internalized our democratic values, thereby combining their influence to build a greater moral support for our political democracy.

Epilogue: New Conflicts and the New Challenge

Although we stop our discourse at this point, the dialectic quality of the evolutionary process continues to operate. The process cannot stop at the desegregated station because this accommodation, carrying its own conflicts, contradicts its own existence and inhibits its own operation as a strong societal force. Already, new conflicts in American race relations are growing out of desegregation; new needs are being formed; and we are now facing the challenge of creating a new kind of interracial accommodation. It seems that this new stage must be one of racial integration, a process of socialization that will render the Negro American psychologically capable of becoming a functional and integral part of the larger society.* Though desegregation has been instituted by legislation, racial integration must come about by socialization. This is a critical command, for the survival of desegregation is dependent upon racial integration. Without the latter, the former cannot long endure.

A process of "withdrawal to resegregation" has been growing out of desegregation, and it is creating new needs which only racial integration can accommodate. The Negro's movement toward the status of desegregated citizen could not be matched by corresponding growth in individual achievement within the race itself. Negro education was strong enough to produce leaders who successfully directed the course of desegregation, but was too weak to produce students who, when placed within the mainstream of American life and education, would show no effect of having grown up outside of it. One of the subtle ironies of our day is the fact that the privileges that desegregation brings to Negroes expose their inadequacies with such force as to drive them back into the protection and security of the segregated world they have always known. Sometimes the force is compulsory; at other times it is voluntary. But in each instance it brings about what we choose to call "withdrawal to resegregation." Pending no basic change in his preparation, it seems safe to predict that the Negro American's voluntary or compulsory withdrawal from the desegregated opportunities now open to him

---

* The concept of integration employed here also implies that the socialization process must be broad enough to develop popular acceptance of the Negro American as an integrated citizen.

will keep many areas of American life segregated in fact for a long time to come.

One can see the withdrawal at work in strategic areas where desegregation has been most distinct and clearly defined. Immediately after the pupils were placed in racially mixed classes, teachers and school officials began to experience the shocking realization that the Supreme Court was right after all, that years of unequal educational opportunities at both the formal and informal levels had severely blocked the development of Negro children.[1] Of course many of these children have been able to withstand the shock of their transition.[2] But most to whom desegregated opportunities have come, feeling their own inadequacies, either return to the protection of their former schools or never take advantage of the privilege at all. Not all the Negro children who are still in a segregated school are there by compulsion. All too many are there because of the feeling of protection and security it brings.

This pattern of withdrawal operates to contradict the desegregation process with even greater force at the college level where Negro high school graduates must meet ever rising standards of college admissions like all other college-bound youths. The potentials of this operation were first revealed during the 1953–1954 school year, when, aided by a grant from the Fund for the Advancement of Education, the National Scholarship Service and Fund for Negro Students, called NSSFNS, began its Southern talent search among the seniors of 81 segregated high schools of the region's 45 leading cities.[3] During that year and the year that followed, 3,178 seniors who represented the upper 10 percent of the classes of these schools were examined through a modified version of the Scholastic Aptitude Test of the College Entrance Examination Board. In the judgment of NSSFNS, "the results were amazingly good, considering the start from scratch." More than half the seniors made at least the minimum qualifying score set by the fund as the lowest possible indicator of success in college.[4] The qualifying score was set at 600 (combined verbal and mathematical sections) with the verbal section given double weight. When judged against the standard rate of all public school boys and girls, however, the 1,461 Negro students tested in May 1953 averaged below the 78th percentile in verbal aptitude and the 66th in mathematical.[5]

Of greatest importance is the amount of withdrawal from desegregation exhibited by these Negro high school graduates. Although 700 of the early group were accepted by interracial colleges, only 399 of them completed their applications for admission. They refused desegregation to this degree despite the fact that NSSFNS would have helped to finance their schooling at the racially mixed colleges.

This early experience was merely a kind of straw in the wind, a warning that the lag between desegregation and integration would be of significant magnitude. In the fall of 1961, there were 67,828 Negro students registered at colleges located in seventeen Southern states, but only 5,388 of these had enrolled at predominantly white colleges. Obviously some of this lag was due to inability to meet admissions standards. A goodly portion, however, was due to an unwillingness to be lonely, a fear of being unable to meet or maintain academic standards, and the general insecurity that accompanies the thought of having to shift from familiar to unfamiliar cultural standards. The trend over the last decade has shown a significant increase in the number of Negro high school graduates who enter mixed colleges and stay there. Nevertheless the Negro college continues to be the main source of higher education for the race.

The operation of the withdrawal process can be expected to go on outside the schools. It threatens to overflow into the area of employment where the growth of equal job opportunities is already placing pressure upon the Negro's technically trained labor supply. In the fall of 1955, Vice President Richard Nixon called fifty-five key businessmen to Washington to discuss job equalization. It was the candid opinion of these men that the problem of Negro workers, even at that time, was no longer one of getting hired; it was one of getting promoted. They urged Negroes to equip themselves for the better jobs that were beginning to open before them.[6] Robert Smuts, Research Associate for Columbia University's program in the Conservation of Human Resources, had warned Negroes about this possible difficulty six years before. "Negroes will not be able to take advantage of these opportunities," he had said, "unless they improve their preparation for work." [7] The pressure had become considerably more visible by 1963. Hampton McKinney, acting director of the Department of Employment for the Chicago Urban League, made this lament in his report to the *Christian Century,* of April 10, 1963: "Unless they can accept these new openings, the task of securing equal job opportunities for Negroes will become more difficult." [8]

Certainly it is easy to understand this difficulty. Naturally, a labor force whose employment opportunities have been as limited as those previously available to Negroes cannot be expected to have a ready-trained and highly motivated group of workers all prepared to take advantage of new opportunities that burst almost suddenly before them. But this fact merely creates the necessity for compulsory withdrawal from desegregated employment. It will not alter one bit the occupational distribution of Negro workers that years of segregation have shaped.

Now we face a new kind of withdrawal to resegregation — one that is more deliberate in its methods and more opposed to the accommodation of racial integration that is so necessary. The success of national legislation in raising the aspiration of Negroes and its failure in providing for the realization of these hopes and needs may be considered a cause. The "open occupancy" phase of President Lyndon B. Johnson's proposed Civil Rights Bill of 1966 failed to gain congressional approval, and the debates of that year added little to prevent the continuation and enlargement of black ghettos that had been encouraged by the refusal of real estate agents or individual owners to sell or rent to Negroes who sought residence in white-occupied areas. Also, the Voting Rights Act passed in 1965 and the voter registration program that had been pushed so diligently by civil rights leaders who operated in the area of Selma, Alabama, and other regions of the Deep South that year, failed to place enough sympathetic voters at the polls to stem a segregationist tide that had not quite receded. Although, in the 1966 elections, the program succeeded in placing some Negro candidates in public offices not held by members of the race since Reconstruction, it could not prevent the reelection of segregationist George Wallace to the governorship of Alabama — a feat accomplished through a pretense election of his wife, Lurline, to the same office; neither could it prevent the election of Lester Maddox, another segregationist, to the governorship of Georgia.

It was after this that racial discontent, born of frustration, flared anew. A movement known as "black power" developed under the leadership of Stokely Carmichael, national chairman of SNCC, and Floyd B. McKissick, national director of CORE. Launched by a splinter element of the civil rights group, the movement spread to disconcert a large portion of the American public who had thought that the race problem was nearing its solution.

The "black power" movement was a withdrawal to resegregation. As Dr. Robert Coles has properly interpreted, it was a separatist movement that rejected racial integration as an immediate goal and aimed to push the Negroes into withdrawal — into consolidation along political and economic lines   until, having gained such independence, they "will exert their new presence as the new form of power it will in fact turn out to be." [9] In his interview of June 17, Carmichael, himself, emphasized this interpretation. He insisted, "I'm not anti-white." Comparing his strategy for Negroes with that used by other ethnic groups, he added, "We're going to elect sheriffs . . . where we're in the majority." [10] Through its dramatic interpretation by mass media, however, "black power" came to mean "black supremacy" and to function as a force that alienated a large number of Americans who had become friends of the civil rights movement. As the power of this newly inherited imagery developed, "black power" leaders gradually inserted tones of violence into the speeches they made and the interviews they granted.

Though probably not intended, the "black power" movement was a withdrawal from desegregation that Negro Americans could little afford. It presupposes a "black economy" that is not feasible in our existing economic order, and it assumes, for a minority, a "black-bloc-vote" that will not consolidate a white majority against it. But even more, it moves in the face of recent research in American education that shows that Negro children achieve best where they have a greater variety of peer aspirations from which to choose; that "the inequalities imposed on children by their home, neighborhood, and peer environment are carried along to become the inequalities with which they confront adult life at the end of school." [11] Notwithstanding the criticisms that have been directed against the Coleman study,[12] separatism, as did segregation, would allow the Negro child to grow up outside of a setting within which he must eventually make a life.

We have used education, employment, and "black power" to illustrate the new conflicts growing out of desegregation because these aspects of our national life are so closely connected. We could, however, show the operation of withdrawal in the use of public facilities now desegregated or even in federally aided housing which has begun to open for Negroes in the South. The conflict is clear. In its present form desegregation inspires a force that becomes its own barrier. If the barrier is to be removed and the evolutionary cycle is to be freed to spiral upward to racial integration, the Negro American must be creative in developing methods by which he can shed the "garment of race" he so unwillingly wears. It may be that this is what Charles Silberman calls "Self-Improvement." [13]

Some methods have already been developed, but they are at best remedial. They try to glean some degree of adequacy from the debris left by previous years of cultural isolation and deprivation but only serve in part the big job in socialization that must be done.

One class of these methods is built around programs aimed at raising the standards of those colleges that are still all-Negro. Negro educators, recognizing the need for change in the colleges they administer, made their first step toward the improvement of their institutions by taking a new look at their purposes. This effort came in 1957 on the occasion of the 125th anniversary of the American Baptist Home Mission Society. On November 12, 1957, a convocation of these educators was held at Virginia Union University in honor of this occasion. The utilization of this convocation to discuss new purposes was altogether logical. The society had dedicated long years of service to the development and support of colleges for Negro youths, and through this service it had made an indirect but significant contribution to the advancement of the race toward the status of desegregated citizenship. However, the educators composing the convocation did not choose to enjoy the luxury of recalling a glorious past. They chose, instead, to turn their attention to the future prospects of their kind of college and the problem of making it an acceptable and integral part of the general scheme of American higher education.

Despite the warning of some educators that the Negro student, no less than the white, must be prepared to live and compete as a mature and responsible member of a free society,[14] there was concurrence in the feeling that the Negro college could continue as before to cater to those Negroes who would attend them and that its function would continue to be remedial. This, too, was a psychology of withdrawal whose effect would keep the quality of many of their graduates below the national average. That such an effect was already operative was apparent in the evidence presented by S. M. Nabrit, who had experienced a chance to observe the inadequacies of Negro college graduates as they competed with those of white colleges for fellowship grants.[15]

Probably the best of these remedial programs is the scheme that *Time* designated as "The Adopt-a-School Plan." Encouraged by the American Council on Education and supported by foundation grants, more than a dozen Northern colleges have been exchanging faculty members and students with Southern partners. These are the kinds of partnerships that have been reported: California's Pomona has been matched with Nashville's Fisk University; Pennsylvania's Haverford and Bryn Mawr with North Carolina's Livingstone College; Cornell with Virginia's Hampton Institute; the University of Michigan with Alabama's Tuskegee; Rhode Island's Brown University with Mississippi's Tougaloo College; and the University of Wisconsin with North Carolina's Agricultural and Technical College, its State College for Negroes, and Texas Southern University at Houston.[16] The aim is simple: to allow the Negro institutions and their students to see and participate in the operation and function of larger institutions in the hope that many qualities of the larger and more mature ones will be transferred to the smaller and less mature.

Despite the effectiveness of such movements as these, they are at best remedial and do little in the area of prevention. As far as the Adopt-a-School Plan is concerned, though better than some, it is a method that comes too late and touches too few. Not very many faculty members and students of the Negro colleges are involved in the exchange, and, in many instances, they are usually the ones among the faculty and students who least need the experience. Another aspect of this program renders it inadequate to meet the needs generated by the serious conflicts which desegregation has inspired: It comes too late in the developmental history of Negro faculty members as well as their students. It is good, however, that the medicine comes at all. It is even better that it carries some remedy. It is a fact, nevertheless, that it must be repeated for each generation of young people who are still allowed to grow up inadequately under conditions that the Adopt-a-School Plan can touch only softly and indirectly.

Seeking to remove the inadequacies of high school students (many of whom are Negroes) by working at a deeper level in the developmental process is the Upward Bound program. Originated by Educational Services, Inc., and initially supported by the Carnegie Foundation as a pilot project for seventeen colleges, the program is now federally funded to the amount of $25,000,000 from the Office of Economic Opportunity and directed by the Department of Health, Education and Welfare. It is operating in some 250 colleges and universities serving poverty areas throughout the country. Its aims are three-fold: to build aspirations for a college education among high school students who have the ability to profit from college experience but lack the finances to buy the opportunity, to enrich and advance their high school development, and to help them make the transition from high school to college.[17]

The program whose orientation seems to best meet the needs generated by the conflicts inherent in desegregation is Project Head Start, which, through the leadership of Mrs. Lyndon B. Johnson and many professionals associated with child development programs, was launched at a White House meeting in February 1965. Supported by OEO, the project aims at the physical and mental development of disadvantaged children, ages three to five, in an effort to provide them with adequacy for normal public school participation. When the final grants for the project's support were made in the late spring, more than 560,000 children were enrolled in the program — in

13,400 classrooms in 2,400 communities, in all fifty states and the territories.[18]

The effects of the exposure of these children to the enrichment experiences that the project provided were phenomenal. Scientific testing showed marked improvements in the children's self-confidence, self-reliance, sense of responsibility, and ability to relate to a group. The small classes, with individual attention from experienced and interested teachers, resulted in as much as a year's progress in two months. Project Head Start, having drawn so many Negro children and their parents under its influence, had found the answer to the blocking force of Negro withdrawal. It had begun the growth of "integrated personalities" where "segregated personalities" would otherwise develop. Its limitations? It, too, does not go far enough. It leaves the child when he is still at the most critical stage of his development

Despite the limitations of these various programs, one must say that they lead in the right direction. When examined in the light of the trend toward resegregation, these programs show clearly the lack of "integrated" socialization in the Negro child but indicate that a solution is still possible. Project Head Start, apparently true to its name, does seem to give preschool children greater readiness for normal public school participation. Upward Bound, the next great personalizing thrust, picks up far later, after conditions of deprivation have eroded the Head Start effect. There is need for an interim program that will establish greater continuity after the experiences of Head Start and push the child's socialization toward the normal level now required by a society that has become desegregated. One can envision that this would be a design which, operating on a home-demonstration basis, would involve parents and children in a sustained relationship with experts in the area of child development. It would require a sustained commitment on the part of parents, and it could create an influence that would go to the heart of the critical areas of the Negro child's socialization.

But even when this continuity is established, whether by visiting parent-surrogates or others who are experts in parental counseling, the Negro child's world of social isolation must still be penetrated. Desegregation did not completely remove the black island in the white sea. Negro children who still spend the most of their lives in a black ghetto must be more widely exposed to national cultural influences. It seems that "salt and pepper" housing would do just this; it seems, too, that the next civil rights act may attack the problem of spatial isolation that Negroes still face. Whether this happens voluntarily through an instituted plan or evolves naturally, the possibility of resegregation will be permanently inhibited only when Negro Americans are socialized into the next stage — the integration of all Americans. Only then will American society be unfragmented by racial difference. Only then will the historical process that guides the relations between the races have run its benevolent course.

NOTES · INDEX

NOTES

CHAPTER I · INTRODUCTION: A PRELUDE TO CHANGE

1. *The Journal of an African Slaver 1789–1829* (Worcester, Mass.: Antiquarian Society, 1930); Nicholas Owen, *Journal of a Slave Dealer* (London: George Routledge and Sons, 1930); and Wendell Holmes Stephenson, *Isaac Franklin: Slave Trader and Planter of the Old South* (Baton Rouge, La.: Louisiana State University Press, 1938), pp. 40–41.

2. Ulrich B. Phillips, *American Negro Slavery* (New York: Appleton-Century-Crofts, 1940), pp. 361–390.

3. William D. Postel, *The Health of the Slaves on Southern Plantations* (Baton Rouge, La.: Louisiana State University Press, 1951).

4. William Massie Papers, 1838–1849, Southern Historical Collection, University of North Carolina Library.

5. Diary and Other Records of Francis Terry Leake, 1841–1862, 5 vols., Southern Historical Collection, University of North Carolina Library.

6. William B. Hesseltine, *The South in American History* (New York: Prentice-Hall, Inc., 1943), pp. 39–40.

7. Frank Tannenbaum, *Slave and Citizen* (New York: Alfred A. Knopf, Inc., 1947); Stanley M. Elkins, *Slavery: A Problem in American Institutional and Intellectual Life* (Chicago: University of Chicago Press, 1962), pp. 117, 128–133; and Roger Bastide, *Sociologie et Psychoanalyse* (Paris: Press Universitaires de France, 1950), pp. 241–243.

8. Walter Firey, "Sentiment and Symbolism as Ecological Variables," in R. W. O'Brien, C. C. Schrag, and W. T. Martin, *Readings in General Sociology* (Boston: Houghton Mifflin Company, 1964), pp. 103–108.

9. For vivid reminiscences concerning this aspect of early Southern life, see the John Hampden Hill Papers, 1883 (?), Southern Historical Collection, University of North Carolina Library.

10. W. J. Cash, *The Mind of the South* (New York: Alfred A. Knopf, Inc., 1946), p. 6.

11. This involvement certainly is reflected in the Letters of Guy M. Bryan to Moses A. Bryan, 1830–1839, University of Texas Archives.

12. Diary and Other Records of Francis Terry Leake, 1841–1862.

13. Taken from Stephenson, *Isaac Franklin,* p. 292.

14. A. T. Walker Account Book, 1851–1861, Southern Historical Collection, University of North Carolina Library.

15. *Birmingham News,* May 8, 1847, as quoted in James B. Sellers, *Slavery in Alabama* (Tuscaloosa, Ala.: University of Alabama Press, 1950), p. 27.

16. Abigail Curlee, "A History of Slave Plantations," *Southwestern Historical Quarterly* 26:261 (July 1922–April 1923); Belle Kearney, *A Slaveholder's Daughter* (New York: The Abbey Press, 1900), p. 3; and The Iven Lewis Brookes Papers, 1793–1865, Southern Historical Collection, University of North Carolina Library.

17. Orland K. Armstrong, *Old Massa's People* (Indianapolis: The Bobbs-Merrill Co., Inc., 1951), p. 96.

18. Frederick L. Olmsted, *A Journey in the Seaboard States, 1853–1854* (New York: G. P. Putnam's Sons, 1904), pp. 54–55.

19. John P. Corry, "Education in Colonial Georgia," *Georgia Historical Quarterly* 16:141 (June 1923); Sellers, *Slavery in Alabama*, p. 121.

20. For examples of laws prohibiting masters from allowing slaves to hire their own time, see V. Alton Moody, "Slavery on Louisiana Sugar Plantations," *Louisiana Historical Quarterly* 7:1–112 (April 1924); H. M. Robinson, *A Digest of the Penal Laws of the State of Louisiana* (New Orleans, 1841); and Oliver H. Prince, *A Digest of the Laws of the State of Georgia* (Athens, Ga., 1837).

21. Booker T. Washington, "Industrial Education for the Negro," in W. E. B. Du Bois, *The Negro Problem* (New York: James Pott and Company, 1903), p. 11; and Booker T. Washington and W. E. B. Du Bois, *The Negro in the South* (Philadelphia: George W. Jacobs and Company, 1907), p. 24.

22. Ulrich B. Phillips, "The Slave Labor in the Charleston District," *Political Science Quarterly* 22:434–435 (1907).

23. Sellers, *Slavery in Alabama*, p. 88.

24. Amstrong, *Old Massa's People*, p. 34.

25. Austin Steward, *Twenty-one Years a Slave and Forty Years Freeman* (Rochester, N.Y.: Allings and Cory, 1859), p. 28.

26. William Alexander Hoke Papers (undated), Southern Historical Collection, University of North Carolina Library.

27. Nehemiah Adams, *A Southside View of Slavery* (Boston: T. R. Marvin Sanborn, Carter, and Maine, 1855), pp. 31–32.

28. "Reminiscences of Glenblythe," Thomas Affleck Papers, 1847–1866, Rosenberg Library Archives, Galveston, Texas.

29. Carter G. Woodson, *The Education of the Negro Prior to 1861* (New York: G. P. Putnam's Sons, 1915), pp. 208–209.

30. Letitia Burwell, *A Girl's Life in Virginia before the War* (Nashville, Tenn.: American Methodist Episcopal Sunday School Union, 1909), pp. 7–22.

31. As reprinted in Catherine H. Birney, *Sarah and Angelina Grimke* (Boston: Lee and Shepard Publishers, 1885), pp. 11–12.

32. *The Experiences of Thomas H. Jones* (Worcester, Mass.: Henry J. Rowland, 1857), pp. 13–15.

33. Benjamin Quarles, *Frederick Douglass* (Washington: Associated Publishers, Inc., 1948), pp. 6–7; also, F. M. Holland, *Frederick Douglass* (New York: Funk & Wagnalls, 1891), p. 15.

34. *The Annual Report of the American Foreign Anti-Slavery Society* (New York, May 7, 1850), p. 128; Woodson, *Education of the Negro*, p. 207; Edward A. Johnson, *School History of the Negro Race in America* (Raleigh, N.C.:

Edwards and Broughton, 1891), pp. 21–22; and Olmsted, *Journey in the Seaboard States,* pp. 196–197.

35. Armstrong, *Old Massa's People,* p. 104.

36. Nehemiah Adams, *Southside View of Slavery,* p. 32.

37. George C. Smith, *Life and Times of George F. Pierce* (Macon, Ga.: 1888), pp. 474–475.

38. Paul Monroe, *A Cyclopedia of Education* (New York: The Macmillan Company, 1913), p. 405; and C. C. Jones, *The Religious Instruction of the Negro in the United States* as quoted in W. P. Harrison, *The Gospel among the Slaves* (Nashville, Tenn.: Publishing House of the Methodist Episcopal Church, 1893), pp. 38–39.

39. Luther P. Jackson, "Religious Development of Negroes in Virginia," *Journal of Negro Education* 16:174 (January 1931); John Rankin, *Letters on American Slavery* (Boston: Garrison and Knapp, 1833), p. 31; Charles C. Jones, *A Catechism of Scripture and Doctrine Practice for Familial and Sabbath Schools Designed Also for the Oral Instruction of Colored Persons* (Philadelphia: Presbyterian Board of Publications, 1853). Though planned for oral instruction, Jones's *Catechism* was used by slaves who were learning to read secretly.

40. For a very thorough report on this educational movement, see Edgar Legare Pennington, *Thomas Bray's Associates and Their Work among Negroes* (Worcester, Mass.: The Society for the Propagation of the Gospel, 1939).

41. Woodson, *Education of the Negro,* pp. 113–114.

42. Bureau of the Census, *Negro Population, 1790–1915* (Washington, D.C.: Government Printing Office, 1918), pp. 53–57.

43. David Walker's *Appeal* as quoted in Carter G. Woodson, *The Negro in Our History* (Washington, D.C.: The Associated Publishers, 1922), p. 93.

44. Herbert Aptheker, "Militant Abolitionists," *Journal of Negro History* 26:446 (October 1941).

45. Despite the difference in opinions expressed by historians who attempt to account for the origins of the Civil War, contrasting political, social, and cultural values seem to constitute causes on which there is general agreement. See Kenneth M. Stampp, "What Caused the Civil War," in Richard W. Leopold and Arthur S. Link, eds., *Problems in American History* (New York: Prentice-Hall, Inc., 1952), pp. 372–425.

46. For difficulties experienced by the Confederacy along these lines, see Francis Butler Simkins, *The South Old and New* (New York: Alfred A. Knopf, Inc., 1951), p. 148; Charles W. Ramsdell, "The Confederate Government and the Railroads," *American Historical Review* 22:794–810 (July 1917); Leland D. Baldwin, *The Stream of American History* (New York: American Book Company, 1953), p. 823; Lawrence Henry Gipson, "The Collapse of the Confederacy," *Mississippi Valley Historical Review* 4:437–458 (March 1918); and Bell Irvin Wiley, *The Plain People of the Confederacy* (Baton Rouge, La.: Louisiana State University Press, 1944), pp. 41–44.

47. Nathaniel W. Stephens, *The Day of the Confederacy* (New Haven: Yale University Press, 1919), pp. 165–182.

48. Charles H. Wesley, *The Collapse of the Confederacy* (Washington, D.C.: The Associated Publishers, 1937), pp. 82–83.

49. William Howard Russell, *Pictures of Southern Life* (New York: James G. Gregory, 1861), p. 76.

50. P. L. Rainwater, "Letters of James Lusk Alcorn," *Journal of Southern History* 3:198, 202 (1937).

51. Elizabeth H. Botume, *First Days amongst the Contrabands* (Boston: Lee and Shepard Publishers, 1893), p. 15.

52. Vincent Colyer, *Brief Report of the Services Rendered by the Freed People of the United States Army in North Carolina, 1862* (New York, 1864), p. 34; and Allan Nevins, *The Emergence of Modern America, 1865–1878* (New York: The Macmillan Company, 1927), p. 9.

53. *Southern Cultivator,* July 1865, as quoted in Mildred Thompson, *Reconstruction in Georgia* (New York: Columbia University Press, 1915), p. 48.

54. As quoted in Botume, *First Days,* pp. 16–17.

55. N. P. Banks, "Emancipated Labor in Louisiana," an address substantially as delivered before the Young Men's Christian Commission at Boston, October 30, 1864, and at Charleston, November 1, 1864 (New Orleans: Department of the Gulf, 1864), p. 6; and John Eaton, *Grant, Lincoln and the Freedmen* (New York: Longmans, Green and Company, 1907), p. 19.

56. For a rather complete account of the role of these organizations in helping solve the problems of the freedmen, see Luther P. Jackson, "The Educational Efforts of the Freedmen's Bureau and Freedmen Aid Societies in South Carolina, 1862–1872," *Journal of Negro History* 8:1–40 (January 1923); and A. D. Mayo, "The Work of Certain Northern Churches in the Education of the Freedmen," *Report of the Commissioner of Education for the Year 1902* (Washington, D.C., 1903), pp. 285–314.

57. Banks, "Emancipated Labor in Louisiana," p. 6.

58. Asa H. Gordon, *Sketches of Negro Life and History in South Carolina* (Hammond, Ind.: W. P. Conkey Publication, 1929), pp. 87–88.

59. See the report of Captain Horace James, Superintendent of Negro Affairs in North Carolina as quoted in the *Freedman's Record* 1:142 (September 1865).

60. *Ibid.,* p.146.

61. *Report of the General Superintendent of Freedmen,* Department of Tennessee and Arkansas, December 31, 1864 (Washington, D.C.: Government Printing Office), pp. 20–21.

62. E. Merton Coulter, *The South During Reconstruction, 1865–1877* (Baton Rouge, La.: Louisiana State University Press, 1947), pp. 71–72.

63. Thompson, *Reconstruction in Georgia,* pp. 56–57; and Donald Henderson, *The Negro Freedmen* (New York: Henry Schuman, 1952), p. 29.

64. Benjamin Quarles, *The Negro in the Civil War* (Boston: Little, Brown and Company, 1953), p. 283.

65. *Preliminary Report Touching on the Conditions and Management of Emancipated Refugees,* made to the Secretary of War by the American Freedmen's Inquiry Commission, June 30, 1863 (New York: John F. Trow, Printer, 1863), pp. 23–24.

66. For a complete story describing the establishment and function of this

agency, see Paul S. Pierce, *The Freedmen's Bureau* (Iowa City: University of Iowa Press, 1904).

67. Some good examples of the traditionalists' interpretations of the Reconstruction period my be found in William A. Dunning, *Reconstruction: Political and Economic* (New York: Harper and Brothers, 1907); James F. Rhodes, *History of the United States* (New York: The Macmillan Company, 1906), Vol. VII; Claude G. Bowers, *The Tragic Era* (Boston: Houghton Mifflin Company, 1929); Coulter, *The South During Reconstruction*. The traditionalist interpretation of the "unsavory" impact of radical Reconstruction upon education is well represented in Wallace Knight, *The Influence of Reconstruction on Education in the South* (New York: Teachers College, Columbia University, 1913).

68. The revisionist view is clearly revealed in such works as W. E. B. Du Bois, "Reconstruction and Its Benefits," *American Historical Review* 15:781–799 (July 1910); Horace Mann Bond, "Social and Economic Forces in Alabama Reconstruction," *Journal of Negro History* 23:290–348 (July 1938); Vernon L. Wharton, *The Negro in Mississippi, 1865–1890* (Chapel Hill, N.C.: University of North Carolina Press, 1947); Simkins, *The South Old and New;* Guion G. Johnson, "Southern Paternalism toward Negroes after Emancipation," *Journal of Southern History* 23:483–509 (November 1957); and John Hope Franklin, *Reconstruction after the Civil War* (Chicago: University of Chicago Press, 1961).

69. John Eaton, *Report of the Superintendent of Freedmen, 1864* (Washington, D.C., 1865), pp. 86–87; and Ullin W. Leavell, *Philanthropy in Negro Education* (Nashville: George Peabody College for Teachers, 1930), pp. 28–29.

70. Henry L. Swint, *The Northern Teacher in the South, 1862–1870* (Nashville: Vanderblit University Press, 1941), p. 40; and *The American Missionary* 9:36–37 (February 1865).

71. J. W. Alvord, Bureau of Refugees, Freedmen, and Abandoned Lands, *Fifth Semi-Annual Report on Schools for Freedmen* (Washington, D.C., 1868), pp. 29–30.

72. *Report of the Board of Education for Freedmen,* Department of the Gulf (New Orleans: Office of the True Delta, 1865), p. 45.

73. *The American Missionary* 9:27 (February 1865).

74. *The History of the American Missionary Association* (New York: S. S. Green, Printer, 1874), pp. 11–12.

75. *Third Report of a Committee of the Representatives of the New York Yearly Meeting of Friends upon the Condition and Wants of Colored Refugees* (New York, 1864), pp. 2–23.

76. *The National Freedman* 1:169–170 (June 1865).

77. Leavell, *Philanthropy in Negro Education,* p. 47.

78. *The American Missionary* 14:14 (January 1870).

79. Leavell, *Philanthropy in Negro Education,* p. 48.

80. J. W. Alvord, Bureau of Refugees, Freedmen, and Abandoned Lands, *Fourth Semi-Annual Report on Schools for Freedmen* (Washington, D.C., 1867), p. 76.

81. *Freedman's Journal* 1:19 (May 1865).

82. Ira B. Bryant, *The Development of the Houston Negro Schools* (Houston: privately printed, 1935), p. 8.

83. *The National Freedman* 1:356 (December 1865).

84. *Report of the Board of Education for Freedmen*, pp. 17–24; and Alvord, *Fifth Semi-Annual Report on Schools for Freedmen*, pp. 6–7.

85. More detail in description of teaching methods and procedures employed by Northern teachers is given in Edward L. Pierce, "Freedmen at Port Royal," *The Atlantic Monthly* 12:305 (December 1863); *The National Freedman* 1:154–155 (June 1865).

86. *The National Freedman* 1:214–215 (August 1865).

87. *The National Freedman* 1:192 (July 1865); 1:261 (September 1865); 2:53 (February 1866).

88. *Freedman's Record* 1:93 (June 1865); *The American Missionary* 9:6 (January 1865); *The National Freedman* 2:156, 169 (February 1866); and *Report of the Board of Education for Freedmen*, p. 7.

89. Myron W. Adams, *A History of Atlanta University, 1865–1929* (Atlanta, Ga.: Atlanta University Press, 1930), pp. 1–12.

90. Cornelius Heatwole, *A History of Education in Virginia* (New York: The Macmillan Company, 1916), pp. 349–353.

91. Miles M. Fisher, *Virginia Union and Sons of Her Achievement* (Richmond: privately printed, 1924), pp. 17–24.

92. Benjamin Brawley, *History of Morehouse College* (Atlanta: Morehouse College, 1917).

93. Facts concerning this phase of the history of Howard University were drawn from the *Howard University Bulletin* 32:1–5 (September 1954).

CHAPTER II · THE RISE OF PUBLIC SCHOOLS AND
EQUAL EDUCATIONAL OPPORTUNITIES IN THE SOUTH

1. Walter L. Fleming, *Documentary History of Reconstruction* (New York: Peter Smith, 1950), I, 109–110.

2. *Ibid.*, p. 112.

3. *Ibid.*, p. 117.

4. Robert Selph Henry, *The Story of Reconstruction* (New York: Peter Smith, 1951), pp. 79–80.

5. *The Journal of the Proceedings of the Constitutional Convention of the State of Mississippi*, August 1865, pp. 109–110.

6. For details concerning the Black Codes, see Henry Steele Commager, *Documents of American History* (New York: Appleton-Century-Crofts, 1949), vol. II; Fleming, *Documentary History of Reconstruction*, vol. I; James Garner, *Reconstruction in Mississippi* (New York: The Macmillan Company, 1901); Leland D. Baldwin, *The Stream of American History* (New York: American Book Company, 1951); and Edward McPherson, *The Political History of the United States of America During the Period of Reconstruction* (Washington, D.C.: Phillip and Solomon, 1871).

7. Carl Schurz, *The Condition of the South, 1865* (Washington, D.C.: 1866).

8. Vincent Colyer, *Brief Report of the Services Rendered by the Freed People to the United States Army in North Carolina, 1862* (New York: privately printed, 1864).

9. *Freedman's Record* 1:156 (October 1865).

10. *The National Freedman* 2:44 (February 1865).

11. Frederick Eby, *The Development of Education in Texas* (New York: The Macmillan Company, 1925), pp. 265–266.

12. M. C. S. Noble, *A History of Public Schools in North Carolina* (Chapel Hill, N.C.: University of North Carolina Press, 1930), pp. 270–272.

13. Stuart Grayson Noble, *Forty Years of Public Schools in Mississippi* (New York: Teachers College, Columbia University, 1918), p. 21.

14. Fleming, *Documentary History of Reconstruction*, II, 183.

15. *Freedman's Record* 2:132 (June 1866).

16. *Freedman's Record* 1:119 (July 1865).

17. For this and a more complete account of such cases, see J. W. Alvord, *Fifth Semi-Annual Report on Schools for Freedmen* (Washington, D.C., 1868).

18. *Ibid.*

19. Carl Schurz, *The Condition of the South, 1865*, p. 24. Johnson's personality caused much of his trouble and prevented his being able to utilize fully the conservatives and few Democrats whose strength might have made it possible for him to salvage his plan. Homer Carey Hockett and Arthur M. Schlesinger, *Land of the Free* (New York: The Macmillan Company, 1944), p. 341.

20. Fleming, *Documentary History of Reconstruction*, I, 423; and the *Houston Weekly Telegraph,* October 22, 1866.

21. Henry, *Story of Reconstruction,* pp. 266–267.

22. *Debates and the Proceedings of the Constitutional Convention of South Carolina, 1868* (Charleston, S.C., 1868), I, 47.

23. *Debates and Proceedings of the Convention Which Assembled at Little Rock, January 7, 1868* (Little Rock, Ark.: J. G. Price, 1868), p. 88.

24. Claude G. Bowers, *The Tragic Era* (Boston: Houghton Mifflin Company, 1929), p. 216.

25. For an extensive account of these earlier laws, see Edgar W. Knight, *Public Education in the South* (New York: Ginn and Company, 1922), ch. vi.

26. John Spencer Bassett, *A Short History of the United States, 1492–1920* (New York: The Macmillan Company, 1927), p. 477.

27. W. E. B. Du Bois, *Black Reconstruction* (Philadelphia: Albert Saifer Publishers, 1935), p. 641.

28. *Debates and Proceedings of the Constitutional Convention of South Carolina, 1868,* I, 71.

29. *Ibid.,* p. 100.

30. *Ibid.,* pp. 264–265.

31. *Ibid.,* p. 709.

32. *Ibid.,* pp. 708–709.

33. *Ibid.*, pp. 890–891.

34. *The Constitution of the State of Alabama, As Revised and Amended by the Convention Assembled at Montgomery on the Fifth Day of November, 1867* (Montgomery, Ala., 1874), pp. 24–25.

35. *Journal of the Proceedings of the Constitutional Convention of Georgia, December, 1867* (Augusta, Ga., 1868), p. 558.

36. *Debates and Proceedings of the Convention Assembled at Little Rock, January 7, 1868,* pp. 880–882.

37. *Journal of the Constitutional Convention of the State of North Carolina* (Raleigh, N.C., 1868), pp. 31–44.

38. *Journal of the Proceedings of the Constitutional Convention of the State of Mississippi, 1868* (Jackson, Miss., 1871), pp. 359–360.

39. A. A. Taylor, *The Negro in the Reconstruction of Virginia* (Washington, D.C.: Association for the Study of Negro Life and History, 1926), p. 145.

40. *Debates and Proceedings of the Constitutional Convention of the State of Virginia, 1867* (Richmond, 1868).

41. Virginius Dabney, *Liberalism in the South* (Chapel Hill, N.C.: University of North Carolina Press, 1923), pp. 165–166.

42. Garner, *Reconstruction in Mississippi,* p. 359.

43. Taylor, *The Negro in the Reconstruction of Virginia,* p. 151.

44. *The American Missionary* 14:56 (March 1870).

45. J. L. M. Curry, *Education of Negroes Since 1860* (Baltimore, 1894), p. 19.

46. Arkansas Department of Education, *Report of the State Superintendent, 1868–1870; 1870–1872* (Little Rock, Ark., 1872), p. 15.

47. *Ibid.,* p. 7

48. *Ibid.,* pp. 52–55.

49. Du Bois, *Black Reconstruction,* p. 652.

50. Jesse Thomas Wallace, *A History of Negroes in Mississippi from 1865–1890* (New York: Teachers College, Columbia University, 1819), p. 136.

51. Charles Edgeworth Jones, *Education in Georgia* (Washington, D.C.: Government Printing Office, 1889), p. 33.

52. Mildred C. Thompson, *Reconstruction in Georgia* (New York: Columbia University Press, 1915), pp. 337–338.

53. Jones, *Education in Georgia,* p. 135.

54. Richard W. Thomas, "A History of Public Education and Charitable Institutions in South Carolina During the Reconstruction Period," unpub. master's thesis, Atlanta University, 1933, p. 36.

55. Knight, *Public Education in the South,* p. 373.

56. Fleming, *Documentary History of Reconstruction,* II, 198–199.

57. Taylor, *The Negro in the Reconstruction of Virginia,* pp. 149–150.

58. *The Houston Weekly Telegraph,* December 28, 1871.

59. *The Houston Weekly Telegraph,* February 2, 1872.

60. Knight, *Public Education in the South,* pp. 366–367.

61. *The Houston Weekly Telegraph,* September 5, 1872.

CHAPTER III · THE GREAT DETOUR: A TRANSITION TO NEGRO EDUCATION

1. *Report of the Joint Select Committee* (Washington, D.C.: Government Printing Office, 1872), p. 245.

2. *Ibid.,* p. 300.

3. For a complete record of the objectives and purposes of these associations, see Walter L. Fleming, *Documentary History of Reconstruction* (New York: Peter Smith, 1950), II, 347–359.

4. *Joint Select Committee,* p. 369.

5. Harold Underwood Faulkner, *American Political and Social History* (New York: F. S. Crofts and Company, 1946), p. 385. See also Herbert Aptheker, *To Be Free* (New York: International Publishers, 1948), p. 183.

6. *Joint Select Committee,* p. 264.

7. Fleming, *Documentary History of Reconstruction,* II, 370.

8. *Joint Select Committee,* p. 20.

9. James Elbert Cutler, *Lynch Law* (London: Longmans, Green, and Company, 1905), pp. 151–152.

10. *Joint Select Committee,* p. 21.

11. For an extended treatise of this era of American history as it relates to the Negro, see Rayford W. Logan, *The Negro in American Life and Thought: The Nadir, 1877–1901* (New York: The Dial Press, Inc., 1954), pp. 10–14.

12. For the revolutionary significance of this "Unknown Compromise," see C. Vann Woodward, *Reunion and Reaction* (Boston: Little, Brown and Company, 1951), pp. 3–21.

13. C. Vann Woodward, *The Strange Career of Jim Crow* (New York: Oxford University Press, 1955), pp. 26–47.

14. *Slaughter House Cases,* 16 Wall 36 (1873).

15. For a rather complete analysis of judicial attrition and the contraction of the equal protection clause of the Fourteenth Amendment, see Robert J. Harris, *The Quest for Equality* (Baton Rouge, La.: Louisiana State University Press, 1960), pp. 82–108.

16. Henry Steele Commager, *Documents of American History* (New York: Appleton-Century-Crofts, 1963), pp. 71–75.

17. U.S. v. Reese, 23 L Ed., 563, 566 (1876).

18. U.S. v. Cruikshank, 23 L Ed., 588 (1876).

19. Hall v. De Cuir, 24 L Ed., 547 (1878).

20. Albert P. Blaustein and Clarence Clyde Ferguson, *Desegregation and the Law* (New Brunswick, N.J.: Rutgers University Press, 1957), p. 92.

21. Civil Rights Cases, 109 U.S. 3, 25 (1883).

22. Chase v. Stephenson, 71 Ill. 382 (1874).

23. Ward v. Flood, 48 Cal. 36 (1874).

24. Board of Education v. Tinnon, 26 Kan. 1 (1881); The People ex rel. v. Board of Education, 101 Ill. 308, 40 Am. Rep. 196 (1882); and Knox et al. v.

Board of Education of the City of Independence, 45 Kan. 152, 25 Pac. 616 (1891).

25. Yick Wo v. Hopkins, 118 U.S. 356 (1886), 151.

26. Strauder v. West Virginia, 100 U.S. 303 (1880), 146–147.

27. For citations of cases setting these precedents, see "The Negro Citizen in the Supreme Court," *Harvard Law Review* 52:823–832 (March 1939).

28. Peter Joseph v. David Bidwell, 28 La. Ann. 382 (1876).

29. The Sue, 22 Fed. 843 (1885); Chesapeake, O. & S. R. Co. v. Wells, 4 S. W. 5 (1887); McGuinn v. Forbes et al., 37 Fed. 639, 1889; and Smith et al. v. Chamberlain, 19 L. R. A. 710 (1893).

30. Plessy v. Ferguson, 163 U.S. 1138 (1896).

31. For the various state laws pertaining to the Negro franchise at this time, see Pauli Murray, ed., *States' Laws on Race and Color* (Cincinnati: The Women's Division of Christian Service Board of Missions and Church Extension of the Methodist Church, 1951).

32. Henry Allen Bullock, "The Expansion of Negro Suffrage in Texas," *Journal of Negro Education* 26:370–371 (Summer 1957).

33. C. Vann Woodward, *Origins of the New South* (Baton Rouge, La.: Louisiana State University Press, 1951), p. 355.

34. Henry Allen Bullock, "Urbanism and Race Relations," in Rupert B. Vance and Nicholas J. Demerath, *The Urban South* (Chapel Hill, N.C.: University of North Carolina Press, 1954), p. 208

35. T. M. Logan, "The Opposition in the South to the Free School System," *Journal of Social Science* 9–11:92–94 (January 1878).

36. George W. Cable, "The Freedmen's Case in Equality," *The Century Magazine* 29:410–411 (January 1885).

37. *Addresses and Journal of Proceedings of the National Education Association* (Albany, N.Y., 1872), p. 278.

38. *The Nation,* January 25, 1877.

39. *Proceedings of the National Educational Association,* pp. 175–176.

40. Isabel C. Barrows, ed., *First Mohonk Conference on the Negro Question, June 1890* held at Lake Mohonk Ulster County, New York, June 4, 5, 6 (Boston: G. H. Ellis, Printer, 1890), p. 12.

41. *Ibid.,* p. 14.

42. *Ibid.,* pp. 78–79.

43. *The Journal of Education* 42:332 (November 1895).

44. Barrows, *First Mohonk Conference,* p. 24.

45. *Ibid.,* p. 29.

46. Booker T. Washington, *Up From Slavery* (New York: Doubleday, Page and Company, 1933), p. 62.

47. *Encyclopedia Americana,* XXVIII, 747–748.

48. Anson Phelps Stokes, *A Brief Biography of Booker T. Washington* (Hampton, Va.: The Hampton Institute Press, 1936), pp. 12–13.

49. Samuel R. Spencer, Jr., *Booker T. Washington and the Negro's Place in American Life* (Boston: Little, Brown and Company, 1955), pp. 91–93.

50. Washington, *Up From Slavery,* pp. 220–223.

51. Spencer, *Booker T. Washington,* pp. 56–57.

52. Booker T. Washington, *Tuskegee and Its People* (New York: D. Appleton and Company, 1910), pp. 56–57.

53. *Ibid.,* pp. 60–62.

54. Spencer, *Booker T. Washington,* pp. 64–65.

55. *Ibid.,* p. 63.

56. Max Thrasher, *Tuskegee* (Boston: Small, Maynard and Company, 1901), pp. 79, 87–92.

57. Washington, *Tuskegee,* p. 63.

58. Spencer, *Booker T. Washington,* p. 82.

59. Emmett J. Scott and Lyman Beecher Stowe, *Booker T. Washington* (New York: Doubleday, Page and Company, 1916), pp. 42–43.

60. Spencer, *Booker T. Washington,* p. 82.

61. Washington, *Tuskegee,* pp. 9–10.

62. *Report of the Superintendent of Public Instruction, North Carolina, 1873–1874* (Raleigh, N.C.: Stone and Uzzell, 1874).

63. A. D. Mayo, *Southern Women in the Recent Movement in the South,* Bureau of Education Circular, no. 1 (Washington, D.C.: Government Printing Office, 1892), p. 202.

64. Edwin R. Embree, *Brown America* (New York: Viking Press, 1931), pp. 116–117.

65. Stuart Grayson Noble, *Forty Years of the Public Schools in Mississippi* (New York: Teachers College, Columbia University, 1918), pp. 58–59.

66. Embree, *Brown America,* pp. 115–116.

67. Stephen B. Weeks, *History of Public School Education in Alabama* (Washington, D.C.: Government Printing Office, 1915), p. 197.

68. Horace Mann Bond, *The Education of the Negro in the American Social Order* (New York: Prentice-Hall, Inc., 1934), p. 155.

69. *Ibid.,* p. 158.

CHAPTER IV · DECISIONS AT CAPON SPRINGS

1. For a general description of the initial phases of this movement, see Charles Dabney, *Universal Education in the South* (Chapel Hill, N.C.: University of North Carolina Press, 1936).

2. For their agreement on these issues, see *Proceedings of the First Capon Springs Conference for Education in the South* (Capon Springs, W.Va., 1898), pp. 3–13.

3. *Proceedings of the Second Capon Springs Conference for Education in the South* (Capon Springs, W.Va., 1899), p. 28.

4. *Ibid.,* p. 72.

5. Dabney, *Universal Education,* p. 11.

6. *Columbia State,* April 24, 1903, as quoted in Dabney, p. 46.

7. *Atlanta Journal,* April 24, 1901, as quoted in Dabney, p. 46.

8. *Review of Reviews* 24:645 (June 1901).

9. *New York Herald,* April 27, 1901.

10. *Proceedings of the Second Capon Springs Conference,* p. 9.

11. *New York Herald,* April 27, 1901.

12. *Proceedings of the First Capon Springs Conference,* pp. 11–12.

13. *Proceedings of the Second Capon Springs Conference,* p. 20.

14. *Proceedings of the First Capon Springs Conference,* pp. 24–25.

15. *Proceedings of the Sixth Conference for Education in the South* (Richmond, Va., 1903), p. 38.

16. *Proceedings of the First Capon Springs Conference,* p. 32.

17. For extended remarks pertaining to this topic, see *ibid.,* pp. 17–19.

18. *Proceedings of the Third Capon Springs Conference for Education in the South* (Capon Springs, W.Va., 1900), p. 55.

19. *Ibid.,* p. 60.

20. Dabney, *Universal Education,* pp. 26–27.

21. *Ibid.,* pp. 149–150.

22. *Proceedings of the Third Capon Springs Conference,* pp. 75–85.

23. *Proceedings of the Second Capon Springs Conference,* p. 74.

24. *Proceedings of the First Capon Springs Conference,* p. 5.

25. *Proceedings of the Third Capon Springs Conference,* p. 17.

26. *Proceedings of the First Capon Springs Conference,* p. 31.

27. *Proceedings of the Second Capon Springs Conference,* pp. 7–8.

28. *Ibid.,* pp. 7–8.

29. *Ibid.,* pp. 9–13.

30. *Proceedings of the Fourth Conference for Education in the South* (Winston-Salem, N.C., 1901), pp. 11–12.

31. Dabney, *Universal Education,* pp. 58–59.

32. *Proceedings of the Fifth Conference for Education in the South* (Knoxville, Tenn., 1902), pp. 38–39.

33. *Proceedings of the Second Capon Springs Conference,* pp. 25–26.

34. *Ibid.,* pp. 25–26.

35. *Ibid.,* pp. 27–28.

36. *Proceedings of the Fourth Conference;* see G. S. Dickerman's Report on the South, pp. 25–26.

37. Charles D. McIver's report on the Greensboro Conference in the *Proceedings of the Fifth Conference,* pp. 23–25.

38. Robert Frazier's report in the *Proceedings of the Fifth Conference,* p. 37.

39. For other reports on progress, see *Proceedings of the Sixth Conference,* pp. 36–74.

40. Reports of the enthusiastic response of other local areas appear in *Proceedings of the Sixth Conference,* pp. 49, 58, 86–87.

41. Hollis B. Frissell's report to the Sixth Conference, p. 54.

42. *Proceedings of the Twelfth Conference for Education in the South* (Atlanta, Ga., 1909).

43. *Proceedings of the Fifth Conference,* pp. 7–8.

44. Reports of each Southern state may be found in the "Meetings of State Superintendents of Education" in the *Proceedings of the Ninth Conference for Education in the South* (Lexington, Ky., 1906).

CHAPTER V · DEEDS OF PHILANTHROPY

1. C. Vann Woodward, *Origins of the New South* (Baton Rouge, La.: Louisiana State University Press, 1951), p. 401.

2. Albert Z. Carr, *John D. Rockefeller's Secret Weapon* (New York: McGraw-Hill Book Company, 1962), p. 18.

3. Andrew Carnegie, *Autobiography* (Garden City, N.Y.: Doubleday and Co., Inc., 1923); Matthew Stephenson, *The Robber Barons* (New York: Harcourt Brace and Company, 1934); Allan Nevins, *John D. Rockefeller: The Heroic Age of American Enterprise* (New York: Charles Scribner's Sons, 1940); John G. Brooks, *An American Citizen: The Life of William Henry Baldwin, Jr.* (Boston: Houghton Mifflin Company, 1910); and Louise Ware, *George Foster Peabody* (Athens, Ga.: University of Georgia Press, 1951).

4. Henry D. Lloyd, *Wealth against Commonwealth* (New York: Harper and Brothers, 1894).

5. Charles Nordhoff, *The Cotton States in the Spring and Summer of 1875* as quoted in Richard W. Leopold and Arthur S. Link, eds., *Problems in American History* (Englewood Cliffs, N.J.: Prentice-Hall, 1952), pp. 460–462.

6. Ullin W. Leavell, *Philanthropy in Negro Education* (Nashville, Tenn.: George Peabody College for Teachers, 1930), pp. 59–61.

7. Edwin R. Embree and Julia Waxman, *Investment in People* (New York: Harper and Brothers, 1929), p. 38.

8. Benjamin Brawley, *Doctor Dillard and the Jeanes Fund* (New York: Fleming H. Revell Company, 1930), pp. 68–69.

9. *Proceedings of the Trustees for the Education of Freedmen* (Baltimore, Md.: The John F. Slater Fund, 1901), p. 13.

10. Brawley, *Doctor Dillard,* pp. 56–57.

11. Arthur D. Wright and Edward E. Redcay, *The Negro Rural School Fund, Inc.* (Washington, D.C.: The Negro Rural School Fund, Inc., 1933), p. 11.

12. *Ibid.,* pp. 44–46.

13. Edwin R. Embree, *Julius Rosenwald Fund: Review of the Two-Year Period, 1938–1940* (Chicago, 1940), p. 5.

14. Embree and Waxman, *Investment in People,* pp. 30, 33.

15. Leavell, *Philanthropy in Negro Education,* pp. 84–85.

16. For other expenditure activities of this fund, see *ibid.,* pp. 86–94.

17. Edward E. Redcay, *County Training Schools,* pp. 6–7.

18. Will W. Alexander, *The Slater and Jeanes Funds: An Educator's Approach to a Difficult Social Problem,* an address delivered at Hampton Institute, Va., April 27, 1933, pp. 4–6.

19. *Proceedings of the Trustees of the John F. Slater Fund* (Baltimore, 1901), pp. 12–13.

20. For reports on income and expenditure of the Fund for the various colleges, see *Proceedings of the Trustees of the John F. Slater Fund, 1905–1906* (New York, 1906).

21. Redcay, *County Training Schools,* pp. 28–32.

22. Brawley, *Doctor Dillard*, pp. 75, 78.

23. Leavell, *Philanthropy in Negro Education*, pp. 118–119.

24. Brawley, *Doctor Dillard*, pp. 59–62; and Wright and Redcay, *The Negro School Fund*, pp. 16–20.

25. Lance G. E. Jones, *The Jeanes Teacher in the United States, 1908–1933* (Chapel Hill, N.C.: University of North Carolina Press, 1937), pp. 52, 62.

26. For a full account of the rise of these agencies and their agents, see Wilson Gee, *The Social Economics of Agriculture* (New York: The Macmillan Company, 1932), pp. 512–527.

27. Embree, *Julius Rosenwald Fund*, pp. 8, 13–14.

28. Embree and Waxman, *Investment in People*, pp. 47–61.

29. These figures have been compiled on the basis of Wright, *The Negro Rural School Fund*, p. 172, and Embree, *Julius Rosenwald*, p. 18.

30. *Proceedings of the Trustees, 1905–1906*, p. 54.

31. Embree, *Julius Rosenwald*, p. 18.

32. John F. Slater Fund, *Proceedings and Reports of the Year Ending September 30, 1930* (New York, 1931), p. 13.

CHAPTER VI · NEGRO EDUCATION AS A WAY OF LIFE

1. Bureau of the Census, *Negro Population in the United States, 1790–1915* (Washington, D.C.: Government Printing Office, 1918), p. 115.

2. E. Franklin Frazier, *The Negro in the United States* (New York: The Macmillan Company, 1957), p. 204.

3. Charles S. Johnson, *Patterns of Negro Segregation* (New York: Harper and Brothers, 1943), p. 8.

4. Charles S. Johnson, *Shadow of the Plantation* (Chicago: University of Chicago Press, 1934), pp. 13–14.

5. Johnson, *Patterns of Negro Segregation*, p. 9.

6. Henry Allen Bullock, "Urbanism and Race Relations," in Rupert B. Vance and Nicholas J. Demerath, *The Urban South* (Chapel Hill, N.C.: University of North Carolina Press, 1954), p. 211.

7. Lorenzo Greene and Carter G. Woodson, *The Negro Wage Earner* (Washington, D.C.: Association for the Study of Negro Life and History, 1930), pp. 37–43.

8. Robert C. Weaver, *Negro Labor* (New York: Harcourt, Brace and Company, 1946), p. 5.

9. Sterling D. Spero and Abram L. Harris, *The Black Worker* (New York: Columbia University Press, 1931), pp. 32–33.

10. Gunnar Myrdal, *An American Dilemma* (New York: Harper and Brothers, 1944), pp. 247–248.

11. Ray Stannard Baker, *Following the Color Line* (New York: Doubleday, Page and Company, 1908), p. 96.

12. Charles S. Mangum, *The Legal Status of the Negro* (Chapel Hill, N.C.: University of North Carolina Press, 1940), pp. 166–169.

13. For a thorough study of these codes of social usage, see Bertram Doyle, *The Etiquette of Race Relations in the South* (Chicago: University of Chicago Press, 1937).

14. *Ibid.*, p. 143.

15. Lewis C. Copeland, "The Negro as a Contrast Conception," in Edgar T. Thompson, *Race Relations and the Race Problem* (Durham, N.C.: Duke University Press, 1939), pp. 152–179.

16. Booker T. Washington, *Story of the Negro* (New York, 1909), I, as quoted in Thompson, *Race Relations*, p. 159.

17. See Johnson, *Shadow of the Plantation*, for anecdotal accounts pertaining to these themes.

18. T. J. Woofter, *The Basis of Racial Adjustment* (Boston: Ginn and Company, 1925), p. 80.

19. Edward E. Redcay, *County Training Schools and Public Secondary Education for Negroes in the South* (Washington, D.C.: John F. Slater Fund, 1935), p. 42.

20. For a description of the movement and act out of which these teachers originated, see Wilson Gee, *The Social Economics of Agriculture* (New York: The Macmillan Company, 1932), pp. 469–530.

21. Redcay, *County Training Schools*, pp. 45–49.

22. *Annual Report of Superintendent of Public Instruction, North Carolina, 1870* (Raleigh, N.C., 1871), p. 53.

23. *Biennial Report of the Superintendent of Public Instruction for the State of Arkansas, 1893–1894* (Morrilton, Ark., 1894).

24. *Commissioner of Education Report for Year Ending June 30, 1904* (Washington, D.C.: Government Printing Office, 1904), pp. 2177–2188.

25. W. E. B. Du Bois, *Some Efforts of American Negroes for Their Own Social Betterment*, Report and Proceedings of the Third Conference for the Study of Negro Problems held at Atlanta University, May 25–26, 1898, pp. 42–95.

26. Myrdal, *An American Dilemma*, p. 862.

27. *Catalog of Tuskegee Normal and Industrial Institute* (Tuskegee Institute, Ala., 1899–1900).

28. *Annual Catalog of the Agricultural and Mechanical College for the Colored Race* (Greensboro, N.C., 1903–1904).

CHAPTER VII · THE FAILURE OF AN EXPERIMENT

1. The tremendous influence that Booker T. Washington exerted over the formation of national policy concerning the Negro American is very well reflected in the large number of letters that passed between him and national leaders. For example, see President Theodore Roosevelt to Booker T. Washington, October 8, 1906. Booker T. Washington to Wm. H. Taft, November 22, 1906; June 11, 1904; December 12, 1906. Booker T. Washington to William H. Baldwin, January 19, 1904; January 22, 1904; January 28, 1904.

Robert J. Harlan to Booker T. Washington, October 28, 1907. **Booker T.** Washington to Andrew Carnegie, November 9, 1907. Booker T. Washington Papers held by Library of Congress.

2. *The Crisis*, June 1911, p. 49. President Taft's view on industrial education for Negroes was very strongly brought out in his Fisk University Address of May 22, 1908.

3. Bureau of the Census, *Negro Population, 1790–1915* (Washington, D.C.: Government Printing Office, 1918), pp. 378–379.

4. Bureau of the Census, *Census of Population: 1950* (Washington, D.C.: Government Printing Office, 1952), vol. II.

5. W. E. B. Du Bois, *The College-Bred Negro* (Atlanta, Ga.: Atlanta University Press, 1902), p. 16.

6. Charles S. Johnson, *The Negro College Graduate* (Chapel Hill, N.C.: University of North Carolina Press, 1938), p. 105.

7. For a full description of the community functions as performed by the early Negro college graduate, see Du Bois, *The College-Bred Negro*.

8. Johnson, *The Negro College Graduate*, p. 105.

9. This kind of evidence is very clearly demonstrated in Ina C. Brown, *Socio-Economic Approach to Educational Problems* (Washington, D.C.: Government Printing Office, 1942).

10. Monroe N. Work, *Negro Year Book, 1916–1917* (Tuskegee Institute, Ala.: 1916), p. 235.

11. Monroe N. Work, *Negro Year Book, 1931–1932* (Tuskegee Institute, Ala.: 1931), p. 204.

12. W. E. B. Du Bois, *The Common School and the Negro American* (Atlanta, Ga.: Atlanta University Press, 1911), pp. 107–115.

13. *Ibid.*, p. 103.

14. T. J. Woofter, *The Negro Problem in Cities* (New York: Doubleday, Doran and Company, 1928), p. 204.

15. Charles S. Johnson, *The Negro in American Civilization* (New York: Henry Holt and Company, 1930), p. 243.

16. Work, *Negro Year Book, 1916–1917*, p. 250; *1931–1932*, pp. 232–233.

17. Jessie Parkhurst Guzman, *Negro Year Book, 1952* (New York, 1952), p. 220.

18. Lorin A. Thompson, "Urbanism, Occupational Shift and Economic Progress," in Rupert B. Vance and Nicholas J. Demerath, *The Urban South* (Chapel Hill, N.C.: University of North Carolina Press, 1954), pp. 39–41.

19. Sterling D. Spero and Abram L. Harris, *The Black Worker: The Negro and the Labor Movement* (New York: Columbia University Press, 1931), p. 47.

20. For the role of the "matriarchy" in the Negro family, see E. Franklin Frazier, *The Negro in the United States* (New York: The Macmillan Company, 1957), pp. 316–321.

21. For the dynamics of segregation as related to homicides among Negroes, see Henry Allen Bullock, "Urban Homicide in Theory and Fact," *Journal of Criminal Law, Criminology and Police Science* 45:565–575 (January–February 1955).

22. Gunnar Myrdal, *An American Dilemma* (New York: Harper and Brothers, 1944), p. 355.

23. These facts were compiled from various state reports of the Bureau of the Census, *Characteristics of Population, Part II, 1950* (Washington, D.C.: Government Printing Office, 1952).

24. Johnson, *Negro in American Civilization,* p. 170.

25. John C. Rose, "Negro Suffrage: The Constitutional Point of View," *The American Political Science Review* 1:17–43 (November 1906).

26. Johnson, *Negro in American Civilization,* pp. 339–340.

27. Bureau of the Census, *Negro Population, 1790–1915,* p. 419.

28. These figures were compiled from *ibid.,* p. 578; and Bureau of the Census, *Negro Population, 1920–1932* (Washington, D.C.: Government Printing Office, 1932), pp. 260, 461.

29. These facts were presented in Paul Lewinson, *Race, Class, and Party: A History of Negro Suffrage and White Politics in the South* (London: Oxford University Press, 1932), pp. 218–220.

30. Ralph Bunche, "The Political Status of the Negro," as quoted in Myrdal, *An American Dilemma,* p. 488.

CHAPTER VIII · IN QUEST OF EQUALITY

1. Newbell Niles Puckett, *Folk Beliefs of Southern Negroes* (Chapel Hill, N.C.: University of North Carolina Press, 1926), p. 50.

2. Arnold Rose, *The Negro's Morale* (Minneapolis: University of Minnesota Press, 1947), p. 19.

3. Joel Chandler Harris, *Uncle Remus* (New York: Appleton-Century-Crofts, 1895), p. xiv.

4. Monroe N. Work, *The Negro Year Book, 1916–1917* (Tuskegee Institute, Ala., 1916), p. 41.

5. *Ibid.,* pp. 46–47.

6. *The Houston Chronicle,* June 22, 1917.

7. E. Franklin Frazier, *The Negro in the United States* (New York: The Macmillan Company, 1957), p. 510.

8. *The Houston Informer,* October 11, 1919, as quoted in Robert T. Kerlin, *The Voice of the Negro* (New York: E. P. Dutton and Company, 1920), p. 34.

9. *The Crisis,* May 1919, as quoted in Kerlin, *Voice of the Negro,* pp. 35–36.

10. Kerlin, *Voice of the Negro,* pp. 40–41.

11. Records of these incidents are described in Work, *The Negro Year Book, 1916–1917,* pp. 42–44.

12. Monroe N. Work, *The Negro Year Book, 1921–1922* (Tuskegee Institute, Ala., 1921), pp. 54–55.

13. Roi Ottley, *Black Odyssey* (London: John Murray, 1949), pp. 251–252.

14. V. F. Calverton, *Anthology of American Negro Literature* (New York: The Modern Library, 1929), pp. 16–17.

15. W. E. B. Du Bois, *Dusk of Dawn* (New York: Harcourt, Brace & Company, 1940), pp. 37–38.

16. *Ibid.,* p. 39.

17. W. E. B. Du Bois, *Dark Water* (New York: Harcourt, Brace & Co., 1920), p. 27.

18. James Weldon Johnson, "O Black and Unknown Bards," in *St. Peter Relates an Incident* (New York: The Viking Press, 1917). Copyright 1917 by James Weldon Johnson. All rights reserved. Reprinted by permission of The Viking Press, Inc.

19. Ottley, *Black Odyssey,* pp. 252–254. For extensive reviews of the Negro American literature of this period and evidence of the dominance of the protest themes that characterized it, see Alain Locke, *The New Negro* (New York: Albert and Charles Boni, 1925); Robert T. Kerlin, *Negro Poets and Their Poems* (Washington, D.C.: The Associated Publishers, 1923); V. F. Calverton, *Anthology of American Negro Literature*; Sterling Brown *et al., The Negro Caravan*; and Herman Dreer, *American Literature by Negro Authors* (New York: The Macmillan Company, 1950).

20. Claude McKay, "If We Must Die," in *Harlem Shadows* (New York: Harcourt, Brace & Co., 1922), p. 53.

21. "America," in *Harlem Shadows,* p. 6.

22. Countee Cullen, *Copper Sun* (New York: Harper & Brothers, 1927), p. 3. Also *On These I Stand* (New York: Harper & Brothers, 1947).

23. *Ibid.*

24. These lines from Langston Hughes come from *Selected Poems* (New York: Alfred A. Knopf, 1959), pp. 160, 175; *The Weary Blues* (New York: Alfred A. Knopf, 1926), p. 51; and "Let America Be America Again," *Esquire,* July 1936.

25. Several comprehensive works dealing with this literary movement have been published. Two of them are Alain Locke, *The New Negro* (New York: Albert and Charles Boni, 1925) and Sterling Brown, Arthur P. Davis, and Ulysses Lee, *The Negro Caravan* (New York: The Dryden Press, 1948).

26. Gunnar Myrdal, *An American Dilemma* (New York: Harper & Brothers, 1944), pp. 751–752, includes an extensive account of the Negro history movement.

27. Carter G. Woodson, *The Negro in Our History* (Washington, D.C.: The Associated Publishers, 1922); Edward A. Johnson, *School History of the Negro Race in America* (Chicago: W. B. Conkey Company, 1897); Merle R. Eppse, *The Negro, Too, in American History* (Nashville, Tenn.: National Publication House, 1949); Carter G. Woodson, *Negro Makers of History* (Washington, D.C.: Associated Publishers, 1928).

28. The educational background of these and other scholars associated with the Negro history movement is freely outlined in Harry W. Greene, *Holders of Doctorates among American Negroes* (Boston: Meador Publishing Company, 1946).

29. William T. Fontaine, " 'Social Determination' in the Writings of Negro Scholars," *American Journal of Sociology* 49:312 (January 1944).

30. For very good examples of this type of research, see Eli S. Marks, "Skin Color Judgments of Negro College Students," *Journal of Abnormal and Social*

Psychology 38:370–376 (1943); and Kenneth Clark and Mamie P. Clark, "Racial Identification and Preference in Negro Children," in Theodore Newcomb and Eugene L. Hartley, eds., *Readings in Social Psychology* (New York: Henry Holt and Company, 1947), pp. 169–178.

31. For accounts of the Negro press during these early years, see I. Garland Penn, *The Afro-American Press* (Springfield, Mass.: Wiley and Company, 1891).

32. W. E. B. Du Bois, *The Negro in Business* (Atlanta, Ga.) pp. 73–77 as quoted in Frazier, *The Negro in the United States*, p. 503.

33. Work, *Negro Year Book, 1916–1917*, p. 38.

34. For the aggressiveness and militancy shown by the various Negro papers soon after World War I, see Robert T. Kerlin, *The Voice of the Negro;* and Frederick G. Detweiler, *The Negro Press in the United States* (Chicago: University of Chicago Press, 1922).

35. Myrdal, *An American Dilemma*, p. 909.

36. Herbert Aptheker, *A Documentary History of the Negro People in the United States* (New York: The Citadel Press, 1951), pp. 880–881; Du Bois, *Dusk of Dawn*, pp. 61, 69–72; John Hope Franklin, *From Slavery to Freedom* (New York: Alfred A. Knopf, Inc., 1952), pp. 384–388. The Du Bois-Washington controversy has been more fully developed in Samuel R. Spencer, Jr., *Booker T. Washington and the Negro's Place in American Life* (Boston: Little, Brown and Company, 1955), pp. 145–161.

37. Du Bois, *Dusk of Dawn*, p. 65.

38. For important documents pertaining to these organizations, see Aptheker, *A Documentary History*, pp. 886–927.

39. *Ibid.*, p. 901.

40. For an account of the merger of the Niagara Movement with this new program and the new organization that followed, we have drawn upon Robert L. Jack, *History of the National Association for the Advancement of Colored People* (Boston: Meador Publishing Company, 1943), pp. 1–9.

41. Maddox v. Veal, 45 Ark. 121 (1885).

42. Cummings v. Richmond County Board of Education, 175 U.S. 528, 20 Supreme Court 197, 44 L. Ed. 262 (1899).

43. W. A. Lowery v. School Trustees, 140 N.C. 33 (1905).

44. William J. McFarland v. Robert Goins, 96 Miss. 67, 50 South 493 (1909).

45. D. E. Williams v. D. B. Bradford, 158 N.C. 37 (1911).

46. Trustees of Colored Schools, Mayfield v. Trustees of White Schools, 180 Ky. 574 (1918).

47. Florence Murray, *The Negro Handbook, 1942* (New York: The Macmillan Company, 1942), pp. 39–40.

48. Florence Murray, *Negro Handbook, 1949* (New York: The Macmillan Company, 1949), pp. 62–63.

49. For accounts of these examples of subterfuge, see *The NAACP Bulletin*, December 1942; *The Crisis*, August 1943.

50. *The NAACP Bulletin*, March 1944.

51. *The Crisis*, June 1943.

52. Cases of this period are reported in Work, *Negro Year Book, 1932*, pp. 99–106.

53. "Constitutional Validity of States Barring Negroes From Primary Elections," *Michigan Law Review* 23:279 (January 1925).

54. *Eighteenth Annual Report for 1927 of the National Association for the Advancement of Colored People,* pp. 7–8.

55. *United States Reports,* 313 (1941), p. 318.

56. Alison Reppy, *Civil Rights in the United States* (New York: Central Book Company, 1951), p. 174.

57. *The Crisis,* March 1945.

58. *The Crisis,* September 1945.

59. *The Crisis,* November 1945.

60. Reports of the various cases leading up to the restrictive covenant decision may be found in *The Twentieth Annual Report of the NAACP;* and Murray, *The Negro Handbook, 1949.*

61. *NAACP Bulletin,* August–September 1941.

62. *NAACP Bulletin,* April 1942.

63. *NAACP Bulletin,* January 1943.

64. *NAACP Bulletin,* March 1943.

CHAPTER IX · THE BID FOR DESEGREGATION

1. For our description of the legal strategy employed by Charles H. Houston, we have relied heavily upon Jack Greenberg, *Race Relations and American Law* (New York: Columbia University Press, 1960), pp. 34–37.

2. Donald G. Murray v. The University of Maryland, 169 Maryland 478, 488 (1936).

3. Missouri *ex rel.* Gaines v. Canada, 83 L. Ed. 211 (1938).

4. State of Missouri at the Relation of Lloyd *Gaines, petitioner v. S. W. Canada, Registrar of the University of Missouri and the Curators of the University of Missouri,* 305 U.S. 337, 83 L. Ed. 208, 59 S. Ct. 232 (1938).

5. State *ex rel.* Bluford v. Canada, Registrar of University, 153 S. W. 2d. 12 (1941).

6. State *ex rel.* Michael *et al.* v. Witham *et al.,* 165 S. W. 2d. 378 (1942).

7. *Statistical Summary of School Segregation-Desegregation, November 1961* (Nashville, Tenn.: Southern Education Reporting Service, 1961), p. 47; and Sipuel v. Board of Education, 332 U.S. 631, 68 Sup. Ct. 299, 92 L. Ed. 604 (1948).

8. Sweatt v. Painter, 339 U.S. 629, L. Ed. 1114, 70 S. Ct. 848 (1950).

9. For a running summary of cases won during this period, see Jessie P. Guzman, *The Negro Year Book, 1952* (New York, 1952), pp. 283–285.

10. Mitchell v. United States *et al.,* 313 U.S. 80, 85 L. Ed. 1201, 61 S. Ct. 873 (1941).

11. Morgan v. Virginia, 328 U.S. 373, 90 L. Ed. 1317, 66 S. Ct. 1050, 165 ALR 574 (1946).

12. For a summary of the development of these cases, see Albert P. Blaustein and Clarence Clyde Ferguson, Jr., *Desegregation and the Law* (New Brunswick, N.J.: Rutgers University Press, 1957), pp. 45–49.

13. *Ibid.,* p. 275.

14. For an account of the NAACP opposition to segregation in housing, see Clement E. Vose, *Caucasians Only* (Berkeley, Calif.: University of California Press, 1959), pp. 50–73.

15. Blaustein and Ferguson, *Desegregation and the Law,* pp. 130–134.

16. For the views of social scientists as presented before the Court, see *The Effects of Segregation and the Consequences of Desegregation,* Appendix to Appellant's Brief, made available through the courtesy of John W. Davis.

17. Facts pertaining to dates of desegregation for the various states may be found in Southern Education Reporting Service, *Statistical Summary,* November 1961.

18. Facts concerning the St. Louis plan were drawn from "Desegregation of the St. Louis Public Schools," St. Louis Public Schools Instruction Department, September 1956.

19. U.S. Civil Rights Commission, *Public Schools North and West, 1962* (Washington, D.C.: Government Printing Office, 1962), pp. 260–263; for problems of desegregation growing out of population shifts, see pp. 270–274.

20. Incidents around which this phase of the St. Louis story has been built were reported in *Southern School News,* May 1963; July 1963; September 1963; November 1963; and March 1964. For similar problems of *de facto* segregation in other Northern cities, see *Time,* February 7, 1964, p. 49; March 6, 1964, p. 82; and May 22, 1964, p. 76.

21. The Louisville plan has been reported largely on the basis of Omer Carmichael, "The Louisville Story," *The New York Times Magazine,* October 7, 1956. Reprint supplied through the courtesy of the author.

22. Personal letter of July 12, 1957, received from Dr. Omer Carmichael, Superintendent of Public Schools in Louisville, Kentucky.

23. U.S. Commission on Civil Rights, *Public Schools Southern States, 1962* (Washington, D.C.: Government Printing Office, 1962), pp. 25–26.

24. Personal letter of May 29, 1957, received from Dr. Hobart M. Corning, Superintendent of Schools, Washington, D.C.

25. *Washington Post,* June 11, 1953.

26. *The Journal of the Columbian Educational Association,* May 1953, p. 13.

27. Don Shoemaker, *With All Deliberate Speed* (New York: Harper and Brothers, 1957), p. 147.

28. *Ibid.,* p. 149.

29. *Ibid.,* pp. 82–83.

30. "A Plan for Beginning Integration in the San Antonio Schools," made available through the courtesy of Superintendent Thomas B. Portwood.

31. *Southern School News,* May 1957.

32. Shoemaker, *With All Deliberate Speed,* pp. 85–86.

33. *Houston Informer,* April 8, 1958.

34. *Houston Informer,* April 1, 1958.

35. *Houston Post,* May 2, 1957.

36. John B. Martin, *The Deep South Says "Never"* (New York: Baltimore Books, 1957), pp. 79–83.

37. A full account of this case may be found in Roscoe Griffin, *A Tentative*

Description and Analysis of the School Desegregation Crisis in Sturgis, Kentucky, August 31–September 19, 1956 (New York: Anti-Defamation League of B'nai B'rith, 1956).

38. John Griffin and Theodore Freedman, *What Happened in Mansfield* (New York: Anti-Defamation League of B'nai B'rith, 1957).

39. Anna Holden and Bonita Valien, *A Tentative Analysis of the School Desegregation Crisis in Clinton, Tennessee* (New York: Anti-Defamation League of B'nai B'rith, 1956).

40. This summary report of the Little Rock incident was taken from the very complete account reported in *Southern School News*, October 1957.

41. James M. Nabrit, Sr., "Legal Inventions and the Desegregation Process," *The Annals of the American Academy of Political and Social Science* 304:36 (March 1956).

42. Various patterns of legislative resistance in the various Southern states have been reported serially by the *Southern School News*. For the ineffectiveness of these laws in their efforts to block desegregation, see Southern Education Reporting Service, *Statistical Summary*, November 1961, p. 3.

43. Erwin Knoll, "10 Years of Desegregation," a series of articles published in the *Houston Post*, May 13–18, 1964.

44. *Southern School News*, June 1964.

45. James S. Coleman, *Equality of Educational Opportunity* (Washington, D.C.: Government Printing Office, 1966), p. 3.

46. For this summary, see *Southern School News*, October 1965.

47. Harry W. Ernst and Andrew H. Calloway, "Reverse Integration," *The New York Times Magazine*, January 8, 1957, reprint.

CHAPTER X · THE MOVE TO CHANGE A SOCIAL ORDER

1. For facts pertaining to the various Presidential orders and the employment of Negroes by Federal agencies, see *A Five-City Survey of Negro American Employees of the Federal Government* (Washington, D.C.: President's Committee on Government Employment Policy, 1957); U.S. Commission on Civil Rights, *Employment* (Washington, D.C.: Government Printing Office, 1962); *The Goals of the President's Committee on Equal Employment Opportunities*, brochure issued by the committee; and John Hope, II, and Edward Shelton, "The Negro in the Federal Government," *Journal of Negro Education* 32:368 (Fall 1963).

2. This statement is verified in a report by Herman P. Miller and taken from Walter G. Daniel, "The Relative Employment and Income of American Negroes," *Journal of Negro Education* 32:352–354 (Fall 1963).

3. Wallace Mendelson, *Discrimination* (Englewood Cliffs, N.J.: Prentice-Hall, Inc., 1962), pp. 117–130.

4. Preston Valien, "Demographic Characteristics of the Negro Population in the United States," *Journal of Negro Education* 32:334–335 (Fall 1963); and Marian P. Yankauer and Milo Sunderhauf, "Housing: Equal Opportunity to Choose Where One Shall Live," *Journal of Negro Education* 32:402–403 (Fall 1963).

5. Louis E. Lomax, *The Negro Revolt* (New York: Harper & Row, Publishers, 1962), pp. 133–143 contains an account of the role of CORE and other organizations in the sit-ins.

6. W. Haywood Burns, *The Voices of Negro Protest in America* (New York: Oxford University Press, 1963), p. 42.

7. George McMillan, "The South's New Time Bomb," *Look,* July 5, 1960, pp. 21–25.

8. C. Eric Lincoln, "The Strategy of a Sit-in," *The Reporter,* January 5, 1961, pp. 20–23.

9. Lomax, *The Negro Revolt,* pp. 144–159. Southern Regional Council, *The Freedom Ride,* A Special Report, May 30, 1961.

10. Martin Luther King, Jr., "A Letter From Birmingham Jail," *Ebony,* August 1963, p. 28.

11. *Houston Post,* August 12, 1964.

CHAPTER XI · EPILOGUE: NEW CONFLICTS AND THE NEW CHALLENGE

1. For reports on the academic inadequacies of Negro children who were desegregated to mixed schools, see H. Harry Giles, *The Integrated Classroom* (New York: Basic Books, 1959), p. 687; *Southern School News,* December 1955, February 1956, March 1956, and July 1956.

2. For evidence of the adjustability of some of these students, see *Southern School News,* May 1959; and Kenneth B. Clark and Lawrence Plotkin, *The Negro Student at Integrated Colleges* (New York: National Scholarship Service and Fund for Negro Students, 1963), p. 21. See also appendix C, pp. 58–59, showing that the academic records of these students were achieved largely in leading American colleges.

3. For a complete report of this survey, see Richard L. Plant, *Blueprint for Talent Searching* (New York: National Scholarship Service and Fund for Negro Students, 1957).

4. *Ibid.,* p. 11.

5. *Interim Report-Southern Project* (New York: National Scholarship Service and Fund for Negro Students, November 1954), p. 19.

6. *Time,* November 7, 1955.

7. Robert W. Smuts, "The Negro Community and the Development of Negro Potential," *Journal of Negro Education* 26:458 (Fall 1957).

8. "New Jobs Open to Negroes," *Christian Century,* April 10, 1963, p. 454.

9. Robert Coles, M.D., "Two Minds About Carmichael," *The New Republic,* November 12, 1966, p. 20.

10. Reported in *Facts on File,* June 23–29, 1966, p. 236.

11. James S. Coleman, *Equality of Educational Opportunity* (Washington, D.C.: Government Printing Office, 1966), p. 325.

12. For example, see Floyd McKissick, "Is Integration Necessary?" *The New Republic,* December 3, 1966, pp. 33–36.

13. Charles E. Silberman, *Crisis in Black and White* (New York: Random House, 1964), pp. 123–144.

14. William H. Hastie, "Some Pains of Progress," *Journal of Negro Education* 27:151–158 (Spring 1958). See also Howard Thurman, "The New Heaven and the New Earth," *Journal of Negro Education* 27:115–119 (Spring 1958).

15. S. M. Nabrit, "Desegregation and the Future of the Graduate and Professional Education in Negro Institutions," *Journal of Negro Education* 27:415 (Summer 1958).

16. *Time,* May 29, 1964, p. 63. Greater details of the nature of this project are available in "A Proposal for Texas Southern University Participation in the Wisconsin Exchange Program," and in "Report on the Conference on Programs to Assist Predominantly Negro Colleges." This conference was held at the Massachusetts Institute of Technology, April 18–19, 1964.

17. It should be noted that Educational Services Incorporated (ESI) was one of several pilot efforts which led to the development of Upward Bound. For a more detailed account, see from the Office of Economic Opportunity, *A Nation Aroused: First Annual Report* (Washington, D.C.: Government Printing Office, 1965), pp. 49–50. An excellent survey of programs of this nature is reported in Edmund S. Gordon and Doxey A. Wilkerson, *Compensatory Education for the Disadvantaged* (New York: College Entrance Examination Board, 1966).

18. "What's Happened to Head Start," Public Affairs Circular, Office of Economic Opportunity, Washington, D.C., January 28, 1966, p. 1.

INDEX

Index

Crawford, James, 5
Credit arrangement: of sharecropper, 152–153
Credit system: of Southern economy, 15
Crime rates, Negro, 190
Crisis, The, 198, 212
Croom, Isaac, 5
Crop-lien system: and sharecroppers, 74; condemned by Frissell, 92; and work of Jeanes teachers, 137
Crozer Theological Seminary, 269
Cullen, Countee, 201, 202
Cummings, J. W.: and maintenance of schools for Negroes, 214
Curriculum: in freedmen's schools, 29–30; in Southern schools, 115–116, 123; special, for Negroes, 145; emphasis of, on rural life, 158; Negroes want same type as whites, 162
Curry, J. L. M., 105; and Negro education, 51; and white supremacy, 93; on educational progress in South, 108; as agent for Slater Fund, 130
Curtis, Florence: and Negro college libraries, 141
Cypert, J. N.: and atypical representation at Arkansas constitutional convention, 46

Dabney, Charles W., 107; and lack of uniformity in Southern public schools, 98; reports on Southern public education, 110
Dallas, Texas: and school desegregation, 277
Danville, Virginia: and freedom riders, 276
Davis, Allison, 206
Davis, Dorothy E., 231
Davis, Jackson, 133, 134
Davis, Jefferson: cabinet of, 16
Davis, Ronald N.: as Federal judge during desegregation at Little Rock, 256–257
Davis, T. Hoyt: and white primary, 221
Deaveaux, Miss: and underground Negro education in South, 25
De Grees, J. C.: as state superintendent of Texas school system, 57–58
Delaware: school officials of, sued, 231; school desegregation in, 232, 235, 261
Delaware State College for Negroes, 262

Delaware, University of: desegregation of, 262
Democratic party: Southern, 64; shift in image of, 65; and white primaries, in Texas, 220, 221
Demonstrations, civil rights, 269–273
Department of Housing and Urban Development, 206
Dependency rate, Negro, 190
Depression, Great, 190
Desegregation, school, 266; after Supreme Court decision, 234–239; economic advantage a factor in, 235; resistance to, 251–262; Southern progress toward, 260–261; and public colleges in South, 262–265; and higher and professional education in South, 263; and faculty of Negro colleges, 265
    Lunch counters, in South, 273–274
    Acceptance of, 278
Detroit, Michigan: and Sweet case, 223; job discrimination in, 224
Dickerman, George S., 106, 107; on counterfeit education, 96–97; on lack of competent Negro teachers in South, 103; on Southern white contributions to Negro education, 109
Dillard, James Hardy, 134, 142; and Rural School Fund, 126; and Slater Fund, 130; and county training school movement, 132; and Jeanes Fund, 133
Dillard University, 205; and New Orleans center, 142; Rosenwald Hall built at, 142
Disenfranchisement, of Negroes, 87, 168, 191–193, 207, 267
District of Columbia: proportion of Negroes in school enrollment, 235; school desegregation in, 235, 244–246, 261. *See also* Washington, D.C.
Douglass, Frederick, 10, 17, 205
Doyle, Bertram, 206; on interracial etiquette, 155
Dreher, Julius D., 91
Du Bois, W. E. B., 85, 173, 206, 207, 269; and efficiency of Negro teachers, 182; founds literary movement, 199–200; controversy with Booker T. Washington, 209–210; and Atlanta conferences, 210; and Niagara Movement, 211; and NAACP, 212
Duncan, B. O.: opposes mixed schools, 49
Dupree, Anna, 249

Index

Durham, North Carolina, 164; and sit-in, 271

Duvall, Viola: and salary equalization for teachers, 218

Dyer, Mrs. Frank: and resistance to desegregation in Houston, Texas, 249

Eaton, John: builds school system for Negroes, 23

Economic reconstruction in South, 151

Economy, Southern: and Negro labor, 148–149

Education: slave, 6; planters' tolerant attitude toward, 11; need for higher, among freedmen, 31; Southern whites' need for, 94; as social ladder for Negroes, 95; progress of, in South, 108–110; for rural children, 142–143; special, purpose of, 147–148; Negro scholars in, 206; equality in, sought, 214

Negro: beginnings of, 11; before Civil War, 13; support of, through public funds, 36; and Southern view, 75; needs to be special, 76, 77; intellectual, 78; tradition of superficiality in, 96; for elite, 99–100; for masses, 100; inferior to white, 176–185

Public: for all Southern children, 37; for Negroes in South, 75; study of conditions in South, 105, 110; unequal apportionment of public funds for, 226

Educational level, median: of Southern Negroes and whites, 173

Educational opportunities: and Civil War, 15

Educational Services, Inc., 286

Educational test. See Literacy test

Eggleston, Joseph D., Jr., 107

Eisenhower, Dwight D.: and school desegregation in Little Rock, 257

Electricians, Negro, 188

Elementary schools: desegregation of, in St. Louis, 237

Elizabeth City, North Carolina: and sit-in, 271

Elkins, Stanley M., 9; and Negro personality, 3

Ellis, Pauline, 222

Emancipation, personal: unwittingly aided by South, 15

Emancipation Proclamation: and movement of slaves away from plantation, 17; meaning of, 24

Emergency program: for freedmen's relief, 19–20, 22

Emory College, 101

Emotional needs: of slaveholders, 4, 7, 16

Employment: equal opportunity in, 168; desegregation in, in St. Louis, 236; in St. Louis schools after desegregation, 237; opportunities for Negroes, 267. See also Job opportunities; Job restrictions

Employment Office, United States: racial discrimination by, 224

Enrollment of public schools: in Georgia, 56; in South Carolina, 56; in Louisiana, 57

Entwistle Tract, Los Angeles: residential segregation in, 222

Environment: influence on Negro community life, 206

Environmentalism: of Negro social scientists, 205

Eppse, Merle, 205

Equalization movement, 216

Equality: racial, Southern attitude toward, 52; Negro, 195, 207, 213

Equalization program: for Mississippi public schools, 260

Ethridge, Mark F.: and Fair Employment Practices Committee, 224

Evans, Roscoe: and Better Conduct Program, 245

Expenditure: per capita, for Negro and white pupils in South, 87, 179–180

for Southern public education: racial differentials become smaller, 116; portion for teaching force, 182

Faculties, public school: desegregation of, in Baltimore, 252

Fair Employment Practices Committee: NAACP becomes watchdog for, 224

Fairchild, George F., 91, 97

Familial contact, between slave and master, 7–8

Family life, Negro, 190

Farm agents: in rural South, 138; Negro, 188

Farm demonstration program, 138

Farmer, B. H.: and *Arkansas Journal of Education,* 53–54

Farmer, James: and CORE, 275

Farmers, Negro: as percentage of total Negro college graduates, 175

Index

Index